The Life and Thought of H. Odera Oruka

Bloomsbury Introductions to World Philosophies

Series Editor:

Monika Kirloskar-Steinbach

Assistant Series Editor:

Leah Kalmanson

Regional Editors:

Nader El-Bizri, James Madaio, Sarah A. Mattice, Takeshi Morisato,
Pascah Mungwini, Mickaella Perina, Omar Rivera and
Georgina Stewart

Bloomsbury Introductions to World Philosophies delivers primers reflecting
exciting new developments in the trajectory of world philosophies.
Instead of privileging a single philosophical approach as the basis of
comparison, the series provides a platform for diverse philosophical
perspectives to accommodate the different dimensions of cross-cultural
philosophizing. While introducing thinkers, texts and themes emanating
from different world philosophies, each book, in an imaginative and
path-breaking way, makes clear how it departs from a conventional
treatment of the subject matter.

Titles in the Series:

A Practical Guide to World Philosophies, by Monika Kirloskar-Steinbach
and Leah Kalmanson
Daya Krishna and Twentieth-Century Indian Philosophy, by Daniel Raveh
Māori Philosophy, by Georgina Tuari Stewart
Philosophy of Science and The Kyoto School, by Dean Anthony Brink
Tanabe Hajime and the Kyoto School, by Takeshi Morisato
African Philosophy, by Pascah Mungwini
The Philosophy of the Brahma-sūtra, by Aleksandar Uskokov
Sikh Philosophy, by Arvind-Pal Singh Mandair
The Philosophy of the Yogasūtra, by Karen O'Brien-Kop

The Life and Thought of H. Odera Oruka

Pursuing Justice in Africa

Gail M. Presbey

BLOOMSBURY ACADEMIC
LONDON · NEW YORK · OXFORD · NEW DELHI · SYDNEY

BLOOMSBURY ACADEMIC
Bloomsbury Publishing Plc
50 Bedford Square, London, WC1B 3DP, UK
1385 Broadway, New York, NY 10018, USA
29 Earlsfort Terrace, Dublin 2, Ireland

BLOOMSBURY, BLOOMSBURY ACADEMIC and the Diana logo are
trademarks of Bloomsbury Publishing Plc

First published in Great Britain 2023

Series design by Louise Dugdale
Cover image © Garry Killian / Adobe Stock

A catalogue record for this book is available from the British Library.

A catalog record for this book is available from the Library of Congress.

ISBN: HB: 978-1-3503-0385-0
       PB: 978-1-3503-0386-7
       ePDF: 978-1-3503-0387-4
       eBook: 978-1-3503-0388-1

Series: Bloomsbury Introductions to World Philosophies

Typeset by RefineCatch Limited, Bungay, Suffolk
Printed and bound in India

To find out more about our authors and books visit www.bloomsbury.com and
sign up for our newsletters.

Figure 1 Image of H. Odera Oruka, from Uppsala University days, *c.* 1967. Photographed by Tommie Zaine.

*Dedicated to the memory of my
father, Harry Presbey
Who gave me early encouragement in philosophy
and academic pursuits broadly
And who avidly read all the letters I wrote home while
I was living in Kenya*

Contents

Figures

Acknowledgements

This book was thirty years in the making. I first met Odera Oruka in 1993, and since then I have been working on many aspects of his philosophy. And so it is very hard to sum up all the help which I have received over these many years.

I very much want to thank all the Kenyans who helped me in this work. They are too numerous to name all of them. A warm thank you to the now deceased Olivia Phoebe Odera Oruka for giving me the permission to quote and publish from her late husband's unpublished work and correspondence, including the use of photographs. Thank you to Chaungo Barasa, Humphrey Ojwang, and Daniel Sasine as my main helpers in interviewing sages. Chaungo Barasa, who had worked with Odera Oruka as a researcher and interviewer on the sage philosophy project, helped me identify and interview several sages, and also helped me to understand the earlier phases of the sage philosophy project in the 1980s. Humphrey Ojwang, who was for many years a Senior Research Fellow and Thematic Unit Head of Linguistic Anthropology at the Institute of African Studies of the University of Nairobi, Kenya, helped me to locate and interview Luo sages for this and other related scholarly works. Thank you to Oriare Nyarwath and John Ouko, as well as Robert Vincent Okungu and Shadrack Wanjola Nasong'o who all helped with translation and transcription of interviews. Thank you to the sages, including Nyando Ayoo, Filida Okaya, Saulo Namianya, and others who helped me to further understand sage philosophy through first-hand experience.

Thank you to colleagues in the Philosophy Department (now Department of Philosophy and Religious Studies) at University of Nairobi, who hosted me in 1994–95 during my sabbatical from Marist College, and in 1998–2000 as a J. William Fulbright Senior Scholar. Special thanks go to the department Chair at the time, Solomon Monyenye, and to department faculty who especially helped me research Prof. Oruka's works such as Oriare Nyarwath, Patrick Dikirr, F. Ochieng'-Odhiambo, Joseph Situma, F.E.A. Owakah, and Jackson Wafula.

Thanks to Lucius Outlaw for being the first to suggest that I should go to Kenya and pursue research on Odera Oruka's philosophy. My ideas could not have developed without the feedback I received from scholars who would attend my conference presentations and freely give their feedback at such times, or later with lengthy conversations and correspondence. I want to thank scholars Anke Graness, Kai Kresse, and Bruce Janz for their generosity, as well as D.A. Masolo, Sam Imbo, Omedi Ochieng, Workineh Kelbessa, Ademola Fayemi Kazeem, Robin Attfield, Betty Wambui, Eddah Mutua, and many others who helped to clarify my ideas and my writing. Series editor Monika Kirloskar-Steinbach has also been very supportive and encouraging. Thank you to Jennifer Gariepy and Laura Dewey for help in editing.

Thank you to Astrid Hedenius for permission to cite her father Ingemar's writings and correspondence, and for being able to include the photo of her father and Odera Oruka. Profound thanks to Tommie Zaine, for sharing his memories and photos of his friend Henry Odera as well as manuscripts left with him for safekeeping. Thanks to Kaj Hansen, Svante Nordin, Lennart Nordenfeldt, Tore Nordenstam, David Felder, and the late Ann-Mari Henschen-Dahlquist, Harrison Muyia, Taban lo Liyong, and Sjef Donders for helping me to piece together the narrative of Oruka's early years of study. Thanks to Jennifer Hultén for translations from Swedish for Hedenius' correspondence.

Thank you to the J. William Fulbright Foundation for supporting my work in Kenya in 1998–2000. Thank you to Marist College for the sabbatical year support in 1995–96, and to University of Detroit Mercy for research leaves in the academic year 2006–07, as well as semesters of Winter 2013, Winter 2015, Fall 2020, and Winter 2022. This book was not my sole activity during all those years or semesters, but it was always part of my activity during those times. University of Detroit Mercy also supported my travel to Kenya on five occasions. I also thank the University of Detroit Mercy's Professors Union for research support.

I would like to thank some of the previous publishers of my articles and book chapters for allowing me to republish some sections of the works. Some parts of Chapter 3 came from an article, "Odera Oruka and Mohandas Gandhi on Reconciliation," *Polylog: Forum für interkulturelles Philosophieren*, 34/2 (2015), 187–208. Parts of chapters 4 and 5 were summarized and published in an encyclopedia article, "Sage Philosophy," *Internet Encyclopedia of Philosophy*, September 2014, found online at http://www.iep.utm.edu/afr-sage/; Some of the ideas of chapters 4 and 5 were shared earlier in print in "Oruka and Sage Philosophy: New Insights in Sagacious Reasoning," in *Handbook of African Philosophy*, edited by Toyin Falola and Adeshina Afolayan. New York: Palgrave Macmillan, 2017, 75–96.

Parts of Chapter 6 has been previously published as a book chapter: "Odera Oruka on Culture Philosophy and Its Role in the S.M. Otieno Burial Trial," in *Odera Oruka in the Twenty-First Century*, edited by Reginald M.J. Oduor, Oriare Nyarwath, and Francis Owakah. Washington, D.C.: Council for Research in Values and Philosophy, 2018, 99–118. Chapter 8 contains some excerpts from the earlier article, "H. Odera Oruka on Moral Reasoning,"

Journal of Value Inquiry, 34:4 (December 2000), pp. 517–528. I acknowledge these earlier versions and thank the publishers for permission to republish them here as part of this text.

Thank you to those who have repeatedly encouraged me to finish this book, including several mentioned above, as well as my partner Tim, and historians Sue Gronewold and Renee Bricker.

Series Editor's Preface

The introductions we include in the World Philosophies series take a single thinker, theme or text and provide a close reading of them. What defines the series is that these are likely to be people or traditions that you have not yet encountered in your study of philosophy. By choosing to include them you broaden your understanding of ideas about the self, knowledge and the world around us. Each book presents unexplored pathways into the study of world philosophies. Instead of privileging a single philosophical approach as the basis of comparison, each book accommodates the many different dimensions of cross-cultural philosophizing. While the choice of terms used by the individual volumes may indeed carry a local inflection, they encourage critical thinking about philosophical plurality. Each book strikes a balance between locality and globality.

The Life and Thought of H. Odera Oruka: Pursuing Justice in Africa provides a fascinating philosophical portrait of the life and work of the proponent of sage philosophy H. Odera Oruka (1944–1995). Gail Presbey puts into the spotlight a thinker who strove to develop a philosophical standpoint that would accomplish both, account for the particular experience of individual societies within the African continent as well as their common experience under imperialism and colonialism. Presbey sets the formation and mature development of Oruka's philosophical thought in relation to his contemporaries at home in Kenya and abroad, while simultaneously further honing the concepts with which he operated. The result is a book that uses Oruka's philosophy in intriguing ways to understand some pressing problems of our times.

Monika Kirloskar-Steinbach

Part One

An Introduction to the Person of Odera Oruka

Introduction

Henry Odera Oruka[1] impressed many people with his dedication to Africa's betterment and his constant drive to learn and do more. He would take me and, on other occasions, other visiting philosophers like Michael Krausz of Bryn Mawr[2] off the beaten track down rural roads in Kenya in order to provide us with experiences quite unlike the usual conference presentation. Without telephones, there was always a matter of chance in these meetings— would the sage we sought be at home or traceable in the area? Once we found the place, we might be met by family members or neighbors who would fetch the sage. Wives would prepare tea for us as we sat at the feet of a wrinkled old man wearing worn clothes and beaming with character. News of our arrival would travel by word of mouth, and in some cases many elder neighbors as well as many curious youth would gather to overhear our conversations. Tape-recorded during our visit, the discussions would be transcribed later to be shared with a larger academic world and a general reading audience. Many interviews just like this were conducted by UON professors and graduate students from both Philosophy and Religious Studies.

Oruka certainly spent much time on the University of Nairobi's campus, where he organized a philosophy department independent of the Religious Studies Department. He chaired the Philosophy Department from 1980 to 1986, engaged his students on many topics, and oversaw many Master's theses and doctoral dissertations.[3] Oruka founded and chaired the Philosophical Association of Kenya. Always dedicated to issues of justice and cultural identity in Kenya, he submitted articles to Kenyan newspapers, appeared on television,and trained District Officers of the Kenyan government in cultural sensitivity. He served as a consultant on environmental studies in Machakos District (Oruka 1997: 280n13).[4] Oruka interviewed sages and other residents of rural Kenya regarding their attitudes toward family planning (Oruka 1995) and served as an expert witness on Luo customs during high-profile court cases involving customary law.[5]

Oruka was not only found in Nairobi or out-of-the-way rural places in Kenya. He could also be found globetrotting, attending university in Sweden and the United States, spending sabbaticals at Ibadan, Nigeria, and presenting papers at conferences around the world. Oruka attended the 1973 World

Congress of Philosophy in Varna, Bulgaria, and later noted that he had attended all the World Congresses since then. (Oruka 1997: 155)[6] In Bulgaria, he met Claude Sumner, the only other participant addressing a topic in African philosophy. He got to know Sumner better when he went to a conference in Addis Ababa in 1976, which included such leading figures in the field of African philosophy as Paulin Hountondji, Cheikh Anta Diop, Ali Mazrui, and E. A. Ruch (Oruka 1997: 155). Oruka attended a conference in honor of W. A. Amo in Ghana in 1978, where he presented his paper "Four Trends in African Philosophy." He attended twenty-five international conferences from 1972 to 1993, including conferences in Britain, Hawaii, Turkey, Brazil, Korea, India, and Spain, and held visiting positions at Haverford College (1983–1984) and Earlham College (1988–1989) in the United States. (Unpublished curriculum vitae, 1993)

Oruka not only traveled to other countries but in addition invited people from other countries to come to Kenya. He was a founding member of the Afro-Asian Philosophical Association, and hosted its second conference in Nairobi in November, 1981. He worked closely with Mourad Wahba of Egypt and Ramjee Singh of India. He served as Secretary General of the Afro-Asian Philosophical Association from 1985 to 1992. He hosted international conferences in Nairobi, including the World Conference in Philosophy in July 1991 and the World Future Studies Federation in July 1995. He was on the steering committee of the *Fédération Internationale des Sociétés de Philosophie* (FISP) from 1988 to 1995.

Oruka is often cited, along with Kwasi Wiredu and Paulin Hountondji, as one of the key thinkers in the debate on the existence and worth of African philosophy. He is most known for the project he called "sage philosophy," which involved, in its beginnings, going into rural areas, interviewing the wise elders of their communities, and putting their oral philosophizing into writing. As Oruka explained, sages were valuable not only because of their knowledge of traditions but also because of their ethical commitment to the betterment of society (Oruka 1990b: xxvii). His extensive interviewing of rural sages demonstrated his great interest in and valuing of African traditions and his aversion to the unthinking assimilation process which has encouraged many African youths to turn their interest away from knowledge that is particularly rooted in Africa. However, it must be noted that his interest in the sages was not as living relics of days gone by. He instead was interested in the philosophic sages as critical thinkers engaged in shedding light on and solving the problems of their communities by critically drawing upon their traditions as well as practicing their own form of creative insight.

As he explained in his essay "Traditions and Modernity in the Scramble for Africa," it is good to improve on African resources, but not to discard them. "Progressive modernization" should entail humbly searching to see what is worthwhile in a value system, whether our own or not. After such a search, we can decide what is worth preserving. This may be contrasted with other versions of "progressive modernization" which take for granted that everything African must be discarded. (Oruka 1997: 255–63)

I first met Professor Oruka in 1993, having sought him out on the recommendation of Lucius Outlaw, who had recently visited Oruka in Kenya for the 1991 World Congress of Philosophy, greatly admired the man's work, and enjoyed the country. I had written Oruka to tell him I was coming and would like to meet him, but I never got any reply. I was unsure whether or not I should still go, but having a couple of friends in Kenya who were ready to host me, I thought I would take the chance and go anyway. Upon arriving in the hallways of the University of Nairobi philosophy department, I found Prof. Oruka's door and knocked on it. It did not open, but a door down the hall did. There was the acting chairman of the department, Dr. Jack Odhiambo. I told him I was looking for Prof. Oruka. "You must be Gail Presbey," he said. "We thought you were a man." After that surprise greeting, I found out that Prof. Oruka had indeed received my correspondence, so the department knew I was coming. When I finally met Oruka he explained that he had been carrying important papers in his car but lost the papers when his car was broken into. So he had no way of writing me back. But he was glad that I had arrived. And I'm glad that I took the chance to go.

Oruka spent those six weeks in the summer of 1993 showing me around Nairobi, taking me to hotel gardens to sip sodas under shade trees and talk about sage philosophy. He also had to show me where the best bands playing African music were performing. He was not your typical stuffy professor, but he was very pensive and reflective most times. He encouraged me to pursue sage philosophy as a research topic and to come back to Kenya to do some in-depth research. He also asked me to arrange a visit for him to the United States. He had already been to Earlham College once and enjoyed it. At the end of six weeks, I had written my first article on sage philosophy, which he read, writing many comments in the margins. Not being a mere sycophant, I was already quite critical in my first article of aspects of his project. I wasn't sure how he would react. Would he think I had imposed on his hospitality just to criticize him? But he took my work as I could only hope he would. He thanked me for my insights and said that criticisms like this would help sage philosophy to become stronger. This is just one of countless examples of Oruka enthusiastically engaging his critics in a mutual dialogue that would advance the field.

Since he was interested in visiting the United States, I tried to arrange a faculty exchange between him and me for the 1994–1995 academic year. He wrote me, "I hope you succeed in your struggle to get our exchange effected. Indeed, I can sense you are a fighter–I am too in certain ways! But do not be surprised–almost all bureaucracies are the same. They usually frustrate or derail straightforward creative thinking." (Pers. comm. from HO to GP, December 6, 1993) Our first attempt did not work out because the University of Nairobi faculty went on strike in 1994 in an effort to have the university administration recognize their union. In early 1995 he wrote to me of an upcoming visit I arranged for him to Marist College in Poughkeepsie, New York, "I hope the plans for my visit to Marist are on. I very much look forward to being there by January [1996]. Indeed this period abroad would be good both for my work and health–since I have had a very hectic period here in the last 1 ½ years." (Pers. comm. from HO to GP)[7] I was able to come back to Kenya in the 1995–1996 academic year to work with Oruka further. I had also arranged, as he had requested, a visiting professorship to begin in January 1996 at my home institution. Little did I know that he would never be able to take up the visiting position. While I was very appreciative of the fact that I was getting to know Oruka's philosophy better, even going with him on his journeys to interview sages, I had no idea that it was in fact a last opportunity, since he would soon be killed by a truck on the streets of Nairobi. He died on 9 December 1995, while he was still fifty-one years old.

Henry Odera Oruka was loved and revered by so many people. Many eulogists praised him for his character and accomplishments and expressed how much they would miss his presence.[8] Newspapers described the keen sense of loss many felt at his passing. This monograph and any further studies in sage philosophy I have done are small attempts to continue his work in his absence.

It's important to keep in mind that sage philosophy was just a part of Oruka's philosophical interests. In a broader sense, he was most interested in issues of global justice. He was acutely aware that Kenya's current context was shaped by a colonial inheritance and that the nation continued to suffer in a climate of domination and dependence, subjected to a world order that put profits before people. His interest in philosophy was due to his seeing it as a tool to expose injustices and to fight for people's rights using reason and argument. Oruka saw sage philosophy as a key aspect of his larger interest in justice; the project could challenge and upset European and American misconceptions about Africans, thereby challenging a system of exploitation. By focusing on sages who had a commitment to the betterment of their communities, he could popularize role models who had something important to offer contemporary Kenyan society, which too often idolized the West. (Oruka 1990b: 9–10) In the present work, I explore Oruka's contributions to ethics and political philosophy, many of which have up to now received less attention than his work in sage philosophy. I also cover his early development as a philosopher and his studies with Ingemar Hedenius to an extent not heretofore accomplished, drawing on drafts of his early work, his Master's and licentiate theses, and correspondence between him and Hedenius.

In an essay in which he reflected upon his life's calling as a philosopher, "My Strange Way to Philosophy," Oruka discussed his own interests in philosophy. He saw his goal to be to clear current and future obstacles to philosophy, wisdom, and justice. He did this by exposing and analyzing three evils: socio-economic deprivation, cultural-racial mythology, and the illusion of appearance. He places an emphasis on the evil of socio-economic deprivation because poverty and hunger are, according to him, the greatest constraint on mental development and creativity. The evil of the illusion of appearance concerns people who pursue style over substance and are distracted and fooled by the glitter of surfaces. Oruka shows a readiness to wage "philosophic war with factors and values which promote social and economic disadvantage and oppression of people." (Oruka 1997: 284) On the positive side, he names three vehicles to a fruitful philosophy: freedom of thought, inspiration, and destiny—the latter referring not to some preordained state-to-be, but to a concern with Africa's origin and future that guides personal and community self-definition. (Oruka 1997: 283–84) Oruka was a philosopher dedicated to a cause. While some have argued that philosophers in general, and Oruka in particular, should be more aloof and not so committed to political goals, it was Oruka's commitment that drew me to his work.

Sage philosophy continues to gain the attention of many in the field of African philosophy. Anthony Oseghare of Nigeria came to Kenya to study with Oruka, completing his PhD under Oruka's supervision in 1985 (Oseghare 1985) and publishing an article about sage philosophy in *International Philosophical Quarterly* in 1992. G. R. Hoffman (Leipzig, 1984) and C. Neugebauer (Vienna, 1987) did PhD work on African philosophy that included information about Oruka. (Graness and Kresse 1997: 117n21) Kwasi Wiredu has said that sage philosophy is "one of the most important developments in post-colonial African philosophy" and that the sages "are the present-day exemplars of our ancestral philosophers." (Wiredu 1996: 150, Bell 2002: 34) Wiredu was one of many scholars, along with Dismas Masolo, F. Ochieng'-Odhiambo, Sophie Oluwole and others, who contributed essays to a collection entitled *Sagacious Reasoning: Henry Odera Oruka in Memoriam.* (Graness and Kresse 1997) In addition to reprinting some key essays by Oruka that might be hard to find otherwise, the collection highlights the work of Oruka's former colleagues, including D. A. Masolo and F. Ochieng'-Odhiambo, and the junior faculty at the University of Nairobi, including Patrick Dikirr and Oriare Nyarwath, who are following in Oruka's footsteps.

Oruka's supporters are not the only ones talking about sage philosophy; the critics have also been talking. Right from the start, Oruka encouraged debate on his ideas and included both supportive and critical essays in his book *Sage Philosophy: Indigenous Thinkers and Modern Debate on African Philosophy.* (Oruka 1990b) Lansana Keita and Peter Bodunrin were some of the more critical essayists included. Since then, D. A. Masolo has noted in his history of African philosophy that Oruka's sages do not make theoretical claims with enough elaboration to satisfy the definitions of philosophy held by Taita Towett and Kwasi Wiredu. (Masolo 1994: 236–38) In an interview, Emmanuel Eze suggested that, while sage philosophy was helpful in some ways because "Oruka's contribution was to break some of the anonymity that produce [*sic*] illusions of 'unanimous' communal African thought," it had its methodological flaws in that the choice of questions and the impetus to systematize came from Oruka. (Eze and Lewis 2000: paragraph 19) The present text will look at these many criticisms of sage philosophy as well as add more. I will then outline a future strategy for sage philosophy that will take its best attributes forward while modifying it in light of past criticisms.

Oruka's interview with sage (and Luo *ker* which means spiritual and cultural leader) Paul Mboya Akoko was covered in the Nairobi press (Oruka 1981); it was also included in a collection edited by Fred Lee Hord and Jonathan Scott Lee, *I Am Because We Are: Readings in Black Philosophy.* (Hord and Lee 1995: 32–44) Oruka's work is prominently mentioned by Segun Gbadegesin in his article, "Current Trends and Perspectives in African Philosophy," in Blackwell's *A Companion to World Philosophies.* (Gbadegesin 1997) Richard Bell's recent book devotes an entire section to Oruka's sage philosophy, and in fact, Bell wants to take Oruka's project further by exploring oral philosophies as examples of narrative and Socratic discourse found not only in the text of sages but also in everyday discourse and village palavers. (Bell 2002: 32–35, 111–12)

Contemporary thinkers find Oruka's methodology especially helpful.

Bagele Chilisa champions sage philosophy interviews as a way to practice indigenous research methodologies. (Chilisa 2012) Boaventura Santos considers the sage philosophy approach an important part of epistemologies of the global South and an example of intercultural translation that he calls "diatopical hermeneutics." (Santos 2012: 59) Santos describes diatopical hermeneutics as struggling to find an answer to the question "How can I keep alive in me the best of modern and democratic Western culture, while at the same time recognising the value of the world that it designated autocratically as non-civilised, ignorant, residual, inferior, or unproductive?" (Santos 2012: 60)

A special issue of *Thought and Practice: Journal of the Philosophical Association of Kenya* is dedicated to Oruka's philosophy. (Oduor 2012) Harzing's *Publish or Perish* calculated that Oruka's works had been cited almost 2,000 times as of August 2022. Google Scholar shows over 450 citations of Oruka's *Sage Philosophy* (1990b) by August 2022, not to mention the citations of his many other works. As of May 2022, there is one monograph in German by Anke Graness analyzing Oruka's work on ethical topics. (Graness 2011). There is also a dissertation published as an online monograph that covers both Oruka and Wim van Binsbergen (Mosima 2016; see also Presbey 2017a; 2017b). As we ready to go to press, two more books on Oruka has been published. There is a monograph by Michael Kamau Mburu, *Odera Oruka and the Right to a Human Minimum: An African Philosopher's Defense of Human Dignity and Environment*, and the edited collection *Rethinking Sage Philosophy: Interdisciplinary Perspectives on and beyond H. Odera Oruka* (June and November 2022). My book intends to address a current gap in the African philosophy literature by covering Oruka's personal genesis as a philosopher, and giving context to the development of his differing topics of interest and the positions he held in the field of philosophy.

I also offer this book, humbly, as just one (hopefully important) contribution to scholarship on Odera Oruka. I look forward to future studies by Kenyans and others who may have a different and better perspective on his life and work than I do. I also want to say that, this book is not all that I want to say on the topic of Odera Oruka. This book includes my correspondence with and interviews of some Kenyans, Europeans and Americans who interacted with Oruka. I have interviewed other Kenyans who do not appear in this book but appear in some articles of mine, and even more who will hopefully be included in a future book more particularly aimed at sage philosophy. With those cautions in mind, I invite readers to join me in learning about a fascinating thinker who has shaped decades of discussion and debate in the field of African philosophy.

1

Reflection on Oruka's Early Years

Not a lot has been written about Oruka's early years. And yet it does not seem right to me to begin the book only with Oruka's formal studies of philosophy at Uppsala University. He told me personally that the sages he knew as a child had a big influence on him. When he and I first met, we went together to interview an old sage who Oruka said he knew as a child, Nyando Ayoo, near his rural home in Sega. This chapter discusses Oruka's childhood and the cultural context of his youth. I will draw upon what he has said about his life and about the sages he knew as a child and young man, and who he interviewed when he was much older. By doing so we will be introduced to key themes that Odera Oruka will fully investigate in his later career as a scholar, such as, the need to address poverty, injustice, and oppression, and to provide people with a human minimum, and the need to go beyond compassion to reform institutions. He argued, and demonstrated by his own scholarly works, that cultural background influences philosophical priorities. He championed people's local traditions and bemoaned their destruction by so-called forces of modernization. Yet, he always emphasized distinguishing one's own views from prevailing opinion, and gravitated toward wise persons who could critique the erroneous thinking prevalent in their society, including superstitious religious beliefs.

Oruka recounted the little we know about his childhood in his article "My Strange Way to Philosophy." (Oruka 1997: 281–87) Oruka was the son of Peter Oruka Rang'inya. His father had ten wives, and Oruka's mother Dolphine Nyang'or Oruka was his father's second wife. (Ogutu 1995–96: 7) By custom, Oruka called all of his father's wives "mother." Oruka's biological mother died when he was eight years old. At the time, Oruka had three younger siblings, but the youngest, only six months old when his mother died, did not survive. Oruka explained that upon his mother's death he stopped attending school to look after his siblings, and so, the youngest one, named Okoth (the rain), "died almost on my lap." (Oruka 1997: 282) After Okoth died, Oruka returned to school, and he and his remaining siblings (his sister Gaudencia and his brother Maurice) (Ochieng'-Odhiambo 1995–96: 13) were raised "as the multi-mothered motherless children of all my father's wives." (Oruka 1997: 282) The description is filled with ambiguity; on the one hand there are a plethora of mothers, but at the same time he also refers to himself and his siblings as "orphans" and suggests that they were sometimes at the mercy of those who did not care for them. While his father was certainly well-off in the rural context—his ten wives and thirty-six children[1] were evidence of his wealth—nevertheless the family lived in rural Kenya, where lack of medical care and proper nutrition contributes to a high mortality rate for mothers and infants—"statistics" which directly impacted Oruka's family.

Oruka's father passed away in 1979 at the age of seventy-nine. (Oruka 1991b: 118) But before he had passed, Oruka had a chance to interview his father in the mid-1970s as part of the sage philosophy project. In that interview we can get some inkling of the early intellectual influences on the child, Henry Odera. It is also fitting that we start by considering this interview, since Oruka dedicates the *Sage Philosophy* book to his father specifically, as well as to "all the sages of Africa." (Oruka 1991b: dedication page) Also, by getting to know his father's ideas, we can get some glimpse into what it must have been like to grow up with such a father as an influence.

Joseph Donders, a White Father and philosophy professor who would be Oruka's colleague at the University of Nairobi, remembered that he had been with Oruka for the interview with Oruka's father. Donders died on March 7, 2013, but earlier, in 2007, he shared this memory with me:

> I still remember about the interview with Odera's father. He was a very old man. He was sitting under a tree. It was a very nice day. . . . He said that death in some way does not exist, but exists together with everything else. And then, there was a bit of wind in the tree, and he said—he pointed at the noise of the tree—he said, it is there, they are there! But they [the ancestors] remained surviving; it was obvious. That was the only thing I remember of that interview because it really struck me.
>
> Joseph Donders, interviewed by the author,
> April 13, 2007, Washington, D.C.

In fact, this is a very interesting aspect of the interview with Oruka Rang'inya. It is not a surprise that it is the part that stuck out in Fr. Donders' mind, because it is the part of the interview that comes closest to saying there is a God and an immortal aspect to humans which has presence and agency. Other statements of Rang'inya's go against this trend (and thereby against religiosity and, more specifically, Christianity), arguing that God is "only" a "useful" idea and that death is the end of human life. In fact, Rang'inya's ambiguous claims about God and spirits were mirrored by Oruka later in his career.

Rang'inya mentions that Africans thought of God before Europeans ever came to Africa. The Luo people (Oruka, Ayoo, and Rang'inya's ethnic group) had their own religion, in which they worshiped *wang chieng*, that is, the face of the sun. They also referred to God as *Were Hagawa*, a name referencing the sun and moon. But Rang'inya distinguished his own beliefs from these religious beliefs of the Luo. He says clearly that "the Luo were quite wrong to think of God in physical terms," that is, to think that the sun and moon were somehow the abode of God. He also says that it is wrong to personalize God. (Oruka 1991b: 119, 120).

Indeed, Rang'inya argued that God is an idea, "The Idea which represents goodness itself." (Oruka 1991b: 119) And God is a useful concept. Rang'inya is not exactly clear. Is God a useful concept because the idea of God as goodness serves as a moral compass for life? Rang'inya says God is "the concept of open-heartedness" and suggests that a person who is not greedy and sacrifices for others "is God." (Oruka 1991b: 119) He has other examples of the "usefulness" of the concept of God that are not clearly related to goodness and open-heartedness. For example, he says that men on both sides of a war pray to God for victory; medicine men pray to God that customers will be directed their way; and even thieves pray to God for help avoiding capture. (Oruka 1991b: 119–20, 126)

Not directly related to the topic of "God's" power, but on the related topic of the power of magic, Rang'inya argues that with a typical married couple, the wife believes in the power of magic, and the husband does not. But, if the husband is smart, he will invite the *ajuoga* to the house when his wife is sick because, practically, based on psychology and due to the wife's faith, the *ajuoga* will help her cope with stress and give her confidence that she will get well, and this in itself will help her to become well. (Oruka 1991b: 126) It is just such arguments, which would base the seeming results of faith and God's action on the physiological effects of human action, that suggest that there is no literal "God" in the sense of a power that can help humans. And yet, Rang'inya says he is against the secular view that discards religion because, after all, religion is useful.

The most difficult aspects of the interview are claims that seem to contradict each other. At the beginning of the interview Rang'inya says, "my own thinking leads me to the conclusion that God resides both in this world as well as in 'heaven.'" Rang'inya adds "God lives in the wind. Thus he is everywhere." While he cautions people against personalizing God, Rang'inya himself uses personal pronouns for God, and says God lives and resides. (Oruka 1991b: 119) Later in the interview, Rang'inya says, "What about heaven? Well, the very idea is fictitious: It is an illusion. From all that we know so far, upon death man's existence simply ceases, it comes to an end." But he quickly follows this with a variation of his earlier statement, "The dead are in the wind," explaining that he means the dead are not in heaven but here on earth with us, if only we would pay attention. "The dead are with us here and now." He pointed to the wind in the tree, and explained that since the dead are in the wind, it is the dead who are shaking the tree. This is the moment that impressed Donders. It would seem that Rang'inya was noticing and acknowledging the presence of those who are dead, when Donders had neglected such presence up to then. Perhaps it is that calling of people to profound contemplation upon mortality and attention to presence that impresses others as a sign of a truly wise person. But at the same time, there can be frustration among those who philosophize—is there a heaven or not? What does it mean to say heaven is here and the dead are here, in the wind, along with God? What does it mean to say that God is not a person but a concept, a useful one that has a presence everywhere?

Wairimu Gichohi wrote her Master's thesis on African philosophy at the University of Nairobi, and in it she grappled with these contradictions apparent in the sage's testimony. She said there was a contradiction involved in Rang'inya's saying that God is a concept, and yet God is in the wind. (Gichohi 1996: 93) Gichohi is looking for critical rationality, not mystical moments, in the shared insights of the sages.[2]

Later in the present book we shall see that Oruka was attracted to arguments by his teacher Ingemar Hedenius that attacked belief in God as irrational. Oruka read Voltaire while at university in Uppsala studying science. (Oruka 1997: 281) It was soon afterward that he took up philosophy studies there. But we see in his own father a precursor to these skeptical ideas regarding religion. On the other hand, Oruka's own position is more agnostic than atheist, and he surprises everyone during his expert witness testimony at the S.M. Otieno trial when he suggests that he may believe in "spirits." (Oruka 1991b: 77–78) An intuition that we are not alone, that we share this world with beings and forces we only obliquely comprehend, is paired with a distaste for the neat and comfortable dogmas of imported organized religions like Christianity. But it's important to note that Oruka gave this testimony in February of 1987. Back in 1983, David Felder, his friend from graduate school at Wayne State University, reunited with Oruka at the World Congress of Philosophy in Montreal. Felder remembers Oruka telling him that his father, who had passed away, returned to Oruka to give him a message on how to divide the family estate. And so, it is with some first-hand experience that Oruka, albeit indirectly, insists that an educated, "modern" world-traveling man can nevertheless believe in spirits.[3]

God and religion were not the only topics of the interview with Oruka Rang'inya. One can't help but notice that Oruka asked his father's opinion on a range of questions which Oruka himself had already addressed in philosophy papers and books. He asks his father about the concept of punishment, about which Oruka wrote a Master's thesis and a book. Rang'inya shares traditional ways of dealing with murder or theft, which usually involve shunning or compensation. The Luo community usually disapproved of capital punishment. In this way father and son find common moral ground. But contrary to the son, the father argued that the modern system of punishment was more just than the old system, since in the old system a whole family suffered when one family member had done some wrong. (Oruka 1991b: 124) In all topics tackled, Rang'inya had a personal opinion which he clearly expressed, often in contrast to the popular opinions of his own community. Perhaps it is the example of his own father, and not training in Western philosophy, that encouraged Oruka to emphasize the ability to distinguish one's own views from the prevailing opinions as a mark of philosophical wisdom and acumen.

Rang'inya asserted that, with regard to race and ethnicity, all humans are equal, and he defended the position in a way that might seem surprising for one so concerned with upholding Luo values and traditions. Rang'inya argued that Luos were arrogant and thought themselves better than others, and that such a prideful attitude was a character defect. (Oruka 1991b: 125) However, Rang'inya insists that men in general have superior intellects to women, since men are ruled by their heads while women follow their hearts, although he admits exceptions to this rule. (Oruka 1991b: 121) Oruka also brought up the concept of "freedom" (in Dhuluo, "fuyanga" or "thuolo")–this was related to the topic of his graduate thesis at Uppsala. Rang'inya gives several concrete examples of what makes someone free according to the Luo context: if they have many sons, so that they are secure from attack; if they work as farmers and their granary is filled so that they can eat and feed others; and if they are well-behaved and show respect to others. (Oruka1991b: 122–23) The emphasis on feeding others is notable in a culture that often suffers crop failures and must survive by sharing food. Rang'inya was able to list quite a few famines that had visited the Luo community. He observed, however, that times had changed, and the communal practice of giving food to others in need was no longer quite relevant because the government had taken over planning and the control of wealth. (Oruka 1991b: 118–19, 121)

While it's not mentioned in the interview included in *Sage Philosophy*, Oruka mentions in the preface to his 1992 book on Jaramogi Oginga Odinga, that his father and Oginga Odinga were close friends and collaborators during the 1940s and 1950s, and due to this, he had first met Oginga Odinga during his childhood. Both men had been founders of the Luo Thrift and Trading Corporation which was founded in 1947, when Oruka was a child. Oruka reminisced about the time he first remembers seeing Oginga Odinga:

> I had seen Oginga Odinga for the first time in 1956 when he visited my
> father at home in Ugenya, Siaya, to solicit my father's influential support
> for his campaign to be elected to the Legislative Council. Odinga had
> arrived in a Land-Rover with one other person and my father had
> welcomed them warmly with the words: '*Wuon Odinga, en mana in.
> Machiegni*' (The son of Odinga, it is really you. Welcome).
>
> Oruka 1992: vii

Why does he focus on the details of this greeting? Surely, this is partly the
vivid memory of childhood. One can still witness in some rural areas of
Kenya the delight of children as a rare Land Rover appears with visitors. But
it is also important for Oruka to explain himself as someone whose household
had personal and longstanding connections to Oginga Odinga. As Cohen
and Odhiambo explain, in Siaya, "You do not in an important sense exist until
you reveal your networks … Identity then is the composition of oneself by
others in a constellation." (Cohen and Atieno Odhiambo 1987: 272) Since
David Parkin noted that Luos in the 1950s had divided loyalties to the
leadership ideas of either Tom Mboya or Oginga Odinga, it is important to
know on which side of this divide Odera Oruka and his family were on.
(Parkin 1978: 219, 222, 239, 278) As Parkin explained, "Odinga ostensibly
stood for the collective defence of the Luo community through both
corporate radical thought and Luo conservatism. Mboya represented
Western-style meritocracy through the transcension of ethnic conservatism
and through individual achievement." (Parkin 1978: 222)[4]

As Cohen and Atieno Odhiambo explain, it was during the 1960s that
Luo identity was debated in association meetings and football clubs, as well
as at branch meetings of the Luo Union. It wasn't just idle, abstract thought.
Issues of identity were connected to legal rights and material concerns. In the
Oginga Odinga camp of radical politics and cultural conservatism, the book
by Paul Mbuya Akoko, *Luo Kitgi gi Timbegi*, defined Luo core values and was
treated as a "canonization of the asserted culture and behavior of this new
nation" and "became part of the regimen for cultural education in the primary
and intermediate schools throughout the 1950s." (Cohen and Atieno
Odhiambo 1987: 278) No doubt Odera Oruka was exposed to this text and
these debates during his childhood. That he still holds such issues as Luo
values and traditions dear is apparent in his including the interview of Paul
Mbuya Akoko in *Sage Philosophy* (both editions). The Kenyan edition of *Sage
Philosophy* has Paul Mbuya's photo on the front cover.

There are some interesting parallels between the themes and positions
that Paul Mbuya Akoko takes during his interview, and the positions
articulated by Oruka's father. For example, Mbuya gives two concrete

examples of a secular, psychological, or demythologized version of events that were popularly thought to be miraculous or the sign of spirits at work. For example, some thought that a jajuok ("night runner") could kill people merely by making a threat. Mbuya asserts that in these cases it was fear that people allowed themselves to feel that was the cause of their death, not the power of the night runner him or herself. Also, there was a famous Luo hero named Gor who people thought could change himself into a goat or a dog to be undetected by his enemies. Mbuya insists that Gor was indeed clever, but rather than actually change himself into these animals, he was successful due to his disguises. (Oruka 1991b: 138–39; 159n13)

Paul Mbuya also commented upon how education through consultation with the wisest men and women elders is being more and more sidelined, in favor of formal schooling. A sign of wisdom is the ability to heed useful advice. Paul Mbuya (in contrast to Rang'inya's insistence on male intellectual superiority) suggests that women who come to him for advice are wiser than men, because they are more able to follow his advice. Despite their superior wisdom, Paul Mbuya nevertheless thinks that women are behind men regarding their formal education and political and social status. But he speculates that in the privacy of their homes, many women may express their abilities and assert their positions more fully. (Oruka 1991b: 138–40)

While Odera Oruka and his family were certainly in the thick of discussions and debates over Luo identity and values, Odera Oruka nevertheless places his family as close to and influenced by neighboring Luhyia concepts and terminologies. For example he notes that during the interview his father discusses freedom by using the word *fuyanga*, which has Luhyia influence, whereas for the same concept, Mbuya would use the term *thuolo*. (Oruka 1991b: 143, 159–60n14)

In *Sage Philosophy* Paul Mbuya is asked about "the old Luo idea of communalism." (Oruka 1991b: 140) Having been introduced in that way, it is no surprise that the discussion centers on how the old practices have been eroding under "the importation of foreign ideas and the process of modernization." (Oruka 1991b: 141) The communal tradition, Paul Mbuya explains, involved ensuring that everyone had enough to eat. For large expensive projects such as marriage, everyone would give a little something to enable it to happen. People would be happier when they shared their food and drink with others. Now the notions of happiness have changed, and selfish individuals find happiness in exclusive material possessions. While the tradition allowed differences in wealth, it did not allow destitution to exist. (Oruka 1991b: 140–42)

John Lonsdale comments upon Oruka's sages, noting that both Paul Mbuya Akoko and Oruka Rang'inya think that wealth is a requirement for freedom. To be able to feed others is freedom, while to depend upon others for food is unfreedom. Lonsdale calls this "plutocratic freedom," since, by being productive oneself and managing a large household, one proves one's fitness to rule others. This is a position that Jomo Kenyatta also held, according to Lonsdale. (2003: 49) It should be noted, however, that Paul Mbuya noted himself that even a rich person is dependent on the cooperation of others. For example, a rich person needs the cooperation of workers. (Oruka 1991b: 144)

This topic leads me to share an interview conducted by myself and Oruka of Nyando Ayoo of Sega, a sage whom Oruka fondly remembered listening to during childhood. I received some insight into Oruka's persistent emphasis on a philosophy concerned with correcting social inequalities and protecting the vulnerable in the world community while visiting his home area with him in 1995 and meeting Ayoo. The wise sages in his community influenced Oruka to emphasize first meeting basic survival needs then dispelling misconceptions and narrow-mindedness to open one's heart before philosophizing.

Ayoo, whom Oruka held in highest esteem for many years, was a 92-year-old man at the time we interviewed him in 1995.[5] He explained to us his philosophy of helping others. As a young man, Ayoo committed himself to the project of giving weary travelers going the many miles on foot between Kampala and Kisumu the food and drink they needed. When he first realized their need, he began carrying a pot of water with a calabash as a ladle to give drink to the thirsty as they went by. In time he built a hotel, where he gave food and drink to all who needed it, regardless of their ability to pay.[6] The town of Sega sprung up around him. In the interview Ayoo used the language of prophecy when he insisted that it was "God's admonition" which told him to start his hotel in Sega. But he also acknowledged his father's example, for his father had assisted many people during a particularly harsh famine in Kenya.[7] Starving people had flocked to his father's house. As Ayoo described,

> … Some were just lying on the floors, others in the open in the middle of the homestead. Porridge of thing' [residue sieved from a local brew made of maize or millet flour] would be prepared for them. They were also fed on milk and cooked blood got from the cattle. And that enabled them to regain strength and preserved their lives. When I saw that, I realized that helping is good.
>
> Ayoo 1995

Ayoo was someone who had reflected on the philosophical implications of his beliefs and actions.

... Indeed there were great sufferings. Living was hard those days. People used to walk without clothes. But patience and persevering are what make one acquire something. Through calm spirit [*chuny mang'ich*] one acquires something. But [impatient] restless spirit [*chuny maliet*] is not good. Humility brings wealth ... The spirit of meanness and jealousy is [brings] poverty.

Ayoo 1995

For Ayoo to think so shows that he could distinguish his own views from those prevailing in his community. Most persons in his society thought he was crazy to give to all who needed. While he was starting his hotel, men from the area would castigate and humiliate him, even beat him, and suggest to him that he was taking on a woman's role of feeding people. Commenting on the young generation who were in Sega in 1995, Ayoo was concerned that the youth just liked "laughing at others" who suffer and fail, rather than helping them. However, he still saw his role as advising everyone on how things *should be*. Ayoo confided his frustrations with the youth to Oruka and me because the youth considered him a foolish person and wouldn't listen to him.

Oruka remarked that he thought Ayoo kept his calm spirit (avoiding *tamaa* or greedy spirit, as it is said in Kiswahili) because he avoided being drawn into the insidious competition for material goods. Where Ayoo spoke of the importance of spiritual wealth, Oruka commented with special emphasis, "That is philosophy he is saying!" In this way, Ayoo was a fellow traveler and role model for Oruka's conviction that consumerism leads to destruction of the planet as well as our moral sensibilities. He also noted that Ayoo had a "heart" [spirit] of development and love that many Luo used to have, but now seems to be "getting finished." Oruka laments about the youth, "They don't see him as an attractive alternative." Ayoo's wife Dorka even mentions that she and other wives don't have Ayoo's "heart" because he was of an older generation. On the other hand, she insists that because she is in a family sharing resources with Ayoo, his acts of generosity are actually the generosity of the entire family.

I think, however, that it is clear that Oruka had taken it upon himself to continue that "heart" and apply it in academia and in the world politics of today. Oruka did not arrive in graduate school in Sweden or the United States completely innocent of philosophy (in the broad sense) and then become a philosopher when he became "Westernized" in his thoughts, as some critics have charged Oruka and others in their critical descriptions of professional African philosophers. Oruka rejected that characterization when he first described professional philosophers in his "Four Trends in Current African Philosophy." There he explained that, among other things, cultural background could "cause disparity in philosophical priority and methodology. . . ." (Oruka 1990b: 13–22) As Ulrich Lölke puts it, "Oruka is not claiming to support a specific 'African' concept of justice, but rather one which is very much related to his 'African experience' and which deals with a perspective from the periphery." (Lölke 1997: 224)

In Oruka's case, we can see that his choice of focus on filling people's basic needs and freeing them from exploitation and political oppression was a reflection of a priority shaped by his experience in Kenya and particularly the Luo cultural value of a "heart" of development and love.

I contend that Oruka saw certain trends develop in his home community in Nyanza Province, Kenya, that troubled him. While he was duly impressed in the days of his youth by people who cared for each other and gave when it was needed, he and others witnessed the erosion of these values, and that was of great concern to him. I had the opportunity to interview several Luo elders with the help of Humphrey Ojwang of the Institute of African Studies, University of Nairobi. Filida Okaya (aged ninety when we interviewed her in 1999) and her grandson George Opiyo explain in this interview what life was like during her youth and what it is like now.[8]

> **Okaya**   During our days business was really good. I think it was graced by God, and we operate on trust for each other. We never broke any business agreements or business conducts like overcharging to reap more profits or cheating in our transactions. I was honest in my dealings, and people came to trust me, and one who is trustworthy can be a great friend . . . .
>
> **Opiyo**   And I would vouch that when we were young people ourselves, I would see people come home here to ask her for water. We've always lived next to a road, and a traveler would come here and say, 'Hey, give me some water.' She always had a very big pot of *ugali* [a porridge made of millet], and instead of water she'd give them porridge, and even that didn't matter to her whether you're from this place, whether you're a fellow tribesman . . . as long as you're in need, she dealt with that problem by providing for it . . . .
>
> **Okaya**   It pleased me, and in those days food was plentiful. My old man had many things; he was rich.
>
> **Presbey**   Is it optional, or would you feel that you're doing something wrong if you didn't give them something?
>
> **Okaya**   That would be a big mistake. My conscience would be troubled.

Opiyo Actually my grandfather never ate in the house except maybe in the evening like now. But all his breakfast, all his lunch, they were outside there, and as he was eating, he'd be checking on passers-by, then say, "Hey, you who's passing, come. . . !"

Okaya Yes! Yes!

Opiyo: ". . . come and eat." And you know you could be called for something that's almost over but he felt so that all along until he died in 1991, that was something he did with pleasure. So it's like they were one in this and she doesn't just feed like you give out of plenty. It was not a question of plenty because when our grandfather would be calling somebody to come and share what he had, it was not because it was much. There were times when she could cut sugarcane and give our grandfather to sell by the roadside so that she could get some money and use for something, but he'd freely give it out and say, "Yes, tomorrow they may come back and give us something." It didn't matter much whether he was giving in return for nothing, "Give," that was the motivation.

Okaya If I fail to give somebody what [he or she] needs, I feel very bad, it's an offence . . . even if it's salt that has been requested from me and I don't have it, I would go to another person who has it, then I'll give the person in need so that [his or her] need is satisfied so that I feel satisfied, too.

Okaya 1999

This was life among the Luo in Nyanza Province, and probably to a great extent across Kenya, during the generation of the present grandparents. But what has become of these traditions of sharing? According to Paulina Otieno, a grandmother herself, the spirit of sharing has been replaced by jealousy, as she explains.

In the past people were kinder as compared to today. These days, jealousy has taken the center stage. So much so that your own brother wouldn't like you to possess anything. He'd want everything for himself and none for you and could even go to the extent of harming you. They even shared food and ate together; they did virtually everything together. . . . And people shared their meals so that toward sunset people would bring together whatever has been cooked from each house: vegetables, fish, potatoes, etc., and people enjoyed the meals, but today this is non-existent. In the olden days people were very united. Times have become so hard in today's life and it's difficult to come by the basic needs;

everyone is struggling to feed their families, and they don't have any extra for another member of another family.

In the olden days life was easy; you could milk cows in the evening; you kept [the milk] in a big gourd in the *abila* [a hut at the middle of a homestead meant for sheep and goats, sometimes used as a resting place for the homeowner], and in the evening people took the milk with cold millet *ugali*, and people were very healthy, very fat; all these are no longer existing.

Life these days is not as it used to be. Take an example: orphans. They used to be properly looked after, but no one cares for orphans today. It's life's hurdles that have brought jealousy. Somebody would not be happy with your achievements. They would be happy seeing your family suffer, and they'd be happy to give your wife an already used soap lather to wash her clothes in because she doesn't have soap and the jealous fellow women rejoice in her deprivation.... People lack money to buy basic needs and they become jealous if a neighbor has something little. That's the most common case of jealousy. They'd only wish you perpetual suffering.

It is a vice in the society. It should be discouraged. Take an example: if a person dies in the neighborhood others would say, "God, that serves him well, he was such a show-off." They would express no sorrow; they rejoice because you're dead, because they are jealous. People should be kind to each other; those who are lucky in life should reach out for the unfortunate.... Jealous members of the family could go to an extent of pretending friendship with you but are only looking for a way to end your life. Jealousy will never end because you cannot inject it with medicine so that it's gotten rid of from the society. It's here to stay.

Otieno 1998

Paulina Otieno here suggests that the sources of jealousy lie deep within the society. Otieno's comments about jealousy and the lack of compassion raise questions on the nature of compassion. Martha Nussbaum notes that many modern philosophical theories considered compassion to be an irrational force with a tendency to mislead or distract us from justice. However, Nussbaum claims that compassion is not just an emotion; rather, it is a kind of "thought about the well-being of others," meaning that compassion is a kind of reasoning. Referring first to Aristotle's notion of "pity," she notes that he says it is based on three beliefs: first, that the suffering is serious and not trivial; second, that the suffering was not primarily caused by actions of the one who is suffering; and third, that the one who pities has roughly the same possibilities in life as the one whom he or she is now pitying. In order for us to experience compassion for others, we need awareness of our own vulnerability; otherwise, our judgments will be harsh. (Nussbaum 1996: esp. 28, 31)

This last point is also expanded upon by Nancy Snow in her article on compassion. In compassion we realize that the other person suffering misfortune is vulnerable in a way that we too could be. The person does not have to be completely innocent of what has befallen them, but their weakness becomes understandable to us. But Snow cautions that "noticing the fact of another's weakness and its role in occasioning his or her plight is compatible with a variety of responses other than compassion, such as morbid curiosity, pity, or malicious enjoyment." (Snow 1991: 195–205, 199) Otieno's examples demonstrate this latter response.

Oruka warned against responding to others' plight with indifference or harsh judgment. Instead, he advocated compassion, even if he did not always call it so in so many words. In an article in the *Sunday Nation*, he warned of the trend when he noted, "It is obvious that many drivers treat road accidents as if they are meant for the cursed and the unfortunate. So they may witness a road accident and pass by without offering help and they may even accelerate while doing so." He noticed callous indifference to those suffering from AIDS: "Many people treat AIDS as a disease meant for some given tribes and not for the majority of Kenyans. . . ." He also showed concern about the street children and "parking boys" who were neglected by Kenyans in the 1990s. Such attitudes he considered to be "displaying such gross ignorance, as well as lack of patriotism and concern for the welfare of others." (Oruka 1994a: 7)

For Oruka, compassion should naturally lead not only to individual and philanthropic acts of compassion but also to institutional and policy change. This is a point agreed upon by Nussbaum. She argues that compassion should inform the structures of public institutions and that moral and civic education should nurture people's abilities to imagine the suffering of others across the boundaries of nation, race, and gender. (Nussbaum 1996: 50, 56) Individual acts of charity are a good start but not enough, for one who feels compassion for the poor, realizing his or her plight might be theirs, must then ask the further question about "the structure of society's allocation of goods and resources." (Nussbaum 1996: 36) As she explains, ". . . there are ways of arranging the world so as to bring these good things more securely within people's grasp; and acknowledging our deep need for them provides a strong incentive for so designing things." (Nussbaum 1996: 45) I therefore see Nussbaum and Oruka in agreement on this issue.

Oruka is also interested in searching for the source of the changes in Luo society. It is not just a local change; the whole world is changing, following philosophical and economic trends that encourage self-centeredness, stinginess, and a neglect of those in need. What are the sources of those changes? David Obuola Nyandiga has this to say about the changes that have come to Luo society:

Nyandiga   Councils of elders are very rare. I think they are not there. Councils of elders were effective in the past because the population was very small, and so it was easy to integrate harmoniously. Today there is a population explosion, and very divergent ideas have emerged so that it becomes impossible to bring such divergent ideas to see sense in a common issue.

There are also external influences which have swayed many to believe that "modern is good, and traditional is ugly." This has completely wiped out the council of elders.... The external influences and the money economy. Everyone, including children today, are in a struggle to get money so much so that no one sits to think of collective societal problems because everyone is assured that a problem belongs to an individual, not society. So this has bred individualism in society.

Children easily acquire negative behaviors of stealing money, and because people have become dishonest, the child would hand over the stolen money to an adult, who will pocket it and then deny any knowledge of stolen money. This creates division in the society.

Presbey   If there are all these new problems brought about by the money economy, why don't the councils of elders meet even more to resolve these problems? ...

Nyandiga   ... Even getting these elders together for a meeting is a big problem since everyone is involved in a struggle for survival, and it becomes almost impossible for one to abandon his work to attend to communal problems. In the past the societal cohesion that enabled one to dedicate all his time to solve societal problems has been replaced by harsh individualism where one only wants things for one's own survival, not communal survival. This is the source of the change in Luo society.
Nyandiga 1998

So changes in Luo society are caught up with larger trends of individualism and the added influence of the role of money. Economic trends have made it harder to practice compassion and caring and to overcome jealousy. These are the same trends that Paul Mbuya Akoko commented upon in his interview for the Sage Philosophy Project. Since Mbuya Akoko died in 1981 (with the photograph included in the interview having been taken in 1974), clearly these problems had been developing in Nyanza for quite some time.

Oruka was worried that large differences in economic status between persons were bringing about a difference in how they were treated. Now the poor could not be guaranteed their basic rights, and the rich were getting more than their fair share. In an article he published in a Kenyan newspaper, Oruka gave the following example of a situation routinely tolerated, when it should not be tolerated at all:

> Take rudeness in office, and disservice to strangers and to "small" people as examples. . . . A "small person" travels all the way from Kitui to Nairobi to receive his PIN. He wanders around at the Income Tax offices for two days without getting any help. In the end, he is told to come back the following month when the relevant person will be available.
>
> On the other hand, an apparently wealthy man takes a public bus from Nairobi to Kisumu. On arrival, the driver takes the man to his residence while all the others are dropped off at the bus station. The other passengers protest and demand the same treatment, but the bus driver refuses to oblige.
>
> Oruka 1994c: 7

Some are denied the basic help to which they are entitled. Others are given extra special help. Such circumstances cannot help but to encourage bitterness and jealousy. Social trends encourage or discourage the development and practice of virtues. Kenyan society, like so many societies around the world, is struggling with the vices and social disharmony that follows in the wake of increasing economic disparity.

When one is engaging in oral interviews, one has to take into account that one's interlocutors might have their own special way of remembering the past. The tricks of memory are not limited to Kenyans; they affect many people when they are asked to remember the past. Many of the elderly interviewed could remember a past time when all had enough to eat, and current problems had not yet arisen. Textbooks on historical method would refer to this backward-looking distortion as "nostalgia." John Tosh explains "generational regret," a common form of nostalgia: "older people habitually complain that nowadays the young are unruly, or that the country is 'going to the dogs', and the same complaints have been documented over a very long period." Raphael Samuel describes the "selective amnesia" at work when we remember the past as a place of "primal bliss" or "enchanted" childhood. (Tosh 2015: 17, 19)

And yet oral historians have done careful studies to understand ways in which earlier food abundance has turned into more recent scarcity. David William Cohen and E. S. Atieno Odhiambo did an in-depth study of Siaya, a county of Nyanza Province that includes Ugenya as a constituency within its borders. (Cohen and Atieno Odhiambo 1989) According to them, memories of a past abundance in relation to current poverty are accurate. They note that European travelers to the Lake Victoria region in the 1870s[9] first witnessed abundant food and self-sufficiency. Any poor areas were attributed to the ravages of the slave trade. While there had been occasional shortfalls of production, there would be markets in times of crisis that would soften the effects of the crisis. Markets were especially located on the interzonal meeting points of drier and moister lands. The markets were managed by members of the dominant lineage of the area.

So how can we explain the transition from abundance to poverty? The authors suggest that it is due to a switch from a subsistence economy to commercial markets. Prior to 1880, each household produced for itself, with some goods to exchange in the Lake Victoria region. But the colonial period brought new tensions: it turned production to the generation of surpluses for colonial and world markets (which would make Britain rich), and it taxed Kenyans to generate cash income to support the local colonial establishment. While historian Bethwell Ogot noted that farmers in Nyanza embraced new crops such as cotton, groundnuts and simsim, and became avid exporters by 1913, making use of the new train station and railroad service at Nyanza, he also noted that forced labor on public works and taxation strained Luo families. Cohen and Atieno Odhiambo noted that Kenyans used their little surplus to buy market goods manufactured in Britain. Through introduction of new tastes, taxes, seizures, forced labor, and quotas of production set for local headmen, Kenyans became impoverished. While colonialists sought to break the habit of subsistence farming, the balance of nature was being disturbed by overplanting, underfallowing, soil erosion, and decimation of forests. Families were exposed to the uncertainties of the markets for cotton, groundnuts, cloves, sugar, sisal, and vegetable oil. When prices went down, the first response was to invest more resources and expand production, but this can lead to environmental deterioration. Combined with labor drain from rural areas, these shifts in production undermined African rural areas' self-sustainability in food. (Cohen and Atieno Odhiambo 1989: 71, 73)

There were struggles over colonial coercion and regulations, exploitative markets, and changes in household production. African producers created forms of overt and covert resistance to the State's plans for extraction of surplus. Some refused to grow cash crops, but some made peace with the colonial state. Some left rural areas to get jobs in the cities; when they came back to the rural areas, they opened their own businesses: shops, bars, hotels, and houses for rental. Due to these businesses the countryside no longer looks like it had. Yet people have little money and there are few sales.

Bethwell Ogot explains that during the decades of British colonial rule of Nyanza when Kenya was declared a Crown Colony, the people in Nyanza organized themselves to fight for their rights. Two religious movements fought against "Westernism" and colonization. John Owalo established his Nomia Luo Mission in 1910, where he set up schools that would be alternatives to missionary education. In 1913 the cult of Mumbo advocated rejecting all things European. During the First World War 165,000 Luos aided Britain in the war effort, mostly as porters; 50,000 of these died. Those who came back had a wider perspective and different views of the British—they saw their weaknesses and were suspicious of their claims to moral superiority. As happened in many places in the colonies, rather than reward loyal soldiers, veterans were neglected as harsh colonial policies were enforced. Ogot mentions that "The Young Kavirondo Association, a political pressure group, was formed in 1921 under the leadership of Jonathan Okwiri, Benjamin Owuor and Simeon Nyende – all 'Mission Boys'." (Ogot 1963: 261) Having been educated formally by the missionaries, they used their skills to challenge colonial government practices. Due to their efforts, taxes were reduced, and forced labor for public works that included women and children was finally abolished in 1922. Archdeacon Walter Edwin Owen, an Anglican missionary, was a champion of social justice, and helped to form the Kavirondo Taxpayers Welfare Association, known as Piny Owacho or "Voice of the People." The group engaged in politics and self-help projects. After the Second World War, The Luo Union was formed, and Oginga Odinga was elected the first Ker or leader of that group. Kenyans began insisting on having a political role. In 1957 the first African direct election was held, and Oginga Odinga won that election, and held a seat in the Legislative Council. (Ogot 1963: 256–71) That was the election that Oruka referred to in his book on Oginga Odinga, when he mentioned that he first met Odinga in 1956 during the election campaign. (Oruka 1992: vii) Oruka would have been twelve years old at the time. This history of Nyanza helps us to understand the intersections of the movement for independence from Britain with Oruka's family life and his own direct experience. The Luo community was ever-vigilant against injustice and cultural imperialism.

Without recapping the entire struggle for independence, with its extreme sacrifices, struggles, and heroes, we can see nevertheless that problems still plagued the newly independent country. In their study of contemporary Siaya District, Cohen and Atieno Odhiambo note that Siaya is not an ecological disaster zone, yet there is hunger. Every year, some people will be hungry for weeks or months. In two out of every seven years, there will be drought which increases hunger. The presence of hunger shows that national and international forces impact food available to households. These forces transform the relations between household members into money exchange relations, affecting gender relations and the physical and mental health of children.

Why is there seasonal hunger? Grain supplies get finished before the next harvest. Too much grain is sold as "excess" for cash earlier in the year. Grain may be sold in a season of abundance when prices are low. Later, during periods of scarcity, prices are high. There is no speculation in grain in Siaya that would encourage people to buy up grain when it is cheap and hold onto it, or to import grain during scarcity. Instead, the practice is to unload risks by selling stock as soon as possible. The common response to repeated episodes of hunger in Siaya is to live through the periods, with visible weight loss and debilitation, and wait for things to get better. (Cohen and Atieno Odhiambo, 1989: 62–63)

The Ministry of Agriculture operates grain boards which severely limit the movement of grain. Cohen and Atieno Odhiambo note that excess grain could rot in the fields of Kakamega while Siaya experiences shortfalls because maize traders are not given permits to transport grain from nearby Bungoma to Siaya. The authors note the irony in claiming that "maize means hunger." Maize meal was first considered white man's food. The colonial authorities demanded that it be grown. It was considered to be a status food because white people ate it. Yet it was light, less nutritious, and less durable compared to sorghum and millet. While switching to maize cultivation was supposed to be "progress," it damaged the environment. The phrase "gorogoro economy" refers to the container in which maize meal is measured. The price stays the same, but the gorogoro has gotten smaller. The phrase is symbolic of how it is harder for rural families to live than it was before the rise of a commercial economy. Meals used to be feasts and were considered social occasions; now they are rations, eaten privately. (Cohen and Atieno Odhiambo, 1989: 64–65, 67)

As in Nyando Ayoo's recollections of his father, a long time ago people in Siaya would help each other during times of famine. Sometimes this help happened under the cloak of darkness. In his autobiography, *Not Yet Uhuru*, Oginga Odinga wrote about childhood memories of Omuodo Alongo's action during the *Kanga* famine of 1918–1919. Omuodo "would fetch me late every night and take me from granary to granary to examine the food stocks. When we found a granary with little left in it he would direct me to a granary which had plenty, and we would replenish the almost-exhausted store. When I asked why he did this, he said we should be kind to those who had nothing. Women with many children had greater need, and to prevent argument over food shares, he thought it best to arrange a redistribution himself, by night." (Odinga 1969: 62–63)

This is the broad context in which Oruka grew up and from which he would then go to Sweden, a country which was known for having tackled the problems of poverty, shortage, and wealth distribution. No wonder that the contrast between the land he came from—a place that once had a robust, if informal, distribution system but later, through colonial dismantling of the old system, found itself socially and institutionally unable to address the growing poverty problem completely—and the land to which he was going, Sweden, would provide him with food for thought that would become a major theme of his philosophical writings.

Part Two

Early Developments as a Philosopher

2

Undergraduate Studies with Ingemar Hedenius

Oruka went to Uppsala University in Sweden to study for his bachelor's degree. He had seen an advertisement in the Kenyan newspapers that scholarships were available for students to study the sciences. Originally having come to Sweden on a scholarship funded by the Swedish International Development Cooperation Agency to study Earth Sciences (geography, geology, and agriculture) in a special course of study designed for English-speakers,[1] he changed his emphasis and studied philosophy under his mentor, Ingemar Hedenius. In Oruka's autobiographical essay "My Strange Way to Philosophy," he explains that Hedenius played an important role in his formation as a philosopher (Oruka 1997: 283). Hedenius oversaw the practical philosophy track of a two-track department. As Bertil Stromberg, Associate Professor of Practical Philosophy at Umea University and a graduate student in Uppsala's program around the same time as Henry Odera, explains, "'Practical philosophy' is in Sweden a label for that area of philosophy which has moral philosophy as its main subject, but which also includes theory of action, game and decision theory, political philosophy, philosophy of religion, and philosophical aesthetics. This is in distinction to what we call 'theoretical philosophy,' with subjects such as general theory of knowledge, metaphysics, philosophy of mind, logic, and philosophy of language." (Stromberg n.d.) The division of philosophical studies into two categories harkens back to Aristotle's distinction between *phronesis* and *sophia,* practical and theoretical wisdom. For Hedenius, the emphasis was on "practical." He wanted to have an influence on his nation and the world. Oruka has his own way of describing what it meant to focus on practical philosophy at Uppsala. He said philosophy "is 'practical' when philosophical concepts and principles are not discussed just for their own theoretical interest, but are discussed and applied to the understanding and improvement of the conditions of human life." (Oruka 1990c: 128)

In correspondence about Oruka's early years in Uppsala, Ann-Mari Henschen-Dahlquist wrote the following:

Hedenius was the incomparably most important of Henry's teachers. . . .
As a young student, Henry came to Uppsala in order to study geology

and meteorology. He knew that Kenya was in great need of people with such education.... But while engaged with them he understood that philosophy was his great interest, and that's why he followed the lectures given by Professor Konrad Marc-Wogau and Ingemar Hedenius. Professor Hedenius was impressed by his strong interest in philosophical questions.... I know that Professor Hedenius had a high estimation of Henry Odera as a very gifted and very noble young man, whom it was important to help so that he could advance to a position where he could display his qualities and accomplish his 'mission.'

Personal communication, Ann-Mari Henschen-Dahlquist to
Gail Presbey, July 17, 2007

She added the following clarification: "I must stress that Marc-Wogau did not have at all the same role as Hedenius in the life of Henry Odera. Marc-Wogau was only his teacher in the elementary studies. Hedenius was also his teacher on the higher level, and he was furthermore Henry's near friend." (Pers. comm., Henschen-Dahlquist to Presbey, 17 July 2007) Since the regular philosophy courses were in Swedish (the science courses he had been taking were in English), Hedenius tutored him individually in English.

In his autobiographical essay, Oruka explains that his first degree from Uppsala was a bachelor of science in the program of the Faculty of Mathematics and Natural Sciences. Although he was on a scholarship, it must have been a scanty one, considering that he worked at a factory while studying. He said that during one of the summers when he went in search of work, he lived in a "wrecked boat resting like a lame duck in one of the gulfs of the Baltic Sea.... There were many people using the ship as a residence, and we did not pay rent." (Oruka 1997: 283) He said that he discovered his interest in philosophy, and more particularly, his conviction that empiricism is the best way to truth, prior to any formal philosophy studies, while working at a paper factory in Sandivicken, Sweden, during which time he had come to the personal insight that there is no knowledge without experience. He muses, "I thought I had a great discovery that I must write down for the world to know before I died. Later, having gone a little deeper into philosophy, I was happy, yet disappointed, to learn that my so-called discovery was a well-known theory associated with British Empiricism." (Oruka 1997: 283)

According to Oruka's personal anecdote, he discovered empiricism on his own. But I want to suggest that there is importance to the point that Oruka had this insight while in a Swedish factory. Perhaps he had imbibed some of the folk philosophy of the area, and was influenced by it. Carl-Göran Heidegren says that as early as the 1870s, even before the influence of Austrian-based logical positivism, there was a certain style or *habitus* of

Nordic thought, and he boils it down to six basic convictions about philosophy and how to philosophize. Philosophy must have its foundation in experience. Philosophy should be based on inductive logic and experimental method, not a priori concepts. Metaphysics should follow or complete empirical knowledge, not be the starting point of philosophizing. Philosophy should have limited research questions rather than search for an all-inclusive system. There is little or no significant difference between philosophy and the special sciences. And philosophy should result in common property for all based on compelling logical arguments, not privileged wisdom for the few (Heidegren 2010).

Oruka wrote in one of his articles that the Swedes did not study the folk philosophies of the Vikings and Visigoths. Rather, they drew upon the ancient Greeks, who had established the scientific method.

It was while reading the Copleston-Russell debate on the existence of God that Oruka said he resolved to study philosophy (Copleston and Russell 1948). He notes that his "longstanding" Swedish friend Tommie Zaine, who received his PhD in aesthetics at Uppsala and was "a great source of books and information," especially in literature, encouraged him to sign up for philosophy studies (Oruka 1997: 282).

Zaine described their meeting and early studies:

When we first met on Friday night 30th of July 1965 he had just arrived in Sweden and was then attending some courses in Agriculture, and I, on my part, was doing evening classes on college-level to be able to enter the University of Uppsala. On that Friday night we randomly met at a students' club ("nation" it is called in Swedish) and found that we were both interested in Literature, and that was what brought us together. When I, a couple of years later, was able to study at the University, I told Henry that I would start with Philosophy, and he joined me there also to read Philosophy. Since the lectures and seminars were held in Swedish (and he spoke very little Swedish) he could not attend the ordinary courses. Prof. Hedenius however designed a special course for Henry with different literature from what I read, and Henry was soon far above me in the subject.

Pers. comm., Tommie Zaine to Gail Presbey, March 10, 2011

Oruka added philosophy as an optional fourth course, and he graduated a year ahead of the rest of his class. When he decided to pursue philosophy and drop the sciences, "I paid the price of losing my scholarship since this 'crazy' philosophy option disappointed my scholarship donors. But the good impression I had made at the Institute of Philosophy helped me to survive." (Oruka 1997: 281) He mentions reading Tolstoy and Voltaire. Certainly his mentor Hedenius was quite famous not only for his works on the Empiricists, an approach that Oruka admired, but also as a famous atheist. On this issue, there is evidence that Oruka still was a believer, but he enjoyed the debate and held his own views with a skepticism characteristic of a philosopher, not a simple believer. Oruka mentions reading Hume's *Dialogues Concerning Natural Religion* and Russell's *Why I Am Not a Christian* early on in his philosophy studies (Oruka 1997: 283).

In an article first published in 1987 and then incorporated into *Sage Philosophy* in 1990, Oruka explains that during his university years he learned nothing of African philosophy. Both at Uppsala and at Wayne State University, analytic philosophy was the dominant influence, and he had only briefly gotten to study Marxism, Existentialism, and Phenomenology. He described his lack of background in African philosophy as a handicap, but on the positive side, he said he learned to treat his analytic training as a tool for helping him to raise criticisms in the field of African philosophy (Oruka 1990b: 3). Interestingly enough, he mentions reading novels by African authors during his time at Uppsala, including works by Chinua Achebe and Kenyan writers James Ngugi (later Ngugi wa Thiong'o) and Okot p'Bitek (Oruka 1997: 282).

Oruka explains that those outside of the profession of philosophy (for example, politicians) often mistook what he was doing for politics. He admits that engaging in practical philosophy, that is, philosophy that is relevant to current social problems and intended to improve "the conditions of human life" can be dangerous (Oruka 1990b: 3). David Felder, currently a retired philosophy professor who had been a graduate student in Wayne State University's philosophy program at the same time as Oruka, remembered Oruka saying to him that he chose philosophy as a field rather than politics because he thought he could be of better help to the world as a philosopher than a politician. I think it is clear from the distinction being made that Oruka himself did not want to rule, that is, hold political office, although it's unclear whether that was due to the opportunities in his circumstances being so limited or compromising, since Kenya had been a single-party democracy for most of his adult life, or whether he preferred the life of the philosopher and would not take up politics even if the situation were different. What is the philosopher's relationship to the state? Here I draw upon Kant, who clarified that he himself did not want to be philosopher-king as Plato had dramatized in his dialogue *The Republic*. Rather, Kant explained, "That kings should philosophize or philosophers become kings is not to be expected. Nor is it to be wished, since the possession of power inevitably corrupts the untrammeled judgment of reason. But kings or kinglike peoples which rule themselves under laws of equality should not suffer the class of philosophers to disappear or to be silent, but should let them speak openly." (Kant 1795) Kant had

Perpetual Peace printed up as a pamphlet for wide distribution, thinking that King Friedrich Wilhelm II of Prussia would come to know of his ideas indirectly. In fact W. B. Gallie calls Kant's publication of his philosophical essay *Perpetual Peace* "a political act," thus showing that there is certainly an overlap between writing philosophy and engaging in politics, at least in the broad sense of political action (Gallie 1979: 8). Oruka saw his life's contribution as exercising his critical faculties to discern what is wrong with our world, why it is wrong, and what should be done instead. Then he wanted to make his critiques well known.

Oruka himself fraternized and philosophized with politicians but eschewed political positions. Mai Palmberg, a student at Uppsala University and a friend of Oruka's during his undergraduate studies, shared that when she had visited Oruka in Nairobi in 1972, he had contacted Oginga Odinga by phone from the Hilton Hotel, since Oruka had stipulated that no one should talk about politics at his residence.[2] Odinga was at that time the ex-vice president of Kenya (having served from 1964 to 1966), whose party, Kenya People's Union, had been banned under Jomo Kenyatta's presidency. Oruka explained in his 1992 book on Oginga Odinga that Odinga and his father, Oruka Rang'inya, were good friends back in the 1940s and 1950s. Oruka said he first met Odinga in 1956 when Odinga came to their home to visit Rang'inya. Oruka wrote that in the 1970s, when he was interviewing other sages as part of his sage philosophy research, it would have been too politically dangerous to arrange a meeting with Odinga. He finally began interviewing him in 1982, but after a coup attempt in August 1982 Odinga was put under house arrest for a year. Oruka's residence and office were searched by Kenyan police. Oruka had already taken the precaution to hide the tapes and transcripts of his interviews with Odinga, for fear of arrest if they were found (Oruka 1992: vii–ix). Considering the circumstances in Kenya, it is no wonder that Oruka did not want to enter politics directly, when even associating with a politician would be enough to have oneself arrested, interrogated, and perhaps tortured—a fate that befell some university professors and students during this time (Mutahi and Theuri 2003: 17–18, 33–41). Books were also seen as dangerous, and Special Branch police ransacked libraries looking for books not only by Marx but also by Frantz Fanon, an author that Oruka admired.[3]

According to Kant, philosophers could get the ear of the ruler indirectly by speaking publicly and by publishing their writings, so that the general public and finally the ruler him- or herself would hear the ideas of the philosophers. It is interesting to note that Kant wrote *Perpetual Peace* during a time when King Friedrich Wilhelm II of Prussia had banned Kant from writing or speaking about his religious views, a ban that went into effect in 1792, several years before *Perpetual Peace* was written in 1795. After the king's death, Kant finally published his views on religion in 1798.[4] Kant's insistence on the king's duty to listen to philosophers definitely may be understood to be his criticism of the political milieu in which he found himself, a milieu that clearly did not appreciate the good sense of listening to philosophers. Oruka found himself in similar, or worse, circumstances in Kenya. He could not count on benign neglect of his writings. He repeatedly spoke up on issues of the day, and he was therefore considered to be meddling in politics in a way that challenged the status quo, even if he were only philosophizing.

The philosopher as outspoken critic of his or her times is a role modeled by Ingemar Hedenius. Remember that Oruka received all three university philosophy degrees under Hedenius' tutelage. But first, let's look at who influenced Hedenius to take up a life of public intellectualism. According to his biographer Svante Nordin, Bertrand Russell was Hedenius' role model. "Bertrand Russell appeared to his Swedish follower not only as the greatest contemporary philosopher but also through his struggle against injustices, prejudices and follies as an almost through and through admirable public figure."[5] Nordin reports on Hedenius' correspondence, which shows his indebtedness to Russell's ideas about and model of the public intellectual. One instance of this connection happened in the spring of 1967, which was right around the time that Oruka began to study with Hedenius in Sweden. The Museum of Modern Art in Stockholm was hosting an arts event to support Bertrand Russell's International War Crimes Tribunal, which intended to expose the United States and other countries' complicity in crimes against humanity in Vietnam. Hedenius spoke at the event, charging the U.S. with responsibility for the Vietnam War. Russell wrote Hedenius to thank him for his support (Andersson 2005: 90).

By the time Hedenius and Oruka met, Hedenius had already been a professor at Uppsala for over thirty years. He began his philosophical career in the 1930s. He wrote books on both Berkeley and Hume that have since been translated into English (Hedenius 1936; Hedenius 1937). His dissertation was on Berkeley. He argued that Berkeley's theory of knowledge influenced the Logical Positivists as well as Hume and Mill. He points out that Berkeley's philosophy had therefore ended up supporting very different ends than those to which Berkeley himself subscribed. Berkeley thought he would convince others of God and the soul's existence, but instead, those who agree with his sensationalism considered his spiritualistic metaphysics as an "inconsistent addition to his system." (Hedenius 1936: 5) He also studied Hume's moral theory, focusing on the role of sympathy and the relationship between virtue and human happiness or utility. These positions may not seem that political or related to contemporary events, but they were.

Johan Strang's historical study places Hedenius and Uppsala philosophy in the context of larger philosophical and political movements (Strang 2010).

Just as the Vienna Circle in Austria was associated with social democracy, freethinking, and the Bauhaus aesthetic movement's emphasis on objectivity, simplicity, and mass production, so the Uppsala philosophy movement was associated with Left politics and secularism. The political circumstances of Austria helped shape the Unity of Science movement and the popularity of the logical empiricists (positivists), who saw themselves as opposed to reactionary and metaphysical philosophies like Heidegger's. Hedenius was involved in building and carrying on an Uppsalan philosophical legacy that started earlier with Axel Hägerström, although Hedenius sometimes subtly changed Hägerström's position even as he claimed to be continuing Hägerström's legacy (Strang 2010: 13, 49–54). Hedenius, along with colleagues Marc-Wogau and Herbert Lars Gustaf Tingsten, denounced other philosophical movements like Hegelian idealism as being too close to Nazism and the origin of totalitarianism. Tingsten reviewed Karl Popper's *The Open Society* in his newspaper, *Dagens Nyheter* (Today's News, August 21, 1947), a leading liberal publication, and allowed Hedenius to publish there as well (Strang 2010: 87–88; Hedenius 1972). Hedenius, in his inaugural lecture as well as in a 1948 essay "Om praktish filosofi," also denounced neo-Thomism and Marxism, claiming that his own tradition was the most scientific. He considered analytic philosophy to be both Swedish and Western (that is, involving Britain and the United States), and he insisted it was also the most democratic (Strang 2010: 58, 73, 87). Many of these quick and politically motivated denouncements of competing philosophical schools are not careful and do not stand the test of time.[6] The line between philosophy and politics is not so easy to draw.

In 1961 Hedenius wrote *Liv och nytta* (Life and utility). An excerpt of this work was later translated into English as "The Welfare State and Its Ideals." (Hedenius 1965: 212–20) In this work Hedenius states that the welfare state, such as the one in Sweden promoted by the Social Democrats, is based on utilitarian ideals. For the past thirty years, he explains, the Social Democrats have had the lessening of poverty as one of their goals, which they reached through legislation and economic planning. He insists that the welfare state is materialistic, in that it prioritizes filling people's material needs, and democratic, in that it wants a wide number of people to share in this economic security. With an increase in economic security, average people can experience an increase in freedom: the liberty to do what they would like with their funds.

Hedenius' ideas on welfare as expressed in this article fit into what Strang calls the general Social Democratic Party's emphasis as an alternative to the polarized positions of Western capitalism and communism. Gunnar and Alva Myrdal, proponents of social democracy, held that "political and social problems can be solved by rational and scientific solutions rather than by ideological confrontation and class struggle." (Strang 2010: 27) It's important to note, however, that Hedenius himself sometimes agreed with the Social Democrats and sometimes with the Liberal Party (Folkpartiet). Hedenius' wife Astrid had held a municipal council position with the Liberal Party (Strang 2010: 74–75; Nordin 2004: 315).

According to Hedenius' contemporary Lars Tragardh, the Swedish system of extensive welfare benefits is due to maintaining a high-trust society (in contrast with the Anglo-Saxon people's high suspicion of the state). Tragardh insists that the Swedish system is not collectivist or communitarian; it's individualist. Swedes consider their state to be a way for them to be liberated from religion and dependence on family. The state provides daycare which helps women to participate equally in the work force. The state also takes care of the elderly. Tragardh explains, "At the heart of this social compact lies what I like to call a Swedish theory of love: authentic human relationships are possible only between autonomous and equal individuals." (Tragardh 2012) While Tragardh is writing today (although he first articulated this view in 1997; see Tragardh 1997: 253–85), he gives us a clue to how Hedenius could be so much in support of material equality and democracy while still emphasizing expansion of personal liberty. What's important for us to keep in mind is that all of this was part of Oruka's environment during his experience abroad.

While Hedenius advocated liberty, he also bemoaned a crisis in his country that he called excessive complacency: contentment with "little playthings," satisfaction with the cheap and ugly. He thought there was the need for a "second revolution" as he called it. He wanted his fellow Swedes to develop artistic taste, to cherish the historical buildings in their midst, to redirect their consumption away from "foolish objects" and toward supporting the artists among them who were neglected. (Hedenius himself played the flute and was an advocate of classical music.) Despite these and other social problems in Sweden, ways in which Sweden did not live up to the ideal of the welfare state, he compared it favorably when contrasted to the slums of the United States (Hedenius 1965: 220). He rebuffs a criticism which he attributes to U.S. President Eisenhower, that the Swedish practice of generous welfare has led to alcoholism, sexual laxity, crime, and suicide.[7] Hedenius does not deny that Sweden has had for a long time and continues to have such problems, but he says that since they were present in Swedish society prior to the implementation of welfare, they can't be attributed to the effects of generous welfare (Hedenius 1965: 218).

He also insists that the welfare state itself is void of ideas such as religious commitments. In fact Hedenius was a famous atheist in a country where belief in Christianity was widespread. He had many debates with Swedish theologians about God's existence. Some credit him and his book *Tro och*

Vetande ("Belief and knowledge" or "Faith and knowledge") with being "instrumental in starting the cultural debate that eventually led to the separating of the Swedish church and state." (Wikipedia n.d.) One Uppsala professor famously said about Hedenius, "There is no God, and Ingemar Hedenius is his prophet." (Andersson 2005: 89) Hedenius thought that a rational and secular approach to social issues could be more humane as well as more correct, since he agreed with the moral injunction elucidated by Russell against believing any proposition that did not have good grounds. Hedenius' various positions influenced Oruka in many ways, some of which will be covered in this chapter; other ways will be covered in other chapters.

Oruka submitted his bachelor of arts 3 betyg (honors) thesis "Political Ethics: Democracy and the Notion of Human Rights" in June 1968.[8] In this document we see many important themes of Oruka's philosophical works mentioned for the first time. The thesis, seventeen pages long, claims to be a reflection on the "Human Rights" chapter of John Hospers' book, *Human Conduct: Problems of Ethics.*[9] Oruka begins by noting that his chosen topics, "democracy" and "human rights," are terms that are often abused in practice. People will give lip service to these concepts while practicing "political demagogy." (Oruka 1968: 1) He also notes that while the Americans claim that they have to fight against communism in Vietnam because the communists are against democracy, the North Vietnamese call their own government a democracy (Oruka 1968: 3). On page two Oruka looks forward to a time when humanity will have a World State, suggesting that before such a thing would be possible, other human goals would have to be reached: "increasing knowledge, on the withering away of irrational beliefs, prejudices, and his fallacious racial anthropology; on rational distribution of the world's property." (Oruka 1968: 2) He further explores democracy noting that it should be understood as a means to promote the rights of the governed, not an end in itself (Oruka 1968: 3). Hospers explains that power should be in the hands of the people and that the people then delegate that power to representatives who will execute the people's will; that is, their representatives are their servants, not their rulers. But Oruka can't help but notice that in practice democracy is very different. Rulers don't serve. Once in power they impose their will, using their position to thwart or crush their competitors for power. Presidents can rank very low in opinion polls (like Johnson in the United States, due to his continuation of the Vietnam War) and still remain in power (Oruka 1968: 5). Oruka notes other hypocrisies of the United States. The U.S. government said in 1948 that Americans have a right to a minimum standard of living, but they only said so to try to diminish the attractiveness of communism. The U.S. welfare system, Oruka points out, is very anemic. The country is not a material democracy. Americans say they uphold freedoms such as freedom of speech, but they are really ruled by Christian dogma. A case in point, Oruka asserts, is that Bertrand Russell was banned from teaching at City College of New York in 1941 due to his opinions (Russell 1969: 320; Dewey and Kallen 1941). All of this leads Oruka to declare that those who say they are advocates of social justice should be against Western democracy (Oruka 1968: 6). Note that he says all of this in his undergraduate thesis, before he has gone to the United States.

As the thesis continues, in a world where both Western/American and communist powers have grave shortcomings, he applauds Sweden for taking a position that tries to reconcile the two extremes by advocating material democracy while still upholding important liberties (Oruka 1968: 7). Oruka comments on the position of newly independent African countries. While they inherit Western democracy from colonial masters, they "badly need" economic democracy (Oruka 1968: 7). So what should Africa do? Oruka states that Africa needs "a well-defined ideology embracing selectively all the traditions that have affected our society." (Oruka 1968: 8) Here we see the theme of selectively embracing traditions that is so central to his later work in sage philosophy, as well as his positions on gender equality and other issues regarding progress and foreign influence.

The thesis goes on to summarize key human rights and comment upon whether his own view coincides with or disagrees with Hospers' treatment. While discussing the right to life, Oruka notes that currently this right is curtailed by governments that practice execution. He states that he is against the death penalty because no one has a right to take away another's life. Murderers may be sick or abnormal, but they don't lose their rights (Oruka 1968: 10–12). Regarding sexual rights, he observed that most nations were too prohibitory (Oruka 1968: 13). It's important to note here that Bertrand Russell's appointment to City College was denied due to a confluence of Episcopal bishops and Catholic clergy who were opposed to Russell's atheism and due to the mother of a student who opposed Russell's position morally allowing sex before marriage (Dewey and Kallen 1941). Given Oruka's admiration of Russell, inclusion of sexual rights is no doubt in part inspired by Russell, although it could more generally be seen as the influence of utilitarianism. Russell was convinced that he was awarded the Nobel Prize in Literature in 1959 for his 1929 book *Marriage and Morals* (Russell 1969: 520; Russell 1929).

Oruka agreed with Hospers that people should have freedom of speech and that they should be able to speak against what they were taught to treat with awe and respect, whether it be God or communism (Oruka 1968: 14). Regarding economic rights, Oruka argued that governments should provide what is possible for them to provide. Since the rich often get their riches by hoodwinking the poor, "a just government should be one which recognizes the robbing of the rich to pay the poor as one of its great duties"—in other words, socialism should be advocated (Oruka 1968: 15). He insisted that people had a right to a minimum standard of living and that people should express a benevolent attitude toward others (and he hoped that such an attitude did not depend on the existence of a God). His survey of important rights and liberties prefigures his later, more in-depth licentiate thesis, and eventually his book based on that thesis, *The Philosophy of Liberty*, especially chapter six, "Six Liberties." (Oruka 1996: 63–84)

He then entertained the question of whether there was a right to religion, that is, a right to engage in and express one's religion. While he begrudgingly admitted such a right, he was more adamant about there being a right to be an atheist. He argued that people were born nonbelievers and were turned into believers by religion. By belief, he stipulated that he meant trusting in something beyond what our five senses can prove. He expressed his view that preachers deter us from our work to make Earth a better place by scaring us with stories about hellfire or irrelevant talk about life after death. He considered religious people to be opponents to sexual rights and economic democracy, which they equated with communism. He exhorted his readers to look forward to the future with the knowledge of the past in mind, not upward to heaven. (Oruka 1968: 16) He further stated that a religious person was deluded and sick, and needed a physician, who in this case would be a rational atheist. He concluded by saying that, while the attainment of human rights may mean something different in London or Nairobi, everywhere they would entail "impartial judgment, social security, education, and work" for every citizen (Oruka 1968: 17).

Where did this hostility toward religion, considering it a repressive force, come from? Clearly, Ingemar Hedenius influenced Oruka, and so did Bertrand Russell, since Oruka had mentioned that reading Russell's book was a key factor in his decision to become a philosopher. But what made him respond so positively to these criticisms of religion? On that, I do not know the answer. But I can fill in a bit of Hedenius' position regarding religion by looking at a journal article Hedenius had published in English in *The Personalist* in 1971 called "Disproofs of God's Existence?" Here he argues against Alvin Plantinga's book *God and Other Minds* (1967). While Hedenius' article came out after Oruka graduated with his licentiate from Uppsala, Plantinga's book came out while Oruka was a student of his at the undergraduate level, so we can presume, especially since he and Oruka were engaged in private one-on-one tutoring, that Hedenius shared his ideas with his student in verbal form before finally writing and publishing them.

In his article Hedenius claims he does not definitely disprove God's existence because he is involved in an empirical study whose conclusions can only be more or less probable (thereby Hedenius already distinguishes his methods from Plantinga's conceptual study) (Hedenius 1971: 25). But he then advances reasons why God's existence is highly improbable, with the problem of evil being a major stumbling block for maintaining that a benevolent and omnipotent God exists, especially if that God is responsible for the creation and sustenance of everything in the world. He argues against the Catholic position that evil is due to God's allowing humans to have free will. He thinks the heart of this position is the claim that we humans are compensated for our suffering (that is, the importance of possessing free will trumps any personal suffering), but he thinks that based on empirical evidence, there is uncompensated evil in our world. Adhering to a utilitarian maxim of increasing overall happiness, he notes, "To create an evil state of affairs which is not compensated by any good state of affairs means to create a more comprehensive state of affairs which, as a whole, is not good but instead evil or indifferent." (Hedenius 1971: 38) Such a scenario counts against the existence of a good God.

Hedenius also adds a bit of social commentary when he critiques God's goodness by highlighting Jesus and others' sayings that God will eternally punish those who do wrong in this life. But he admits that Christians could try to save their arguments for the existence of God by jettisoning their belief in these sayings of Jesus, and he mentions that he meets many people who do exactly that to maintain their belief (Hedenius 1971: 36–37). This may be the core reason why Hedenius is against the idea of God's existence. As we will see in the next chapter, he was a critic of practices of punishment, and he traced this practice of punishment to Christian concepts of the need to punish evildoers. Oruka shows some early signs of sharing Hedenius' thoughts on crime and punishment when, in his BA thesis, he says murderers may be sick or abnormal but should not be executed for this because they still have rights.

When it came to the "3 betyg" grade for his BA honors thesis, Hedenius wrote on June 27, 1968,

> It was with a certain degree of hesitation I gave your work a "3." It has, according to my opinion, several flaws and is not free from mistakes. Personally I cannot agree with you on most of the ideas you have uttered in the paper. On the other hand your paper gives me a clear impression of your high intellectual capacity and your intensity in thinking over essential problems. In these respects you are on the same level as the best of my Swedish pupils. This has to my view to compensate, that your present presentation of philosophical theories in your field and your sense for logical consistency still ought to be improved.[10]

We don't have a record of the specific ways in which Hedenius' own position disagrees with Oruka's. Certainly the topics chosen for the paper show Hedenius' influence.

At this point I would like to present a bit of historical research on the development of the welfare state in Sweden and ask whether it is a secular alternative that rejects the role of the church as destructive (Hedenius' position, which seems to have influenced Oruka) or rather the outcome of a Christian world view (a position that Hedenius does not seem to take into consideration). Various commentators have argued both perspectives. In many accounts of the development of the welfare state, distinctions are made about its history in the various Nordic countries. While there are distinct differences in the histories of these Nordic welfare states, there are also overarching themes and mutual influences.

According to Uffe Østergård, the populations of Western Europe accepted increasingly high taxes, due to their "acceptance of unprecedented intervention in their private lives and families" beginning in 1945 and continuing until about 1974, at which point resistance to increasing taxes arose (Østergård 2011: 81–82). Note that Oruka studied with Hedenius while confidence in the role of taxation still existed. In Swedish a citizen was called a "Medborger," literally, a co-citizen. This spread from Sweden to neighboring countries. The role of the state was broadened so that it encompassed not only a monopoly of violence and security, but also socialization, economic policy, care of the elderly, health policy, and culture and media, resulting in a "well-being" or welfare from cradle to grave (Østergård 2011: 83). Østergård, a history professor, then searches for the earlier history of these results. He emphasizes the influence of institutional religion, as in a national church, in the formation of national identity and acceptance of welfare.

The Pension Act of 1891 in Denmark was the birth of the Scandinavian welfare state. While it was inspired by an earlier German example, it encompassed the entire Danish population as citizens regardless of whether they were active in the labor market. For example, women could get benefits even if they did not have a history of paid employment. The provisions of the Pension Act were financed through taxation rather than by employers, and the amount citizens were granted depended on the current income of the society rather than contributions citizens and/or employers made to a fund (Østergård 2011: 85). As Tim Knudsen explained, "the method of payment implies a higher degree of solidarity in the population since taxpayers are expected to pay tax not in the preparation for their own retirement but for the sake of those who are pensioners now." (quoted in Østergård 2011: 86n28, translation by Østergård) According to Knudsen, this high level of solidarity was "brought about by an extraordinary effort on the part of the State and the Church." (quoted in Østergård 2011: 86n28, translation by Østergård) It is this high level of effort on the part of organized religion in forging the consensus around welfare rights that I find completely missing in Hedenius' account. Østergård considers social democracy as a continuation of eighteenth- and nineteenth-century evangelical pietist movements; in other words, social democracy was due to the influence of a secularized Lutheranism rather than international socialism (Østergård 2011: 93). Østergård also emphasizes that the role of Protestantism in Scandinavia, with its Lutheran influence, is different than that found in the United States, where Calvinism is more prominent (Østergård 2011: 94).

A specific development that helped Scandinavians be generous with their fellow citizens also relied upon Lutheranism. Østergård argues that the Danish king Christian II in 1521 and 1522 upheld the distinction between aiding "deserving" and "undeserving" poor using a Catholic model. But Luther emphasized that one is saved by faith, not by works. Danes were able to erode the strict dichotomy between the "deserving" and "undeserving" poor, a distinction that undermines solidarity (Østergård 2011: 88–89). Where a society holds that only those who have worked hard enough to "deserve" it should be given the sustenance they need, there develops a stingy body public that does not want anyone to benefit from another's work; such stinginess results in a push for low taxes and low public expenditure. But the church and other public figures were able to influence Danes to set aside this distinction and agree to help all members of their society without passing judgment on them. Østergård also argued that Luther's emphasis on the laity, which debunked the idea that clergy are better than laity, and his establishment of procedures to choose their own clergy started practices of democratic self-governance. If it's really true that the church played a role in this change of mindset and practices, then the church should not be considered the cause of all problems. In fact, Hedenius (and by implication, Oruka) would have to admit that the church (e.g., the Lutheran Church) can play a helpful role in bringing about a fully satisfactory state of affairs: sharing societal wealth to cover all people's basic material needs.

This view poses an important challenge to the perceived weaknesses of Hedenius' own position of value nihilism, which he inherited and revised from his precursor, the famous Uppsala philosopher Axel Hägerström. Hägerström was a proponent of value nihilism, the position that claims that value judgments are connected to feelings or sentiments. Hedenius went further and argued that only statements can be true or false. But value expressions, like "this is good," are not actually statements. As Strang explained, drawing upon Staffan Källström's study, *Den gode nihilisten*, "The value nihilistic theory was used as part of a radical and progressive cultural and political rhetoric that aimed to overcome traditional and conservative views in favour of social and political reforms."[11] Strang notes parallels between Hedenius' views and Alfred J. Ayer and Rudolf Carnap's claims that value statements have a deceptive grammatical form (Ayer 1936: 108; Carnap 1935: 24). Strang also sees parallels to Ludwig Wittgenstein's *Tractatus Logico-Philosophicus,* and he notes that "In the beginning of *Om rätt och moral* Hedenius explicitly described Hägerström and Uppsala philosophy as 'a similar and contemporaneous reaction against metaphysics as the Cambridge School and logical empiricism.'" (Strang 2010: 54; Hedenius 1941: 9)

Critics of value nihilism charged that, under such a view, everything would be allowed. They claimed it left humanity with a spiritual void. Hedenius answered such charges in two ways. First, he would assert that the individual had a responsibility to make moral decisions. He would often sound like Sartre or the existentialists in his insistence on responsibility. Second, he often referred to empirical fact: there was indeed already a strong consensus on basic fundamental values (Strang 2010: 78, 81–82). This emphasis on "shared values" was part of the "*volkish*" rhetoric of the Social Democrats at the time. Strang sees a problem in Hedenius' seeming obliviousness to the idea that these values might not be shared everywhere (Strang 2010: 102). He states, "Given the frequent references to this community of shared values, it is striking that the Scandinavian value nihilists seldom tried to specify the values, nor the limits of the society or culture that shared them." (Strang 2010: 82) Among the Swedes it was only Gunnar Myrdal who actually tried to interview people and conduct opinion polls in order to define this consensus on a culture's values.[12] For others like Hedenius, the presence of this value consensus was presupposed or considered obvious. It is exactly this point that I think is a weakness in Hedenius' position of value nihilism. He has neglected the part of Scandinavian history when the current consensus regarding social welfare was purposely forged, due to the efforts of the institutional church. At a later stage, these same values were carried on by the community in an atmosphere of co-citizenship. The source of the values was forgotten or downplayed, but the forged consensus on values continued.

So, does the church deserve credit for this consensus? Some might argue against Østergård that, while the state church played a role in the historical formation of social welfare, the Swedes' transfer of the church's role to the state is evidence that the Swedes wanted to escape the influence of religion while keeping a fully secularized version of what they thought were the best values promoted by the church. Lars Bo Kaspersen and Johannes Lindvall argue this position (Kaspersen and Lindvall 2008: 119–43). They assert that "in the nineteenth century, the secular state had captured the organizational infrastructure that churches used to provide these services," (Kaspersen and Lindvall 2008: 119) thus marginalizing the continued influence of the church and transferring power from the church to the secular state. This led over time to the acceptance, even by church leaders themselves, that "the state, not religious organizations, was the natural provider of poor relief and education." (Kaspersen and Lindvall 2008: 120)

In Denmark, the state nationalized the church in 1536. The Danish king was considered to have responsibility for the sick and the poor. The first poor-relief legislation was enacted in 1539. At that time, the state used local parishes to help the poor. It was in the late seventeenth century and early eighteenth century that, under the influence of Pietism, King Christian VII of Denmark instituted a system of orphanages and schools, taking over this role from the church. In 1739, a bill was passed to establish schools, a departure from dependence on religious schools. By 1814, primary education was free for all persons, that is, supported by the state. Clause 89 of the 1849 Constitution said that the state was responsible to assist any person unable to provide for himself and his family. By 1867, clergy were excluded from poor-relief commissions, making poor relief secular. In the 1870s and 1880s conservative church leaders endorsed state responsibility for poor relief. For example, Bishop H. L. Martensen advocated this position in *Den Social Ethik* (The social ethic) in 1878 (Martensen 1878). In 1891 and 1892, the state funded support for the elderly, unemployed, and sick. By 1933, educated social workers rather than churches were in charge of poor relief (Kaspersen and Lindvall 2008).

The first comprehensive poor-relief legislation in Sweden was enacted in 1847. In 1871, the Poor Relief Act delegated poor relief to municipalities. Clergy were still involved. In the early twentieth century, private social insurance schemes were replaced by state programs. Nationwide primary education was instituted in 1842, but the church continued to dominate primary education; school boards were headed by parish ministers. However, the political liberal movement advocated church-state separation. Teaching began to be considered a profession independent of the church. "Unity schools" in the years between the First and Second World Wars began to emphasize equality and social reform. Educational institutions finally became secularized in 1958. Kaspersen and Lindvall are convinced that the main Swedish religious organizations saw the state as the natural provider of poor relief by the early twentieth century. The church would, in contrast, minister to people's spiritual needs. For example, Per Pehrsson said as much in a speech to the Clergyman's Association in 1916, and Bishop Hjalmar Danell echoed such sentiments in 1920. Otto Centerwall, from 1905 to 1944 the dean of *Samariterhemmet* in Uppsala, said that now that the state takes care of the poor, the church can focus on preaching and increasing the spirit of love.[13]

The Swedes' high trust in their government contrasts sharply with the situation in post-colonial African states. Colonial governments artificially created nations through conquest and then hypocritically claimed they ruled these new states only because Africans were incapable of self-government and needed guidance. Traditional African forms of governance, with their fragile systems of checks and balances, were neglected or else co-opted by having African leaders pledge allegiance to the colonists (Mamdani 1996: 37–108). Colonizers controlled the economy, underpaying African farmers for their produce and using the gains made on the market to fund infrastructure. Almost all of the infrastructure, however, was intended to aid extraction. Such projects as railroads and harbors were built to export produce and other raw materials, not to help Africans or their businesses (Davidson 1992: 209–13). For the most part, colonial governments did not fund education. Religious organizations started schools, but no state religion existed to help shape a common value system as the church had done in Sweden. Instead, colonizers divided Kenya and other countries into many geographic regions and assigned competing missionary societies particular areas in which to focus their efforts.

Colonial states depended on force, coercion, and the capitulation, not the consent, of the governed. Africans who cooperated were rewarded with power, and as Mahmood Mamdani pointed out in his study of Uganda, collaborators often exploited their relationship with colonizers by brutalizing the people and extracting even more resources from them than the colonizers required. The colonial system thus turned local rulers into tyrants. Colonial governments did not build trust; they were imposed, and extraction was their goal (Mamdani 1996: 37–108).

The corruption that existed during colonial rule continued despite the transition to independence. With misuse of resources endemic in government and poverty rampant among the people, citizens did not welcome higher taxation in expectation that their needs would be taken care of "from cradle to grave." Colonial governments never intended to provide such services to conquered peoples, and post-colonial governments proved to be almost as unreliable.

From the time of colonial rule through the time independent states formed within the artificial national borders carved out by colonizers, ethnic groups were thrown together that had never before cooperated with one another to create a government. Beset by scarcity and mutual distrust, various groups vied for power and economic resources. In Kenya, networks of political patronage funneled state resources to some areas, but not others. Civil servants who did not feel much loyalty to the state skimmed off national resources to augment their scanty paychecks. Citizens could not rely on state welfare and therefore did not want to contribute to it. Individuals would rather evade taxes and any other contribution to the state if they could.

At the time Oruka was finishing his studies abroad, there had been only five years of independent rule in Kenya, which got its independence in 1963. After he returned to Kenya, one of the first topics he wrote about (in 1972) was the paradoxes of the first ten years of independence, and how far what happened was from what African liberationists wanted to happen. While I want to leave the fuller description of the critique contained in that article for a future chapter, I mention it now to draw attention to the high contrast Oruka experienced between Sweden and Kenya (as well as between hopes for Kenya's independence and how independence turned out ten years later). Because Oruka had lived in Sweden, a country whose citizens felt enough confidence in their government and enough solidarity amongst themselves to pay high taxes—voluntarily, without coercion or the influence of religion— in exchange for generous benefits and guarantees from the state, which, furthermore, did not limit their freedoms and on the whole respected their rights, he found the dysfunction in other countries glaring indeed. The next country Oruka experienced far differed from Sweden's model society. He went to Detroit, Michigan, soon after it had experienced race riots, and he found city dwellers there caught in economic depression and poverty.

Oruka in the United States and Writings on Punishment

Figure 2 H. Odera Oruka with Ingemar Hedenius, Hallvide, Sweden, in 1975. Photo by Astrid Hedenius.

With his undergraduate scholarship and degree finished, Oruka went back to Kenya, but he longed to continue studying philosophy. In 1968, larger socio-politico-economic forces entered in to bring Ingemar Hedenius to the United States as a visiting professor at Wayne State University (WSU) in Detroit, Michigan. Once in Detroit, Hedenius arranged to get Oruka a job as a graduate assistant at Wayne State, so that Oruka could get his Master's degree in philosophy there. The Master's degree thesis which he Ochieng' wrote bears Hedenius' name as mentor. Oruka's Master's thesis then formed a large part of his first book, which was published in Nairobi when he returned there to take a position at University of Nairobi.[1] In this chapter, I will cite both the thesis and the later book, and I will make note if there is a discrepancy between the two sources.

Richard Brad Angell had come to WSU in 1968 to be acting chair of the department. He explained Prof. Hedenius' visit in this way:

> 1968, I believe, was the year of the riots in Detroit.[2] The faculty found it uncomfortable to live there. Wayne State's Philosophy Department had a very good reputation, and Indiana University's Philosophy Department tried to take advantage of the situation. In effect they raided Wayne State's Department, offering to hire all of the tenured professors, and succeeded eventually in getting five of them I believe. To fill the gaps Wayne hired two visiting Professors, one of which was Dr. Hedenius. . . . I don't know why they chose Hedenius, but he was well known and from a great university in Sweden. . . . It was a good choice.
>
> Pers. comm., Angell to Presbey, May 11, 2007

While in Detroit, Hedenius gave lectures on speech acts (normative and informative sentences) and medical ethics (Nordin 2004: 401).

It may be that the logicians Stig Kanger and Dag Prawicz in his department at Uppsala had connections to WSU, a department that emphasized analytic philosophy (Nordin 2004: 401–2). And while one could hope that Hedenius was drawn to Detroit out of concern for its problems, Svante Nordin notes that the move to Detroit was probably prompted by Hedenius' desire to have a break from student protests in Sweden, where some more stridently leftist students saw Hedenius as too anti-communist. A Marxist working group there had published a bulletin in which they demanded that the philosophy department teach more Marxism and Existentialism, and they discussed plans to occupy the philosophy department in protest. Nordin (2004: 401) quoted a letter dated August 31, 1968, from Hedenius to Anna-Karin Malmstrom, in which Hedenius (presumably with humorous exaggeration) uses metaphors fresh from the riot suppression in Detroit the year before: "I hope you all show the courage and determination about the double-Maoists or others trying to annoy our dear institution. . . . Should it become serious a National Guard should be organized under your command."[3] Already in 1967, foreseeing these kinds of student requests, Hedenius had begun to study Marx again for the first time since the 1930s. Nordin, combing a variety of Hedenius' correspondence as well as newspaper interviews and articles, notes that Hedenius sympathized with Marx's hatred of the bourgeoisie but found it difficult to relate to other aspects of Marx's philosophy. Hedenius did finally teach a course on Marx when he returned to Uppsala in spring 1970 while Oruka was there working on his licentiate degree, but Hedenius was completely frustrated with student response to the course, due to their "ignorance of the philosophy of Marx and Engels" coupled with their "fanaticism in believing that this philosophy is the only true one" (Nordin 2004: 402).

Hedenius wrote home to Ann-Mari that the *Detroit Free Press* called the place he lived in Detroit one of the worst areas "characterized by prostitution and terror," and he took note of a large black policeman that patrolled the philosophy department. Hedenius admired his colleagues at WSU and enjoyed his time there, but he was frustrated to be unable to guide some of his students back home. He wrote his pupil Sven Danielssen, "One has the feeling to be far away from earth and almost as an Apollo 8 on the backside of the moon" (Nordin 2004: 399).[4] When he returned from Detroit he spoke to Swedish newspapers about the poverty, police brutality, and racial tension in the United States (Nordin 2004: 401).[5]

Soon after Hedenius' arrival in Detroit, Oruka wrote him on 4 September 1968, asking Hedenius to try to arrange for him to study at WSU. Hedenius wrote back on 21 September 1968, explaining that he had gotten Oruka a position assisting students in logic for a salary of $2,800 per year. He wrote to warn Odera, "You ought to arrive, if possible, in daylight. Detroit is one of the most law-less cities in the US with 40 hold-ups or murders every night" (Pers. comm., Hedenius to Oruka, 21 September 1968, Uppsala University archive).[6] Odera arrived in Detroit October 3, "quite broke" from having borrowed money for his air fare. When he arrived, he found that there were other Kenyans studying at WSU. They had gotten there due to a big scholarship fund set up right after Kenya's independence. Harrison Muyia (1934–2016) was a "spokesman" for the first group of eighty-one students from Kenya on "Airlift Africa" (Muyia 1962: 55). Muyia was vice president of the African Students Union of Michigan, and through this organization he got to know Odera Oruka, and Oruka came to know other African students studying at WSU (interview with the author, n.d.).

While it might have been just a coincidence of history that Oruka ended up in a suffering and decaying city torn by racial strife and poverty in the heart of the richest nation in the world, the experience certainly played a role in shaping his philosophical trajectory. As he explains in his autobiographical essay,

> The 1960s formed a period of great hope. It was the hope of the end of racism, colonialism and the oppression of the 'wretched of the earth.' In the 1970s and 1980s, that hope had vanished. My reading in literature and philosophy has convinced me that, although some may by chance be

more gifted than others, the great divide between the mentally creative and non-creative persons lies in socio-economic reality.... Socio-economic deprivation with its accompaniments—poverty and hunger—is the greatest constraint to mental development and creativity.

Oruka 1997: 284

He said that he agreed with Karl Marx that "economics controls minds" and that for African philosophy to flourish, Africa and the entire Third World needed to overcome economic deprivation. It is because all was not well with the world, he explains, that he prioritized social, legal, and political philosophy. He does, however, see a crisis situation as a possible motivation to philosophize, since in such a situation we are concerned about our personal or group origin and destiny (Oruka 1997: 286–87).

Having arrived in Detroit on October 3, 1968, he took courses, wrote his MA thesis, "The Concept of Punishment and its Abolition," and submitted it for acceptance in November 1969.[7] Odera explained that he wrote the Master's thesis in response to a paper that Hedenius had presented to the WSU department in February 1969. Hedenius developed these ideas further in his 1972 Swedish-language book *Om människans moraliska villkor* (On the moral conditions of man).[8] However, his paper in English, "Retribution," had been published in 1963 (Hedenius 1963: 35–45), and Oruka discussed this article in his thesis (Oruka 1969: 16–20; Oruka 1985: 19–24). A later paper of Hedenius' in English, "The Concept of Punishment," was published in 1973—perhaps it is related to Hedenius' 1969 WSU paper presentation, since its last reference is dated 1968 (Hedenius 1973: 13–30).

Before turning to Oruka's thesis I would like to visit Hedenius' philosophical works on the topic of punishment. Hedenius thought religious ideas were used to reinforce a certain practice of punishment that he found problematic. What is the view advocated by the religious or "magical" perspective, according to Hedenius? He describes it this way:

Every criminal has acted of his own so-called free will and has thereby brought down on himself a guilt which is in direct proportion to the magnitude of the crime. In order to be exonerated from this guilt it is necessary for the criminal to suffer a penalty, the severity of which is in direct proportion to the weight of his guilt . . . criminals should be treated in this and no other way.

Hedenius 1965: 214

In an address to Uppsala graduates in 1963, later published in English as "Retribution," an article that Oruka (1969: 17–20) discusses in his thesis,

Hedenius explains the wrong-headedness of this usual understanding that a person who has done harm or committed a crime should be made to suffer. He asks his readers to think of a game of billiards. What causes a billiard ball to sink into a pocket? Usually viewers attribute the result to the stroke that the ball received. But in fact, there are multiple related causes for the ball to sink into the pocket, including the weight of the balls, their shape, the table's qualities, and gravity, for example. But those other factors fade from our minds and the entire cause is usually focused on the stroke. Likewise, when a crime is committed, there are multiple factors that play a role: the community, its laws and material conditions, and its traditions and prejudices, as well as the individuals who grow up and find their place within the society. In Swedish culture, Hedenius (1963: 43) would bemoan the "cultural poverty that so often is characteristic of the criminal's environment." In this "game" of watching crimes happen, onlookers don't focus on the strokes the ball receives, but only the properties of the ball, that is, the individual who did the act. Such condemnation of criminals always involves an erroneous reporting of causality that resulted in the act. For that and other reasons, Hedenius preferred that the practices of punishment be abolished altogether. Using a utilitarian approach, he suggested that society use carrots rather than sticks in order to gain the social cooperation desired.

Certainly in some contexts, stealing is encouraged by poverty and lack of opportunity for an honest living. In Sweden the problem of poverty had been addressed, and yet there were still thefts. Hedenius thought it was due to the easy availability of tempting goods. He suggested that Swedes who owned cars should lock them. But he noted some law-abiding Swedes thought that such actions punished the innocent rather than criminals, who should learn to control themselves. But Hedenius was confident that, if people saw his proposal as more rational, in that it would be more likely to protect their property, they would give up these archaic religious notions of guilt and punishment and find satisfaction in living in a safer society (44–45).

Hedenius also addressed the problems of conflating the current law of the land with morality. States often consider their citizens to have a moral obligation to obey the law because the law presumably forbids immoral acts. However, laws often forbid acts that are considered immoral from the government's own narrow perspective, but are considered good acts from other competing moral perspectives. He gives an example from Nazi Germany, where the possession of a radio receiver was punishable by death. This law was due to the concern that radio receivers were used to help Jews escape the death chambers; from the Nazi government perspective, to engage in such acts would undermine their authority and thwart their project. Hedenius (1973: 21) comments that, rather than call these executions "punishments," it would be more apt to call them acts of "deliberate terror."

Hedenius wrote that he approved of an attempt by a committee of experts in the 1950s to re-write Swedish parliamentary legislation such that there was no mention of "crime" and "punishment." But Parliament reinserted the terms because they thought they would be useful in maintaining law and order. Hedenius explained that he disagreed with the use of the terms and the assertion that they were psychologically practical for maintaining law and order (30). Svante Nordin's book on Hedenius goes into more detail on the debate in Sweden, and how Hedenius' views on the topic would later be debated in the pages of *Tiden* magazine in 1979 and 1981, with Olof Kinberg agreeing with Hedenius and Sten Hecksner, who later became national police commissioner, arguing against them. Hedenius called his position the "Behandlingsteorin," the theory of treatment (Nordin 2004: 483–86).

Oruka notes in his MA thesis that Hedenius' February 1969 paper at WSU (which we can presume is related to the published 1973 article) argues that the concept of punishment is unacceptable because engaging in an immoral act requires intention to do so. But laws punish people even if they are ignorant of the law and not knowingly doing wrong. The law also admits that guilt is never determined with absolute certainty. Thus the punishment of a certain number of innocent persons is built into the system of law. Hedenius found that unacceptable. Oruka, however, explains that the reason to abolish the practice of punishment is "not only that a few innocent people are punished, but that all so-called criminals are never responsible for their acts" (Oruka 1969: 7; paraphrased in Oruka 1985: 7).

Oruka explains that his own position diverges from Hedenius' position that there are primary causes of crime (the "criminal forces" present in society) and secondary causes (free will, intentions, and character formation). Oruka confidently counterposes that only the primary causes are determinants of crime, and if they were removed, individuals would never commit crime (Oruka 1969: 19; Oruka 1985: 23). Consistent with this position, he counsels that: 1) both the concept and practice of punishment should be abolished, and 2) that criminal forces be eradicated. Oruka even states boldly that "if they [criminal forces] were removed, no individual would intentionally commit a crime." He thought that utilitarians could be persuaded of his view that attention should be focused on eradicating criminal forces. He even believes that a factor like bad parenting could be socially eradicated, although he doesn't explain the details (Oruka 1969: 19; Oruka 1985: 23). (It's interesting to note that while Oruka (1985: xi) faulted Hedenius for not outlining implementation, Oruka could be similarly faulted.)

Oruka drew upon authors Maurice de Fleury and Harry Elmer Barnes to argue that social circumstances (parents and peers) and heredity shaped the criminal. He also referred to Marx's determinist view of history as further authority for his views (Oruka 1969: 22–23; Oruka 1985: 26). Criminals therefore could not be held morally responsible for their own actions (Oruka 1969: 11; Oruka 1985: 15). Past-experience arguments, such determinist arguments as "heredity," and John Hospers' "soft determinism," which contends that unconscious forces working on conscious individuals make free acts impossible (Oruka 1985: 16) (a point Oruka refers to in his book, not in his thesis), go beyond Hedenius' arguments. I also think it is not an easily tenable philosophical position.

While I would agree that socio-economic factors are constraints on a person's freedom and responsibility, I would not agree that people have no freedom and therefore no responsibility for their actions. Since people often have a tendency to notice only the individual causes but not the underlying social causes of actions, and therefore to punish individuals rather than address social problems that cause crime, it seems to me that Hedenius' position itself was quite radical in assigning social causes primary status over individual causes. But Oruka stressed what was a popular idea at the time (or perhaps at an earlier time, since he referred to works written in the 1930s, which may have been made popular by Clarence Darrow's courtroom arguments): that society had a responsibility to provide a context for citizens in which they would not be driven to criminal activity out of despair or lack of alternatives.

Citing statistics that said that almost ninety-five percent of all crimes are economically motivated, Oruka saw unsatisfied basic needs as the motivator for crimes and the eradication of poverty as the key to stopping crime. He admired theorists who saw private property itself as the cause of crime. Quoting H. E. Barnes again, he argued that it is empirically shown that severe punishment has never reduced crime, and capitalism greatly increased crime (Oruka 1969: 20; Oruka 1985: 24). As grist for his thesis, he referred to statistics from the U.S. Riot Commission Report of 1968 that showed crime to be rampant in impoverished African American neighborhoods. An unsatisfied need leads to pain, and when this pain is coupled with the conviction that the only way to minister to this pain is to commit a crime, the criminal act is done (Oruka 1969: 13–14; see also Oruka 1985: 16–17). Coming to Detroit in 1968 after the race riots, reading the analyses of the causes of the riots, and experiencing himself the problems of poverty and racial discrimination in the U.S. shaped his interests, and he addressed philosophical debates related to the situation he found himself in.

He argued that the long-term goal of punishment was social security. But he felt that social security could only be safely based on social harmony, and that social harmony could only be based on egalitarianism, "when one group is not made to feel too superior or inferior to another, when the gap between the rich and the poor is insignificant or felt by the citizens to be so, when the society is free of hatred, racial, tribal, communal etc." (Oruka 1969: 27; Oruka 1985: 29). He favored "treatment" of both criminals and society over punishment, and looked forward to a time when people would treat criminals not with "indifference, aloofness or cruelty" but instead "feeling a fraternal concern for them" (Oruka 1969: 37; Oruka 1985: 34–35). Critics of the position Oruka articulates, such as H. L. A. Hart in the 1968 book *Punishment and Responsibility,* and others like Francis V. Raab charge that it is absurd to say of someone that they have no control over the shaping of their own character. Raab (1963) is concerned that if such excuses were used for criminals there would be no preventing anyone at all from justifying their criminal behavior using the same kinds of arguments—a scenario that Oruka dismisses as "far-fetched and absurdly conservative" (Hart 1968; see Oruka 1969: 33–42, quote on 38; Oruka 1985: 31–35).

In a section clearly added onto his book's first edition after the thesis, Oruka continues to argue against the position that criminals commit their crimes out of their own free will, and maintains that, if we clearly understood that criminals were suffering from a sickness, we should call for an ambulance rather than a policeman—in fact, the only role for the policeman, Oruka (1985: 80–85) continues, is to help put the criminal in the ambulance. The reference to the "ambulance" is just a humorous way of illustrating the fact that a criminal still needs to be detained so as not to harm others, and must go through individual treatment. But Oruka wants to complement the focus on the individual criminal's treatment with "society treatment" (89). He clarifies that "curing" the criminal "entails removing the conditions that cause people to adopt criminal behavior" (84). One can't just treat criminals as individuals; one has to treat the "community at large" from which the criminal hails (85). Society must change its customs, its values, its political ideologies, and its moral commitments in such a way that criminality is reduced (89).

It is on these issues that I want to engage the critique of Oruka's concept of punishment recently published in a Kenyan philosophy journal by a current member of the University of Nairobi Philosophy Department. Jacinta Mwenda Maweu (2012: 97–109) disagrees with several aspects of Oruka's account of punishment. Maweu says that the criminal has agency and is not a mere victim of circumstances. On this point I agree, but I don't know whether she holds a position, like Hedenius and I do, which regards the presence of both primary and secondary causes, or whether she attributes all of an individual's actions to individual causes. She also claims that Oruka is involved in a contradiction because, although he agrees that criminals can be held and submitted to treatment, he doesn't recognize that this loss of liberty will be interpreted as punishment by the criminal. (Oruka does think he handles this point by saying that the treatment is intrinsically good, and the lack of liberty is only an extrinsic factor of the treatment [Oruka 1969: 43–44; Oruka 1985: 90]). Also, Maweu (2012: 103–106) notes holding a criminal until the treatment is successful could lead to indefinite detention, since it is difficult to discern when a person has been truly cured of criminal tendencies. I would add to Maweu's point here by noting that claiming detention of persons is "treatment" can be abused. For example, the Soviet Union was notorious for labeling political dissidents mentally ill and forcing them to undergo treatment. Recent news articles show that Russia continues such practices today. Critics of these practices say that punishment continues under a thin veneer of humanitarian concern and "treatment" (Rodriguez 2007; van Voren 2016).

However, Maweu (2012: 104) then states, "If the principles cannot be implemented they ought to be abandoned." She thinks these points of hers show that Oruka's substitution of treatment for punishment cannot be implemented and so should be abandoned. While she has good points regarding the difficulty of mandated treatment for individuals, she neglects to take into account Oruka's broader proposal. While she references authors who argue that it is important to change the social environment of the criminal, she later does not give any mention to what Oruka had called treatment of the "community at large" or mitigating the social forces that cause crime. Instead she only argues that treatment of individual prisoners is difficult. Certainly, it is hard to succeed in transforming individuals when they must return to a world full of powerful criminal forces. I think that Oruka's, or at least Hedenius', proposals are possible, and that Maweu has too hastily concluded that they are impossible.

To find evidence that addressing criminal forces in society can lower crime rates, all we have to do is notice that there are certain societies that have much lower crime and imprisonment rates than others. According to statistics from 2016 gathered by the United Nations, Nairobi currently experiences a rate of intentional homicide of 3.7 per 100,000 people (down from 7.2 in 2012), while Sweden and other European (and even East Asian) countries had rates around 0.5 to 1 (UNODC 2018). At the same time, cities in Central America like Guatemala City, San Pedro Sula, La Ceiba, Belize City, and San Salvador had high rates of 60 to 193 per 100,000. It is hard to chalk up such drastic differences to nothing but individual free will, intentions, and character formation. Even a conservative ethicist like John Kekes (1995) argues that external factors sometimes impede character formation, and the extent of control we have had over our character and actions will result in our deserving "strong blame" or "weak blame" for our wrongful actions (55–57, 84–94, esp. 93). If character formation is partly out of an individual's own control, then it will not do to suggest that individuals must wholly and solely be blamed for criminal actions.

What are some of the examples of societies who succeeded in lowering their crime rates by reducing criminal forces? There are societies that make preventive programs (such as after-school sports and activities) and voluntary drug and alcohol treatment more available than others. The United Nations noted successful programs in the United States and Canada, where cities were able to achieve drastic drops in arrest rates by providing free after-school activities, or even paying students to attend them. Such programs showed they paid for themselves several times over in the savings on welfare and unemployment insurance costs, not to mention costs of imprisonment. And yet, the United Nations notes, nations still prefer to spend their money on "building up criminal justice systems rather than preventing crime" (UNODC 2000). While Oruka's particularly deterministic way of focusing only on social criminal forces and not at all on individual forces may be a bit extreme, the Hedenius' more nuanced position, which may have seemed utopian back when he articulated it in the 1950s, is now common parlance. The 2009 United Nations document on crime prevention surveys causes of crime, including macro- and microenvironmental factors as well as individual factors, and among the latter, many of the individual factors (those having to do with heredity, family circumstance, and racial discrimination) are beyond the individual's control. It argues that severe sentences, including capital punishment, don't work to deter crime, and that prison costs five times more than crime opportunity reduction methods, such as reducing poverty and inequality, increasing employment, strengthening the rule of law, and giving people a feeling that they are included in society. The same document notes that there is a big challenge in engaging in crime reduction strategies in Africa due to the extreme poverty there (UNODC 2008: 3–18, esp. 5, 18). And so, positions on punishment like those advocated by Hedenius and Oruka back in 1969 are now the mainstream position at the United Nations, although that does not mean they are the general practice among governments of the world.

A society like the U.S. with a relatively minimal social safety net compared to other member countries of the Organization for Economic Cooperation and Development (OECD) underserves the population of those who would like to have voluntary treatment for their drug and alcohol addictions but can't afford treatment, and there is a long waiting list for people who wish to be placed in government-funded programs (CDC 2002). Other programs that focus on crime prevention, such as "CeaseFire" in Chicago, face constant budget cuts (Kavan 2008; Schmitz 2008). From Oruka's perspective these cuts are foolhardy. The amount of money saved by refusing to provide voluntary treatment to people suffering addiction is eclipsed by the higher costs spent jailing sufferers who turn to crime out of desperation. Treatment is not completely impossible to implement; it can be done much more than it is now. The examples I give are all preventive measures that can reduce "criminal forces" without curtailing individual liberties. But Hedenius (1963: 44–45) himself was stumped by the fact that there was still such petty crime as car theft in Sweden, where people were supplied to a great extent with their basic necessities.[9] Such trends call into question whether punishment can be completely eradicated.

In his thesis as well as the book, Oruka (1985: 90–92) admits that his proposal for a society that rectifies the social forces which create criminals instead of using punishment may seem like a utopian speculation to his readers, but he then asserts, drawing upon Herbert Marcuse's 1969 book *An Essay on Liberation*, that "the time for a Utopian Speculation is come" (Oruka 1969: 43; Oruka 1985: 90). He also clarifies that, insofar as he has recommended abolishing the institution of punishment, he cannot unconditionally recommend immediate abolition of the system, since current criminal forces have become too accustomed to being restrained by their fear of punishment (Oruka 1969: 47).

In the last few pages of his MA thesis he criticizes the idea that an extremely harsh and punitive system will eradicate crime. He uses the Nazis as an example and he calls their draconian ways "terrorism" or "punishment with terror." He doesn't stop to define his terms, and his use of "terrorism" doesn't have any obvious reference to our current ideas of "insurgent terror" or "war on terror," but it is certainly related to ideas of "state terror." These pages seem to me to be a hasty addition; in fact, he calls this chapter "Postscript." With only an anecdotal reference to those who argue against him by claiming that "there were hardly any crimes during the twelve years of Hitler's reign," Oruka argues that, although fear of police brutality or mercilessness might scare people into obeying laws and refraining from crime, it does not cure the problem of criminality, which needs rectificatory measures. He follows with an example that could be confusing without further clarification: a colonized people, criminalized for starting a guerilla war against an intolerable colonial government, does not surrender in response to government-administered terror (Oruka 1969: 45). His point is that terror only constrains actions but does not reform the will.[10] In his thesis, he does not define terror; he sorts out two kinds of punishment, that is, plain punishment and punishment with terror. His only point is to debunk the view that perhaps plain punishment doesn't work, but punishment with terror is really effective. He repeats this point, replete with ambiguous terminology, on page 92 of *Punishment and Terrorism in Africa*, the book about state terror that he developed from his thesis.

Punishment and Terrorism in Africa promotes the concept of "terrorism" briefly covered in the last couple of pages of his thesis to a key theme throughout the book. But his use of the term throughout the book remains unsatisfactory, and he seems to use it as a synonym for excessive use of force, or cruel and unusual punishment. On page 94 he suggests there are three requirements for an act to be considered punishment: it must be done by a recognized authority or the authority's agent; its infliction should not be beyond a reasonable maximum; and it must be inflicted on a person in his or her right mind. He then says that "terror" is any action that, despite being considered by those administering it to be punishment, fails one of the three criteria (Oruka 1985: 94).

He thinks that a distinction like this can explain why governments such as the white supremacist establishment in South Africa call their attackers "terrorists"; such governments think the insurgents don't have the authority to punish them. This seems to me to be a very odd usage, because it's not at all clear that insurgents have punishing the colonizers as their goal. Repelling the invaders or knocking them out of political power is insurgents' strategic goal. Oruka (1985: 47) offers this definition: "Terrorism is the intentional infliction of suffering or loss on one party by another party which has no authority or legitimacy to do so." He says in one sentence, without further explanation, that terrorists try to "coerce or annihilate" others.

He then adds onto this definition, "or else it is punishment beyond a reasonable maximum" (47). The "or else" in his definition is frustrating. Does an action that has either attribute *a* or *b* constitute terrorism? This latter stipulation seems to argue that cruel and unusual punishment is terrorism. He gives as an example cutting off the ear of a man who failed to pay his income tax (44). But he then argues that the problem with this example is that the one punished would never consent to that kind of punishment, which reduces the example to a demonstration of the first part of Oruka's definition of terrorism.

The definitions of terrorism later in his book have the same ambiguity. He refers to "punishment inflicted with or as terror" (92). So, is terror an added ingredient to punishment? Or is it one of many expressions of punishment?

I would argue that there is some overlap between punishment and terrorism, in that excessive punishment can have as its goal the terrorizing of the person punished or a third party that is to witness the punishment. But since not all terrorism is related to punishment, terrorism can't simply be considered a subset of punishment. Sirkku Hellsten (2018) rightly noted that Oruka's goal was to shine a light on state terrorism, when the government terrorizes its own people disguised as motivated by punishment. State terrorism was often downplayed as usual coverage of terrorism focused on insurgents who attacked the state (296–97). I agree that it was important, excellent and brave of Oruka to tackle this sensitive topic, especially while he was still in Africa and his own country practiced this kind of internal state terror. My only point here is that so far Oruka's definition doesn't adequately cover terrorism as a concept.

Sometimes the terrorist is only engaged in actions that he/she/they think will have a longed-for effect on the party terrorized or third parties. The goal is compliance of others, not their punishing. His definition of terrorism lacks a description of the ways terrorists hope to strike fear into a larger population by attacking a few members of that population and fails to take into account the fact that some terrorists have a political goal in mind. Clearly, the person whose ear is cut off as punishment for nonpayment of taxes is used as an example to others who might consider not paying their taxes. By spreading fear, the government hopes to enforce laws on tax payment. Oruka inadequately theorizes the idea that terrorism is manipulative in this way, and that terrorism is used so often and so deliberately by colonial forces in Africa (as well as by dictators in independent Africa).

We can turn to philosopher Claudia Card for a contemporary definition of terrorism. Terrorism is political violence that uses direct harm to ostensible targets to manipulate and change a wider group of people indirectly by intimidation. The direct harm done to the acknowledged victims is often collateral to the ultimate purpose of the terror. Terrorism uses human beings without regard for their humanity, as objects to achieve ulterior goals (Card 2003: 173).

While Hellsten suggests that Oruka's definition of terrorism is similar to that of Primoratz (Hellsten: 296), in fact I don't see any parallels between the two. Primoratz says, after spending an entire chapter reviewing the proposed definitions of terrorism given by many philosophers in recent years, that from his perspective and "for the purposes of philosophical discussion, terrorism is best defined as the deliberate use of violence, or threat of its use, against innocent people, with the aim of intimidating some other people into a course of action they otherwise would not take." (Primoratz 2013: 30). Perhaps Oruka would not disagree with this kind of definition, but he himself did not advocate a definition like this in his book on this topic.

Where does Oruka get his narrower usage of the term *terrorism*? One of his sources is a 1954 article, "On Punishment," by A. M. Quinton. In this article, Quinton explains that the concept of punishment requires that the person on the receiving end is guilty. If they are not guilty, they may indeed be experiencing pain but not punishment. Quinton (1954: 478) goes on to explain that the suffering of innocent people at the hands of those who consider themselves to be punishing others is by definition "not punishment, it is judicial error or terrorism or, in Bradley's characteristically repellant phrase, 'social surgery.'" Hedenius applies this usage in his article "The Concept of Punishment" (1973). For example, he stipulates that the word "punishment" is commonly used even to describe infliction of pain on innocent people, but this is an improper use of the term, for "if what some people call 'punishment' is not in itself justified, we ought not to speak of 'punishment' but of something else which we wouldn't use the honorific term to describe, at best some sort of social engineering involving suffering or sometimes mere harassment or terrorism" (Hedenius 1973: 13). This, I suggest from a careful reading, is the slim basis for Oruka's use of the term. My only complaint is that this is not an adequate definition of terrorism. Neither Quinton nor Hedenius say that punishment of the innocent is terrorism per se, just that such punishment may be terrorism or something else, e.g., judicial error—not every imprisonment of an innocent person is terrorism. Many theorists note the importance of realizing that terror tactics target a certain person or group of people in order to impact the mindset and actions of another group of people or a government (Presbey 2011; Card 2003: 173). Theorists also debate whether "terrorism" is a word that should be used only regarding insurgent groups, or if it should include state terrorism as well.

In his book Oruka clearly criticizes the practice of excessive punishment, and he exposes many laws that protect property to the point of jeopardizing life. For example, in many African countries, he notes, property theft can be punishable by death (Oruka 1985: 96–97). In the second edition of *Punishment and Terrorism* (1985) he refers to his own sage philosophy project, at that time called *Thoughts of Traditional Kenyan Sages,* and notes that the sages he interviewed from 1974 to 1977 said that according to community traditions, theft was hardly ever punishable by death (127). Referring to his second criterion for punishment, he argues that poverty is the main cause of most thefts, so to punish robbery with death is clearly "beyond an ethical maximum" (96). He also complains that in Kenya many poor people are arrested and thrown in jail for making *chang'aa,* an alcoholic home brew. Since those who engage in this informal business do so to survive, they usually rebel against their imprisonment. *Chang'aa* brewers reject the authority of the Kenyan state to imprison them on those grounds, which reflects the first part of Oruka's definition of punishment. In other words, they do not give minimal ethical consent. But Oruka also says their punishment is not proportional to their actions; it is beyond a reasonable maximum (70–72).

Oruka labels such examples dramatic, clearly excessive punishment of the poor, but he fails to theorize how the over-punishment of small crimes is supposed to create a climate of fear intended to uphold an economic and political status quo. In his *Discipline and Punish* Michel Foucault describes the way public executions of poor thieves in seventeenth-century France were intended to instill respect for property among the impoverished onlookers through fear. Foucault (1995: 49) calls the executions spectacles intended to display the dissymmetry between the criminal and the all-powerful sovereign, who breaks the body of the criminal and reduces it to dust thrown to the winds. These ceremonies of punishment were in fact an "exercise in terror." Foucault also notes how the public executions of impoverished thieves provoked backlash and so were not effective in their goal (61–63). "Never did the people feel more threatened by a legal violence exercised without moderation or restraint" (63). Clearly, excessive punishment is experienced as terror, and Foucault explains how that is the case in the French context.

The closest Oruka (1985: 89) comes to mentioning third-party influence is when he calls terror "fake deterrence." A deterrent is intended to prevent crime; it could be interpreted as an attempt to influence third parties beyond the individual criminal in question. Oruka says that small punishments as deterrents to larger future evils could be justified using a utilitarian calculus if the punishments could be kept within reasonable limits. Oruka doesn't discuss whether those limits would be provided by a deontological context, but he says that, in practice, such punishments do not stay within reasonable limits and so are almost always terrorism (79). Oruka also stipulates that deterrence is an aspect of all forms of punishment, including punishments intended as retribution (44, 121), so deterrence does not apply only to terrorism. After showing that deterrence is not morally justified, Oruka makes the tandem point that terror doesn't really succeed in reducing criminal behavior. Referring to rising crime statistics, he concludes terror is an ineffective deterrent.

A recurring aspect of Oruka's book is his reference to minimums and maximums. Citizens or subjects must have a minimal level of consent to government's actions for the actions to count as punishment. But what defines minimal consent? Is it, as Socrates said in Plato's *Crito*, that one has not left? Or that one has not publicly spoken out against the laws or the practice? Oruka does not say. He repeats like a mantra that certain punishments go beyond a reasonable maximum, but he does not provide guidelines for judging whether the maximum has been exceeded, although he gives plenty of easy examples of punishment that, according to our gut intuitions, go beyond the maximum. Does he mean the maximum threshold of pain? Or does he mean proportionality, that is, punishment of a magnitude that fits the crime? Those philosophers and medical doctors who take up the challenging task of defining "torture" engage in fine-line debates about certain procedures and whether or not they are torture (Sutton 2013). But colonial and post-colonial African history is so chock-full of human rights violations, one does not have to struggle to find an example of punishment that without doubt goes beyond a humanistic maximum.

Are these concepts, "torture" and "terrorism," mutually equated? Punishment beyond a certain maximum would most certainly be considered "torture," but Oruka consistently calls it "terrorism." A common tactic of torture is to keep the victim always on the alert, fearing repetition of the pain. In that way victims are "terrorized" by torture: fear and anxiety exhaust them and in some sense wound them for life. It is not just the physical wounds and scars that are important.[11] But even if all torture victims are terrorized, they are not all used in a political campaign to impact a third party. Kidnappers can hold people for ransom without political goals, but kidnappers still have the goal of affecting the action of third parties. They want people with money to give them money. Some people are kidnapped and tortured just because another person likes the feeling of power they have over another individual. Such kidnappings may be hidden for decades; the kidnapper's goal is not to coerce third parties at all.[12] Jay Sloan-Lynch (2012) admits that domestic abuse does not seem to be a good candidate for the descriptor *terrorism* because it lacks a clear political motivation or the creation of a climate of terror. And yet Sloan-Lynch insists that it is helpful to consider domestic violence terrorism because it is not a mere case of assault and battery; it has social and historical narratives and institutions that inform the individual practices, and so the act is also about "cementing advantages and maintaining privileges for men in society while at the same time reinforcing women's inferior status" (785). The conceptual clarity in Oruka's thesis and book could be enhanced by his directly addressing the social and historical factors and community effects of acts of terror as part of his definition of terror.

In the journal which Oruka edited, *Thought and Practice*, an early issue features an article by G. C. M. Mutiso (1975: 49–52) called "The Irrational as a System of Control," which focuses on how governments try to control people through the use of fear—fear of death, fear of losing jobs, fear of the loss of privileges and status, etc. The article draws upon the insights of a book by Soviet dissident Nadezdha Mandelstam. Her husband, the poet Osip Mandelstam, was arrested and killed for writing a poem that criticized Stalin. One may guess that Kenyan authors were drawing on these themes out of fear that something similar was happening in their own country.

In the 1985 second edition of *Punishment and Terrorism*, which includes an eighth chapter first published as an article in 1982, Oruka (1985: 104) merely reiterates his earlier definition of terrorism and adds that all acts of terrorism have a common objective, that is, "they are cruel and aim at the total subjugation of their victims, mostly by the use of violence." In this chapter he explores state terrorism, explaining on page 105 that legal terrorism is always "state inspired." "Legal terrorism" is state terrorism with a veneer of legality to it, insofar as rulers design laws that legitimate such practices as murder and torture. He augments his description of "legal" state terror with generic examples (people shot dead for protesting) as well as specific examples (President Tolbert of Liberia had his troops shoot into a crowd of people protesting the rise in the price of rice, killing forty people) (107). But then Oruka admits that some African governments drop all pretense of legality and engage in state terror to an extent that he describes as declaring war on their own subjects. He gives as examples "Marcias Nguema, Jean Bokassa, Idi Amin, and the Burundi state thuggery of 1973" (109).

In his book, Oruka criticizes African governments that have laws against treason, interpret those laws broadly, and then sentence "treasonous" people to death or life imprisonment. What these governments are really doing is using justice as a pretext for getting rid of their political rivals. Oruka suggests the government of Zaire's conviction and imprisonment of Nguza Karl-I-Bond, a rival to dictator Mobutu Sese Seko, as a case in point (97–99). Again Oruka uses these examples to show excessive punishment (the second requirement of his definition of terrorism) and does not mention the chilling effect these executions have on the general public or how such executions may discourage political dissent or rivalry. I presume that Oruka knew all of this through personal experience. He lived with the effects of terror in his home country. As already mentioned in chapter 1 of this book, in his 1992 book on Oginga Odinga, he recounted how he hid his interviews with Odinga for fear that the police would search his premises and could detain and torture him. The friend he entrusted with the tapes buried them under a kiosk (Oruka 1992: viii). But Oruka doesn't add this aspect of his lived knowledge to his definition of terror in his book. I consider this lack due to the fact he relied only on Quinton and Hedenius as sources for his definition.

Despite this shortcoming, there are other strengths of Oruka's book. A very interesting passage of his thesis describes how the majority of impoverished persons struggling for survival experience the law as a constant threat to survival and therefore a constant temptation to transgress. Using as examples a person called in for questioning, imprisoned, or taken to court because s/he "resembles a criminal suspect" and a person whose right to immigrant status is questioned, he shows that the law interferes with people before they are ever proven guilty of a crime. The only people who can be rather confident that the law will not unpredictably interfere with their lives are those who are well-off and have high social status and power (Oruka 1969: 39–40).

I find his treatment of the topic interesting because in the United States, where the relative security of the middle class is often considered, at least in academic circles, the majority position, temptation to crime is considered only a problem at the fringes of society. Of course, that is because television news programs have caused us to focus on petty property theft as the most visible crime, and we associate such crimes with racial minorities. The average suburban American has not been conditioned to think of the white collar crimes of business fraud and tax evasion as theft. Jeremy Waldron (1991) has shown how simply existing as a homeless person in America puts one in an almost constant position of breaking some law, since one has no legal place to reside. More could be said about how our perceptions of crime are shaped by our own social context and dominant ideology.

But I think that Oruka's description, while perhaps reinforced by his Detroit experience, comes first from his Kenyan experience of living under colonial and post-colonial rule. Oruka's description of one's daily vulnerability to arrest closely parallels Paulin Hountondji's (1992: 344–64) article "Daily Life in Black Africa." Hountondji explains that one couldn't help but be a lawbreaker under post-colonial African rule because there were so many laws that it was impossible not to break some of them almost all of the time, which meant that one was always vulnerable to the law's interference.

Gandhi described similar situations where repressive rules like the Rowlatt Laws in India and pass laws in South Africa made it all too easy to be in violation of a law if you were penniless, jobless, or critical of the government. The British often resorted to draconian measures to quell unrest, rather than give their subjects independence. Ironically, one of the main founders and proponents of utilitarianism, John Stuart Mill, considered British colonial rule in India to be beyond reproach. In his view, despite blunders and excesses of violence, when taken as a whole the good that British rule did for India far outweighed the pain caused (Mill and East India Co. 1858: 94). Don Habibi notes that in this calculus there was little or no room for counting Indians' resentment of foreign rule as serious pain. Looking at Mill's *System of Logic*, Habibi (1999: esp. 131–32) notes that Mill has great confidence in the "science" of character formation, and Mill thought that environmental factors could be controlled so as to mold and shape people for a better human future. The same optimism that motivates Oruka to imagine that we could redesign our world to make crime almost non-existent helped Mill think that Britain could use violence to subjugate India and mold Indians in a new way for their own good.

Europeans practiced genocide in Africa. Germany inflicted genocide on the San in South Africa and the Herero in Namibia (Adhikari 2011; Mamdani 2001: 9–10). Caroline Elkins' (2006) recent book and the BBC documentary based on it (*Kenya: White Terror*, 2002) go into detail about repressive measures, including torture, that the British used in Kenya during their fight against the "Mau Mau" during the last days of British colonial government in the 1960s. These lessons in heavy-handed rule were not lost on newly independent African countries. Oruka and other academics at Kenya's universities had a chance to experience first-hand (on the receiving end) the attempts to enforce compliance to the government through "punishment" and even torture (Mutahi and Theuri 2003: 17–18, 33–41).

In his book Oruka mentioned these same atrocities of British colonizers, who arrested people and detained them "on remand." He cites the study of J. Read, a scholar of the East African legal system, who noted that, of 97,927 people who became prisoners in Kenya in 1961, 52,312 were "committed on remand," and of them, only 7,925 were convicted and sentenced.[13] Oruka's (1985: 72–73) point is that being imprisoned on remand is still a hardship; if one is convicted, one's time in prison should count toward the time served, and if one is on remand too long and later found innocent, one should be able to sue the government. Oruka does not mention why so many Kenyans were being arrested—that in fact, the arrests may have been "white terror," as the BBC documentary calls it, intended to scare Kenyans away from supporting armed opposition to British rule. The British began these imprisonments in earnest in the 1950s. Then again, Oruka also cites high statistics for remand in 1964, the first year of Kenya's independence, showing that the pattern of imprisonment had not immediately changed under Kenyan rule (72).

In *Punishment and Terrorism* Oruka does put forth some important criticisms of colonial rule in Africa, and he includes some defense of those who fight against colonialism. Oruka wrote his thesis and his book at a time when most African countries, with the exception of the Portuguese colonies, had won political independence from Europe. But there was the problem of white rule in Rhodesia (now Zimbabwe) and South Africa, and the larger problem of misrule in independent African countries, which was exacerbated by continued meddling and foreign control by Europe and the United States. Remember that Oruka maintains that a government has to have authority in order for its actions to count as punishment. In order to achieve this authority, it must receive at least a minimum amount of ethical consent from its subjects (44). This by itself is problematic as a key aspect of authority, partly because the "amount" of consent is undefined and subjective and partly Oruka does not outline what factors may or may not influence a person to withdraw or give their consent to be ruled. Despite his argument's shortcomings, Oruka uses specific examples to show that colonialism is rule without authority; therefore, colonial subjects do not give consent to be punished. In this case, rising up against their own government is not to be considered criminality and terrorism.

Oruka points out that the white-run government of South Africa calls those who resist their rule terrorists, but the African liberation forces call the white rulers terrorists due to their lack of legitimate authority to rule and punish. He calls attention to this practice of selectively labeling one's enemies terrorists without judging one's own actions by the same criteria. Critics of white rule within South Africa have made a similar point (Johns and Davies 1991: 157). Since the white regimes have no authority according to Oruka's (1985: 46–47) three-part definition, their acts constitute not punishment but terrorism. A few paragraphs later he mentions that authority erodes when punishment goes beyond a reasonable maximum, which is of course part of what gives a government authority or not, but only part (47). Hannah Arendt (1968a: 38, 41, 92, 160-61, 198, 204-07; 1968b) says political authority is based on the history of the founding moment of a society and the connection of the current government with that society's founding moment, none of which is mentioned by Oruka. Oruka does well to denounce colonialism and continuing white rule in Africa, but to do so he draws upon a rather limited account of what is wrong with colonial rule.

In the material first published in 1982 and later added to the second edition of *Punishment and Terrorism,* Oruka notes that governments which practice "legal" state terrorism often try to justify their excesses by saying their acts are the only way to counter revolutionary terrorists victimizing people and trying to dismantle legitimate rule. However, as Oruka (1985: 110–11) mentions, he thinks revolutionary groups are responding to the legal terrorism that preceded the formation of the revolutionary groups. This may very well be the case (I think it often is so), but ideally it should be argued at greater length.

Oruka contradicts himself when he discusses what to do with deposed African dictators. Consistent with his condemnation of capital punishment, he insists that dictators' lives should be spared and criticizes newly formed governments, some of which gained power through coups, who hastily kill deposed rulers. But then Oruka argues that such rulers could be "incarcerated for life, denied the possession of any property, and tortured" (110–11). Surprisingly, Oruka argues that such treatment could be morally justified if it were "commensurate with the crimes or acts committed by the oppressors during their days in power" (110–11). He suggests that this kind of legal terrorism could be morally justified against "three great sons of God," Francisco Macias Nguema of Equatorial Guinea, Idi Amin of Uganda, and Jean Bokassa of Central Africa. Oruka further suggests imprisonment and torture of these three would not be terroristic but merely punitive if the treatment did not exceed a "reasonable maximum" (110–11). Oruka explains in a related end note that he still intends to argue against punishment as an institution; however, given that in our world punishment is a functioning institution, imprisonment and torture of the three dictators would be morally justified (113, 128n52). My concern is that the rationale in these cases is still clearly retributive. I also find it difficult to imagine what a "reasonable maximum" of torture would be. On the one hand, Oruka's position here looks inadequate from a human rights perspective; on the other, from the perspective of those who want to kill all of yesterday's rulers, he is counseling great restraint.

Another interesting aspect of *Punishment and Terrorism* is his coverage of African traditions dealing with crime. He insists African traditions of compensation were neither retributive nor backward-looking, but forward-looking and therapeutic (48–49). Oruka does admit that there have been some "barbaric" traditions of punishment in Africa which should be stopped. For example, a Sudanese woman who has lost her virginity outside of marriage might be killed (51). He takes the nuanced position that we must realize that some traditions are useful and others are dangerous. Realizing that traditional African culture encompasses both compensation-restitution and inhumane punishments, Oruka argues, we can't simply preserve all traditions (53). If he advocates traditions of compensation, it is because he judges that these traditions are reasonable and helpful today, not because he counsels deference to all traditions because they are traditions (54). Mostly, he explains, he wants to promote reasonable solutions.

Once Oruka returned to Kenya in July 1970, he worked to turn "The Concept of Punishment" into a book. He wrote to Hedenius as early as 1971 saying he had shown it to a publisher who said that it was too specialized and therefore not marketable. (Correspondence of Oruka to Hedenius, October 4, 1971, Uppsala archive). Oruka writes on July 3, 1974, that his book *Punishment and Terrorism* is almost ready to be published. "The 1st part will consist of the work I did with you at Wayne. The 2nd part I have been doing since I came to Kenya."[14] Oruka had prepared his ideas on punishment as a paper to deliver at the Lagos Festival of the Arts and Culture, which was planned for 1975 but postponed until 1977. In that paper he cautioned listeners that Africans should not just champion their cultural practices because they are traditions. Rather, they should use reason to define a philosophy and a practice that "po[r]trays what is genuinely good, dignifying and progressive to those concerned" (Oruka 1977: 1). Oruka mostly repeats points from *Punishment and Terrorism* then concludes, "Punishment and terrorism in much of Africa today are inflicted with fear, hate and ignorance, and in complete disregard or perversion of reason and truth…. The only education or learning which punishment or terrorism imparts on its recipient are fear, hate and the dread of humanity" (46). His ambiguous use of terms like "terrorism" persists. But the important thing to note is that Oruka became a prophet of sorts, a prophet who speaks under the influence of reason, not any spirit or other-worldly revelation. He goes everywhere, even to Nigeria during a violent coup in 1976 and 1977, to speak out against abuses of power and to ask for reform.

On June 29, 1976, Oruka wrote Hedenius, "I sent you a copy of my book on punishment, I hope you have by now received it. I do not consider it my best work but I was very eager to get it published mostly because I believe that what it contains are currently some of the real and pressing issues in Africa." Hedenius later published a review of the book in Swedish. Oruka had it translated and wrote Hedenius back to say how much he appreciated the review.

Hedenius' review of Oruka's book was headlined, "Lawlessness in Today's Africa: Black Pounces upon Black, Terror and Massacres."[15] Hedenius counsels readers of the book to consider Oruka not naïve, but rather a rare example of a "pure-hearted and idealistic" person. He clarifies that Oruka holds a determinist view that would abolish current punishment practices and replace them with "different kinds of care." The only solution to crime brought about by destitution is to reform society so that it becomes harmonious. Hedenius notes how Oruka catalogs pre-colonial practices of compensation as well as cruel punishments such as mutilations and live burials. European penal codes were imposed during colonial times but practiced with cruelty and arbitrariness. Hedenius goes on to say that Oruka then outlines even crueler Black-against-Black practices in post-colonial Africa. Hedenius considers Oruka's main point to be that the twentieth century is a "dark century for Africa" due in large part to the inability of oppressed Africans to resist the abuse of power under which they suffer. Oruka speaks out against the use of capital punishment in both Kenya and the Central African Republic. Hedenius ends with praise for the bravery Oruka shows in writing *Punishment and Terrorism*. He says,

> How infinitely much more courageous and substantial isn't he in his thinking than these hordes of European and American philosophers who never have anything to contribute to the improvement of the world but rather maintain a wall of silence in such contexts. As far as I am concerned, I find some comfort and pride in the fact that he got his

fundamental philosophical training in Uppsala and then returned to his own country to become a leading intellectual.

And that is probably the most significant aspect of the book: Oruka spoke out clearly on an issue from his perspective as a philosopher located in Africa. Most philosophers didn't address these kinds of issues in their writings, and the few who did wrote from the safety of their European or American abodes. Oruka spoke out from the inside, challenging fellow Africans to rethink their ideas and their practices.

On June 21, 1977, he wrote that he'd received seven reviews of *Punishment and Terrorism*.[16] The first edition was nearly sold out, so the publisher planned to issue a reprint. Oruka wrote, "I am surprised at the success of the book, for I never expected that it would do that well" (Pers. comm., Oruka to Hedenius, 21 June 1977, Hedenius papers, Uppsala University archives). The book would be only the beginning of almost twenty more years of public philosophizing for Oruka on concerns ranging from Kenya and Africa to our larger international world of inequalities and injustices.

Sirkku Hellsten has written an article evaluating Oruka's ideas. She agrees that state terrorism is a big problem in many African countries, including Kenya. She likes his emphasis on excessive punishment, but then she goes a step further and says in many cases, it is not too much punishment that is the problem, but rather, the good people are punished while the criminals are set free and rewarded, all because the heads of state are rewarding loyal followers and punishing their internal critics. She gives several cases of this distortion, which she calls "reverse" or "upside-down" ethics. She refers briefly to the "Anglo-leasing and other grand corruption scandals" during which those who exposed the crimes (like John Githongo) or argued for more transparency were punished by the state; and in the "tragic West gate terrorist strike in September 2013" the reporters were punished when they revealed looting by "the rescuers" (Hellsten: 298). Her observations are in line with D. A. Masolo who notes that many African heads of state use the concept of "punishment" as a cover for getting rid of any perceived threats to their power (Masolo 2018: 213). But Hellsten concludes, nevertheless, that we need proper punishment, not that we need no punishment. She thought Oruka did not make a successful case for abolishing punishment. She thinks the state needs the power to threaten proper punishment to lawbreakers (Hellsten: 300). She thinks there is evidence that proper punishment has some deterrent effect, and she disagrees with Oruka's determinism (290). Since Oruka was right to note the danger posed by post-colonial rulers of Africa who terrorize their own people, she thinks that this danger has to be met by citizens practicing "civil action" against leaders who badly govern (300). Indeed as we will soon see, many critics of current practices of punishment engage in such civil action while they theorize about the need to end the practices of punishment currently harming people not only in Africa but around the world.

The issues that Oruka's book raise continue to be highly relevant to our world today. We could ask ourselves, would Oruka be disappointed, or heartened, by developments on this topic of punishment, prisons, and human rights since his passing? Even at the time of his death, his hopes for reform were not met. I think it would be fair to say that he would be disappointed at the slow pace of reforms. Prisons in many countries of Africa continue to be overcrowded and unhealthy. Around the world, too many societies continue to incarcerate at high numbers, while many societies offer little support to address the life conditions that often lead to crime (whether it be due to lack of funds or lack of political will to spend the funds in that way) (Sarkin 2008). Joycelyn M. Pollock (2014) notes that in places like the U.S., earlier plans for rehabilitation have been replaced by a retributive model. According to some theorists and practitioners, poverty exacerbates prison conditions because, for prisons to be a deterrent to crime, they must be worse than the conditions of poverty in the country. And so, if prisoners are harmed physically or psychologically and in need of healing, the current conditions cannot provide that but often further traumatize and damage poor individuals and their families (6, 9).

On the theoretical level there are some advances. Many philosophers, following the work of Angela Davis (2012: 35–51), analyse the "carceral state" with its prison-industrial complex and its school-to-prison pipeline. Theorists like Dorothy Roberts (2022) even show how social services like family protective services, ostensibly put in place to care for children, work with the police and courts to criminalize poor parents for not being able to meet their children's needs, instead of helping eradicate poverty for children and their families. Philosophers like Mechthild Nagel (2006; 2013) interrogate the wrong-headedness of philosophical arguments propping up current punitive systems both globally and in particular in Africa. Philosophers and peace activists have described restorative justice models based on African values of *ubuntu* as well as Native American practices in some ways similar to the African traditions Oruka championed. But not enough countries seem willing to put these into practice. Some faith communities facilitate these alternatives, however (Enns and Myers 2009).

One of the main and more obvious connections to Oruka's work is the development of the Black Lives Matter movement (BLM) and the "defund the police" movement in the U.S. As Patrisse Cullors (2018), co-founder of BLM explained, she was motivated to start the movement because she saw how her brother, who had mental illness but did not have the mental health care he needed, was criminalized and further harmed by the police. He now suffers additionally from post-traumatic stress disorder. She has been part of a movement to enforce new guidelines that would ensure that police can't abuse their power and that they would be accountable for wrong use of force. She and others in BLM want governments to fund programs that would prevent crime or de-escalate conflict.

Other more mainstream Democrats, following President Biden's State of the Union speech of 2022, suggest a "both-and" approach, not wanting to cut police funding but preferring to augment it with programs that have been proven to lower crime, like summer employment programs, better street lighting, reduced access to alcohol and guns, and turning vacant lots into parks. George Lopez (2022) notes that aggressive policing tactics turn communities against police. The best approaches, he suggests, are to address underlying problems and to invest in programs that help people lead healthy and successful lives, including preschool (shown to reduce arrests later in life) and cognitive behavioral therapy for teens. So, is the both-and approach the best?

Advocates of defunding the police point out that police unions across the U.S. are often opposed to any police reforms. Instead, they defend their members against abuse "even when there is ample evidence of misconduct" (Scheiber, Stockman, and Goodman 2020). According to Noam Scheiber, Farah Stockman, and J. David Goodman, police unions collect membership dues and then use their funds on "litigation to block reform" or even to back certain politicians in local and state races, while using "provocative rhetoric" to denounce liberal reforms or discredit progressive candidates and representatives. Some police union presidents like Lt. Bob Kroll of Minneapolis have called BLM protesters "a terrorist movement" and have overtly criticized Barack Obama for suggesting police reforms and praised Donald Trump for criticizing BLM (Scheiber, Stockman, and Goodman 2020). Due to these strident positions, those who want to change policing and the prison-industrial complex are skeptical that the police should be given more financial reserves to come up with ways to monitor themselves or provide a range of services better overseen by social services.

In addition to ample discussions of the need to curb abuse by the police, and to provide support for mental health, there are larger mental health issues hinted at in Oruka's analysis that are left unaddressed. Usually, mental health is discussed in the context of an individual not fitting in with society. What if it's the society that is sick? Karen Horney (1937) first discussed this problem in her early work, *The Neurotic Personality of our Time*. She thought that contemporary American consumer culture was giving rise to particular common neuroses.

The mental illness of whole social groups has been addressed by others. Native American historian Jack D. Forbes (Forbes and Jensen [1979] 1992) decades ago discussed an illness called "the Wetiko Cannibal Psychosis," drawing on the understanding of the *wétiko* by the Algonquin Indians of North America. The illness, considered a mind virus or mental illness, involves cannibalizing the life-force of others, consuming them to secure one's own personal wealth. Transmission of these ideas and behavior patterns is like that of a virus or infection. As explained by Alnoor Ladha and Martin Kirk (2016), "Wetiko short-circuits the individual's ability to see itself as an enmeshed and interdependent part of a balanced environment and raises the self-serving ego to supremacy. . . . It allows—indeed commands—the infected entity to consume far more than it needs in a blind, murderous daze of self-aggrandizement." This *wétiko* illness is seen as the impetus for the destructive treatment of our environment and other humans. It may result in "criminal" acts—but it could also produce behavior that the society, due to norms produced over centuries of colonialism, considers perfectly legal, albeit considered immoral from the perspective of environmentalists and human rights advocates. The problem is that those infected with *wétiko* are not being criminalized or sent to treatment, either. Often they end up as leaders. As therapist and lawyer Bill Eddy (2019) explains, narcissists and sociopaths get elected by using emotional warfare and counting on the media to amplify their voices to reach millions. And so, this account of Oruka's, explaining that criminals should be rehabilitated, is bolstered by accounts like Eddy's that show that dictators in Africa and elsewhere can't be coddled in their narcissism. A vigilant citizenry needs to know the danger signs of such malignant personalities and to avoid catapulting such persons into power.

And yet, even when contemporary psychiatrists see narcissistic egoism, delusions of grandeur, or other psychological problems in prominent Americans, this often does not result in such persons being whisked away in an ambulance (as Oruka described) to receive mental health treatment. Instead, such persons may be promoted to the head of their companies or even elected president of a country. While, as of 2022, certain heads of state like Vladimir Putin have been able to stay in power for a long time, it is in Africa that two heads of state have served the longest, for over forty years now. Others have changed government rules to ensure that they can stay as long as they want. Theorists note that these authoritarian strongmen have their ways of holding on to power, including promising their citizens safety and fast economic development (that may never materialize) (Cheeseman 2020). Oruka would no doubt be frustrated, as was Socrates, with the fact that the strong (as Thrasymachus stated in book 1 of the *Republic*, or as his contemporary Chuang Tzu wrote in "Cracking the Safe," see Merton 2004:

72–75) can write their own rules and evade punishment for their criminal actions. Socrates also thought that tyrants were miserable, owing to their addiction to power and their paranoia about being toppled. Oruka addressed these perennial questions of philosophy, with hopes, like Eddy's, that people could use their reason to become vigilant against such abuses of power, in politics and in our legislative bodies, courts, and prisons.

4

Oruka's Thesis/Book on Liberty and Early Years in Nairobi

After completing his MA degree at WSU, Oruka went back to Uppsala with Hedenius, and by the end of 1970 he received his licentiate in philosophy. It's important to note that in Scandinavia in general, and Sweden in particular, the doctorate degree was basically equivalent to the German "habilitation" (or second doctorate), while the Licentiate or Fil. Lic. Degree is considered equivalent to the American or British Ph.D.[1]

Oruka wrote "Ph.D" in parentheses after the Swedish Fil. Lic. degree in his curriculum vitae to lessen confusion, since the American and British doctorate was more widely known.[2] He also added there a grade of "'Beromlig' (Top)," and noted as well that he received from Uppsala University the Honorary Doctorate (Fil. Dr. Honoris Causa) (which we note would be generally equivalent to the habilitation) in June of 1993. (Unpublished curriculum vitae, 1993)

Odera Oruka had written his Fil.Lic. dissertation under Hedenius' direction in 1970, on the topic of liberty. It was a precursor to his later published work *The Philosophy of Liberty*. While the Uppsala University Philosophy Department does not have a copy of that thesis in its files, a friend and fellow graduate student of Odera Oruka's, Tommy Zaine, had copies of substantial parts of that thesis, given to him by Odera Oruka. The thesis' title is "On Liberty and the Subjection of Mankind." One of the first things that Oruka did upon graduating from Uppsala was to submit part of this thesis (about twenty-five pages, similar to chapter 4 of the book he will publish in 1991) for publication in a new journal, the first issue of *Cahiers philosophiques africains/African philosophical journal* published in Zaire (Oruka 1972a).[3] Much later, in 1991, Oruka finally published the entire thesis along with other related writings in a book entitled *The Philosophy of Liberty: An Essay on Political Philosophy* (Nairobi: Standard Textbooks Graphics and Publishing).[4] The changes he made to the earlier text are minimal. Zaine's manuscripts correspond to pp. 3–31 of the published book, that is, chapters 1 and 2.[5] We can reasonably infer that chapters 3–6 of the published book, that is, up to p. 84 were also part of the original thesis. The other parts (chapters 7 and 8) show signs of having been written later.[6] For convenience's sake I am going to refer to the published book's page numbers, but I will only discuss here the part I think he wrote as his thesis in 1970.

While the ostensible theme of the document is social liberty or freedom, throughout the work, we see the theme of concern for the welfare of the poor. The survey covers key historical figures. Looking at Plotinus and Origen, he criticizes them for their idea of Christianity that ignores the difficult conditions of material existence for the many poor. He disagrees that a slave in chains could be "free" in any relevant sense, or that God could provide liberation apart from material conditions. He asserted that mental and intellectual liberty could not be achieved by ignoring social realities. (Oruka 1996: 8, 10).

Oruka identifies himself as a utilitarian influenced by Marxism. He has a criticism of Kant's idea of a moral law that is indifferent to benefits. "Kant forgot that morality and freedom are issues only in a collective existence, a society. And societies exist only for the sole purpose of ensuring or fulfilling certain human ends or desires." (18) He also criticizes Kant for asserting that there is a universal moral law. He asks the reader to look at our world—filled with multiple moralities. If Kant were to try to introduce his "universal morality" for a basis for world government, it would appear in our current world as one of many moralities competing for political domination. (18)

Oruka then offered his criticisms of Hobbes' *Leviathan*. A government should not only offer security and nothing else to its citizenry, for security itself is conditional upon social welfare. And so, government must concern itself with social welfare.

Oruka is not exactly a utilitarian. He does say that what he likes about Mill is that Mill holds that no opinion can be sure to be the truth. He approves of this criticism of the universality of truth. But he charges that utilitarianism has a key shortcoming. Mill's emphasis on freedom can lead to free trade, free enterprise, monopoly capitalism, and the expansion of the gap between the have and have-nots. (22) Also, a stress on freedom can lead to anarchy and a neglect of community. (22) He also disagrees with James Burnham. Burnham was an American philosophy professor who had been a communist in the 1920s and 1930s but became an anti-communist after 1940, and he claimed that the Machiavellian tradition justified elite control of the masses through use of myth (23).[7] Oruka explains his own view (in contrast to Burnham), that wealth and economic power must first be centralized and then distributed in order to avoid their being concentrated among the few (25). He explains that what he likes about Marxism is its realistic emphasis on the concern over poverty and misery. Unlike the other philosophers who ignore or mystify poverty, Marx addresses it. But he does not like the idea of inevitability of progress and eventual revolution, and he thinks that there is no final stage of history—rather, there is no end to history. (30–32)

Chapter 3 of the book *Philosophy of Liberty* shows signs of either being part of the thesis and later being updated, or being written a few years later than the thesis, in the mid-1970s. It seems related in topic to early papers published by Oruka in 1973 (and it is not unusual for recent graduates to publish part of their theses as articles). Chapter 3 references a book written in 1974. It focuses on Marxism and Existentialism. If you will remember from the discussion in our previous chapter, during this time in 1970 Hedenius was offering lectures on Marxism and Existentialism, not because he wanted to, but because he was capitulating to pressures of Uppsala University students who had demanded that such subjects be offered. So this chapter surveys Marx and Sartre and evaluates the pros and cons of their approaches and insights regarding liberty.

Reflecting further on Marx's idea of historical determinism, and the reasons for his predictions not coming true in history, Oruka explains how he thinks Africa's current situation departs from classical Marxist analysis. In Africa, he explains, there is a difference between the ruling class and the dominant class. While Africans have won independence and have taken political power, that makes them only the rulers. They are not the dominant class, since in most cases, "the dominant class is a non-indigenous commune using the indigenous ruling class as the proxy" for their economic domination. People angry with economic circumstances vent their anger on African rulers rather than the dominant class. On top of this, the foreign-based dominant class treats African rulers like their errand-boys and vents anger if they bungle the errand. If there is too much bungling, the foreign dominant class helps to orchestrate a coup to replace one group of rulers with another. (Oruka does not name names, but keep in mind that Patrice Lumumba was assassinated in 1961 and replaced by Mobutu. Scholars variously pin the assassination on Belgium, Britain, or the USA's CIA (Bustin 2002; Azikiwe 2013; Gilbert and Reynolds 2008: 385-86). While it's possible that a coup could be a genuine popular response of the people to bad rulers, they may find their ability to change government policies hindered by the fact that the "the country was already mortgaged to foreign powers" (Oruka 1996: 38–39, quote 39). Attempts at genuine social revolution end up being short-lived as they are attacked by international pressures. Oruka refers to a Marxist theoretician, Mihailo Markovic, who in a 1974 book says that a successful social revolution needs a closed national market that can defend itself against international pressure, but Oruka notes that in Africa, "this requirement is next to impossible" (ibid., p. 40).

In chapter 4 he begins to delineate the meaning of liberty and what it means to have a right. He refers to Swedish philosophy professor Stig Kanger and his discussion of eight kinds of rights (Kanger and Kanger 1966). Rights help us to fulfill needs. He discusses primary and secondary needs and suggests that in different contexts, some things (like heat) could be considered a need (during Swedish winter) or a luxury (in Kenya). (Oruka 1996:51; see also Oruka 1972a:148–51) He disagrees with Oppenheim's (1961) definition of freedom[8] which Oruka charges with defending a laissez-faire idea of liberty. Oppenheim defended the famous saying that everyone, including the homeless, were "free to sleep under bridges." This use of "liberty" obfuscates the central role of economic liberty in ensuring other forms of liberty (Oruka 1996:54; Oppenheim, online as in previous end note). Oruka argues that Oppenheim is using the word "impossible" too restrictively; lack of opportunity also results in impossibility, according to Oruka. For example (and here Oruka was no doubt drawing upon his personal experience), if one is moneyless and lives in a place where schools are not free, it is impossible for that person to get an education. (Oruka 1996: 55–56; see also Oruka 1972a:157) Oppenheim opposed the UNESCO definition of liberty which said liberty included not only lack of restraint but also "positive organization of the social and economic conditions of the people" (Oruka 1996: 58). Oruka instead agrees with UNESCO's definition, and criticizes Oppenheim for having a suppressed premise to his argument, that is, he has an assumption that liberty has nothing to do with social and economic contexts of individuals (see Oruka 1996: 83, note 6).

In chapters 5 and 6, Oruka outlines humanity's primary and secondary needs, and shows how types of freedom help humans to fulfill their needs. Indeed, he argues in his conclusion that the point about freedom being defined by needs is the "cardinal idea" of his whole book (82). After defining economic freedom in capitalist and socialist contexts, he puts forward his own definition of economic freedom, which is: "freedom to satisfy all one's biological needs and freedom from exploitation from any other person(s)" (66). The second part of his definition is intended to reject capitalist notions of economic freedom, since they are based on contracts and contracts can be exploitative. He admits that his definition is close to the socialist definition (67). He expresses concern that economic dependence can interfere with one having effective political freedom, insofar as the poor may be forced to suppress their opinions in order to receive material help (70). On this point he refers both to international examples, such as poor countries forced to "toe the US line" at the UN so that they could get foreign aid (70), and also to his experience in the United States, where black people have formal but not effective political equality with whites, meaning, they are not able to fulfill their needs through political participation. (71)

Oruka in general supports intellectual freedom, and insists that for it to be realized a society should provide free education for its members (72). However, he gives an example of it being justifiably curtailed in order to meet primary needs, for example, when space research involving sending humans to the moon has to be curtailed in order to fund welfare of poor Americans (73).[9] He also mentions scenarios when two parties disagree but neither holds a position related to a primary freedom, such as the debate between free thinkers and those who hold religious dogma. He asks, which party should we remove? I don't understand why "removal" is the best option here. He has under-described his scenario. But he says that we should remove the party who has a greater probability of being wrong. (73) In his experience, intellectual beliefs (like those of the free-thinker) are to be upheld since they "are often more objective than religious beliefs and political dogmas" (74). Here he explains he is trying to fight against a history where those who challenged religious or political dogmas have been suppressed. (74) The influence of Hedenius (and Russell) is clear here. Likewise when he speaks of religious freedom, he also asserts the freedom to be non-religious. He defines religious freedom as freedom to believe in a supernatural being and to be more concerned about the afterlife than a good life here on earth. He also notes that religions sometimes impinge upon sexual freedom, for example, the Catholic church may have its own stipulations about whether and when a marriage can take place (76–80).

Oruka describes and defends the need for cultural freedom, which he explains is the freedom to choose to maintain or to change one's culture in order to pursue the good life. He gives as an example of the latter the Chinese "cultural revolution" which had as its goal the pursuit of a more "rational culture." He then suggests that Africans could as well shirk the colonial mentality and find a new way to live (75). Here he mentions only freedom from colonial practices. He does not mention maintaining or resurrecting African cultural traditions. He sums up his treatment of the six liberties by suggesting that economic freedom is the most fundamental, which makes political freedom possible, which makes cultural freedom possible; and if one has cultural freedom, then one can have intellectual, religious, and sexual freedom (80).

By July 30, 1970, Oruka was writing Hedenius from Nairobi. He had gone back there both because his funds in Sweden had run out and also because he had hopes of securing a teaching job in the philosophy department. But as he wrote in July, his appointment in the department had not yet been confirmed, because Bishop Neill was on a holiday until September. Oruka thought there was a lot of "confusion" about the position, so he was also applying for another job as the secretary of East African exams.

In the same correspondence Oruka goes on to say: "Despite these disappointments I have a strong feeling that this is my country and I have to fight my way out as far as possible." He also tells Hedenius how much he appreciates all Hedenius has done for him.

"Now that I am home I can tell you that I consider the time I spent studying under you as the most honorable period of my stay abroad. You made me exercise my intelligence . . . you have indeed done more for me than you perhaps are aware of: I don't mean that you gave me grades, I mean that you gave me confidence to try to understand life not to mention study philosophy. Since I started school I had many teachers but none I consider as great as you . . . I mean the greatness which comes from the natural charm, wit, and intelligence of a personality. . . . Please accept my very high appreciation of the effort you have made, both financially and professionally, to make me finish my studies."

Hedenius writes Oruka back on September 4, 1970, saying: "I can never live up to your high appreciation of me as a friend and a teacher . . . I must sincerely tell you, that I have never had a pupil whom (sic) I have liked more. Intelligent and even brilliant people are not rare in the philosophical department. But few have your honesty and sincere interest in what is essential in human problems." (Uppsala archive).

The Uppsala archive is filled with correspondence between Oruka and Hedenius regarding Oruka's chances of being hired to teach philosophy at UON. Oruka explained that when he first met A. S. Neill, the Catholic bishop in charge of the small joint Philosophy-Religious Studies department there, he was immediately questioned about his religious affiliation. Oruka says, "For my survival with him, I answered 'Catholic.'" (corresp. September 29, 1970 Uppsala archive). Upon hearing this, Neill suggested that Oruka go to the priest who was Head of the Catholic Secretariat in Nairobi to see if they would contribute funds to hire him, but Oruka said that the Secretariat was skeptical that Oruka was "still a good Catholic" after having studied at Uppsala since it was a "Protestant town" (ibid). Oruka notes that a Catholic Dutch Father/Priest had already begun teaching at University of Nairobi, and Oruka sensed that the priest was more of a priority to the Secretariat than himself. All of this runaround had Oruka frustrated. He wrote "I am completely unsure as to what is behind all these. I get the impression that Bishop Neill is not interested in employing me and that he is trying to save his face about it" (ibid). No wonder that Oruka was suspicious, with his previous concern about Bertrand Russell's dismissal from teaching at an American university.

Oruka realized that Neill was using lack of funds as the reason why he would not be hired. So Oruka wrote October 30, 1970 with the good news that he had been appointed because of a sympathetic faculty member in the History department deciding to contribute part of their departmental budget in order to hire him. In exchange, he would teach the history of political ideas and philosophy of history. (Uppsala archive). He wrote on April 10, 1971 that although he had been teaching in a temporary position, Bishop Neill did not hire him for a permanent position but instead hired another faculty member in Religion. Out of concern for his future employment he began to submit applications for jobs elsewhere. He was anxious to publish his work so that he could apply for the permanent position at his university, and told Hedenius with pride that some of his writings on liberty would be published in *African Philosophical Journal*. He mentions that he is lecturing first and third year students in Ethics, and that, "I don't want to make the course too academic and theoretical. My aim is to discuss the practical social issues that have a bearing on morality (ibid)."

Oruka wrote about his discomfort in the department in those early years. He and Joseph Nyasani were recruited at the same time. Oruka explained, "Neill himself used to refer to us both as 'Our two assistant African tutorial assistants,'" thereby already reducing their low rank of Tutorial Assistant even lower by repeating "assistant" twice (Oruka 1990c: 126). In 1971, when Neill heard that Oruka only had about ten students sign up for logic, Neill responded by saying he did not think Africans were suited for its study, since "the African mind is intuitive, not logical," whereas the Western mind had a long exposure to logic since the days of Aristotle (Oruka 1990c: 127).

A year passed before Oruka wrote Hedenius again, with the good news that some of his work on both punishment and liberty had been published. Also, he had established the Philosophical Association of Kenya, and had been asked to be co-editor of the *African Philosophical Journal* from Kinshasa. He was teaching Ethics, but still feeling strain with Bishop Neill since for the Bishop, "ethics is religion and religion ethics." (April 14, 1972). He wrote again May 16, 1972, sending Hedenius a news clipping with the public advertising of the post in the philosophy department, proving his suspicions that Neill did not recommend him for the position. Now Oruka would have to apply just like outsiders, and he asked Hedenius to write him a letter of reference. At stake was whether the licentiate from Uppsala was equivalent to an American Ph.D. Hedenius wrote a letter of reference stating with confidence that the degree was equivalent to an American Ph.D.

Oruka was not taking chances. He also applied for a position at Florida State University; it was to be a joint position between them and Florida Agricultural and Mechanical University. But Oruka told his professor, "You know how much I hate American life; but as things stand for me here I am thinking of going there, if they give me a chance. It is impossible to be the only lay man among seven priests and work happily. They seem to be concerned even with the morality of my social life outside the department." (May 16, 1972) Hedenius wrote a letter of reference to the Chairman of the Philosophy Dept at Florida State University on June 7, 1972, recommending

Oruka and stating that the licentiate "roughly corresponds to a Ph.D. in any reputable university in the U.S."

Oruka's letter to Hedenius of June 9, 1972, is jubilant. "The Bishop is defeated!" he exclaims. Oruka had been given the permanent position in the department in Nairobi. He explains that Hedenius' letter, along with a letter from another professor (not named), greatly supported him. Oruka wasted no time in using his academic freedom. In the same letter he says, "Recently I gave a public speech in Nairobi in which I attacked mythologies (religions) as the main factors that hinder African philosophical progress. About 300 people attended and the priests did not like and were infuriated." (ibid) He also mentions that Florida State University assured him of a job. He tells Hedenius that he thinks that nevertheless he should stay in Nairobi. In a letter of September 12, 1972, Oruka mentions that Florida State / Florida A and M offered him a yearly salary of $13,000, and that Prof. Gruender had phoned to Nairobi. David Felder, his friend from Wayne State (a fellow graduate student), now at Florida A and M, had written Oruka to welcome him back to the States. But Oruka explains to Hedenius that he turned down this job offer.

In this letter Oruka also tells Hedenius the inside story of why Neill opposed his permanent appointment, told to him by someone on the Appointments committee. Neill had argued that Oruka's education in philosophy had not been broad enough, because he had only learned Ethics and not other branches of philosophy. Neill also insisted that job candidates had to have six years of hard study, but that Oruka had not had that. For these reasons Neill was favoring two European candidates who had received PhD's, and another Kenyan who was still working toward the Ph.D. With this as a background Oruka had been called in for an interview and was able to point out to the committee that he had already been teaching, in addition to Ethics, logic, Philosophy of Art, Philosophy of History, and Philosophy of Religion. (Remember that these subjects were all part of the Uppsala program in Practical Philosophy.) With publications as well as his founding of the Philosophical Association of Kenya and his co-editorship, all those impressed with his credentials chose him out of the ten finalist candidates. The Chairman of the Board and the Vice-Chancellor agreed with the recommendation and he was hired (correspondence, Oruka to Hedenius, September 12, 1972, Uppsala archive).

So, what more can we learn about this situation, with the benefit of hindsight? If we look at Neill's (1991) autobiography, *God's Apprentice*, we hear straight from Neill his own perspective, and we can see his justifications for his actions as well as some problematic positions that Oruka and others would disagree with. Neill describes himself as someone concerned for education in Africa. His first visit to Africa in 1950 was to survey theological education there. He found seminaries to be "small, under-staffed and ill equipped" and coursework "so unimaginatively Western." (275) As he explained, "few of the teachers, the majority of whom had failed to learn thoroughly any African language, had ever asked themselves how the African mind works, and how students could be helped to rethink Christian truth in their own way." (275) He wanted African Christians to develop their own theology (albeit Christian) based on grappling with their own questions, not by copying Western theologians. Statements like this show a concern to understand Africans, but also a presumption that the African mind is different from the European mind. When Neill agreed to try to help University of Nairobi set up a department of religion, he noted that he was met with suspicion. Kenyan churches were conservative, and were afraid the university would be a source of heretical thought. (279) Even before the project got off the ground, there was tension between the Roman Catholic Archbishop of Nairobi and the Anglican Archbishop of Nairobi over who would have influence over the appointments in such a department (281).

The University College (as it was known then) finally agreed that a department could be supported, but not until after 1973, if Neill could raise funds from religious bodies to begin hiring in 1970. (282) Soon after that (in 1970) the University of East Africa was ended, so that the University College then became University of Nairobi. (286) Neill says as soon as he arrived to take over the task of creating the department, he found out that an Appointments committee had already hired two people, when there were only funds to hire one, and that one of their hires, he found out, had not completed his Master's degree as he had claimed to do. (287) Perhaps these kinds of problems predisposed Neill to be skeptical of Oruka. Neill describes how pleased he was that "Dr. J.G. Donders, the Dutch White Father" was hired with financial help from the Roman Catholic Secretariat. Neill then mentions hiring "Dr. Henry Odera," but after mentioning Oruka's degrees from WSU and Uppsala, he continues that he "was not very well qualified, but he grew to the work, and showed considerable originality and enterprise.... In any case, we felt it essential to have a Kenyan member of staff in the sub-department of philosophy."[10] (292) Oruka had to contend with this under-estimation of his qualifications and abilities for quite some time.

Neill, as his autobiography states, found himself in a situation in the early 1970s where there were a lot of challenges to the standard curriculum at University of Nairobi. On the one hand, Neill felt strongly that the Religious Studies and Philosophy department should have an international perspective. He wanted to teach World Religions, not just Christianity, and he sponsored a series of lectures on world religions ("Religious Communities of Kenya") that also appealed to the general public. His department offered courses on

African traditions in Religion, and created a course on "religions of East Africa" that was required of all first year students. He also created a course called Christianity in Africa that included the study of Ethiopian churches as well as African prophets like Simon Kimbango. He mentioned the changes in the History and English departments, where they emphasized courses on African history and literature to the exclusion of European topics. While Neill said he could only embrace the idea of an African university for Africans "with grave reservations," he thought it was easy to respond to this request in the context of religious studies. But from Neill's perspective, a course on African philosophy would be much more difficult. (291–92)

Neill thought that one could not teach philosophy without discussing its long history in Europe. He thought it was clear that Africans did not have any elaborate or systematic patterns of thought, and if that was what was meant by philosophy, Africans did not have one. But, they do have a Weltanschauung or general outlook on the world, which was a broader sense of philosophy. For example, "The African does not think in abstract terms of being, but of vital force, what a thing does or can do.... An African is not devoid of ideas of right and wrong, but these are related not to offences against an abstract set of laws, still less to transgressions against the love of a holy God; they are seen as actions which enhance the being of the family, or else rend and damage its carefully woven fabric." (294) Here Neill clearly shows his indebtedness to the study of "Bantu Philosophy" by Placide Tempels. He explained that Oruka had designed courses in Ethics that looked at the different ethical views within Africa, for example, the fact that the Kikuyu ethnic group required male and female circumcision, while the Luo ethnic group, being Nilotic, regarded the practice "with a mixture of dislike and contempt" (294)

Joseph Donders, who was a member of the University of Nairobi Philosophy and Religious Studies Department at the same time in the 1970s as Oruka, described his first impressions of Oruka:

He was a typical Luo, straight up like a pencil, dressed like a gentleman. With a flower in a buttonhole, always ... I only know that the final outcome of his studies that he was a typical pragmatist. That's why he was interested in teaching Ethics ... One of his favorite topics was death penalty. He was always fighting against the death penalty.[11]

According to Donders, Oruka did not come to UON knowing anything about the existence of African philosophy. Donders explained that he himself had read works by Placide Tempels, Léopold Sédar Senghor, and other authors in the journal, *Presence Africaine* but that Oruka had not done so.

This lack of background put him at odds, at first, with some of the other faculty members at UON, as Donders explains:

> We were always having inter-faculty meetings ... he also had difficulties with his African confreres, colleagues, who considered him to be studying in a context they did not know about, a foreign context. Of course now he is a kind of representative of African philosophy. But at first he did not believe in African philosophy at all. And that's why he definitely did not relate well to Okot p'Bitek or Ngugi wa Thiong'o. They lived in a completely different context.[12]

Was this a fair estimate of Oruka's background? Oruka himself wrote that little in his education at Wayne State or Uppsala prepared him in African philosophy since both institutions were dominated by "Analytical philosophy" (1990c: 127). But he did think that analytical training could be put to use as a "tool" for investigating African philosophy (1990c: 128). While it may be that Oruka still had much to learn about African philosophy at the start of his time in UON, he had gained some important background during his time in Sweden and the U.S. He delivered a talk on "Black Consciousness" in Nairobi in 1971, which was very soon after his return to Kenya. It was published in a Kenyan journal, *Joliso*, in 1973, and anthologized in his *Trends* book (1990c: 70–87). There, he surveys the works of Frantz Fanon, Léopold Senghor, Kwame Nkrumah, Eldridge Cleaver, Amilcar Cabral, and Steve Biko.

Donders went on to explain that the UON faculty as well as undergraduate students encouraged Oruka to be open to exploring African philosophical perspectives. Donders said:

> He started to get aware that in the French speaking part of Africa, they had been thinking in completely different ways. Then there was one professor in the History department, I forgot his name, but he was giving a course on Africans in the diaspora. He was not a Kenyan, maybe American, but he was black. He stressed that Africans should read their own tradition instead of always reading about others' traditions. Okot p'Bitek called together the medical students and said, "Don't forget that your ancestors had been healing people successfully," that you should not forget about that ... and when you were studying architecture, take care for the African traditions, that the Father should not have to walk through the room of his daughter. The Kikuyus had a hut for the boys, girls, father, hut for the mother, servants and so on. Ngugi wa Thiong'o built his house, I was there once, it was like that. A hut for the boys, a hut for the girls. So you had that whole idea, Kenya got aware of its Kenyaness.

> So that was hanging in the air. Somebody like I came in like a complete stranger. But I think most probably I knew more about African philosophy than Henry Odera. I think so.[13]

Donders explained that he himself had to change his perspective through his experience in Kenya. The Roman Catholic Church was moving away from a "Baltimore Catechism" memorization model to one that closely related to African religious experience. Donders wanted to see "Jesus in the context of the Africans," and he thought that a new approach was needed to avoid the problem of students who, wanting to get in touch with their African identities, would reject their Christian identities as a foreign or colonial imposition. Donders thought that a lot of youths were struggling with questions of identity and belonging. According to Donders, Oruka said he felt alone in Sweden, as if he didn't fit in, but then had similar emotions when he came back to Kenya. So it was a struggle, but also a good challenge, to combine philosophical activity with contemporary African culture.

Taban lo Liyong offered his perspective on how Oruka and the sage philosophy project fit into the larger context of changes spearheaded at the time by the UON Department of Literature and Languages. Born in Sudan, he grew up in Uganda and attended university in the United States. He arrived at UON in 1968, having just received his MFA from the University of Iowa. Makerere University in Kampala had already converted its curriculum away from a Eurocentric emphasis. He and others worked for three years to change the curriculum at UON likewise, famously declaring their goal to abolish the English Department, and in its it place, have a department of literatures and languages that included French as well as English studies. This new department would focus on East African, African, Commonwealth and Caribbean literatures, including oral literatures. They also expanded the curriculum to include song, dance, music, and theater. They also taught literature in the context of political developments (Liyong 1971). Lo Liyong explains that he was first hired into the Cultural Division of the Institute of Development Studies.[14] He was recruited by Ngugi wa Thiong'o to "storm" the English department. He was willing to do it because it fit his overall philosophy of education. In his essay "The Education of Taban lo Liyong," he satirizes and critiques the kind of education he received in American universities. In a place where his professors "don't read Mazrui or Mboya," they "crammed" knowledge into the heads of students "like indigestible food" (Liyong 1966: 17–18). In contrast, education should be meaningful, contextual, and learnable through experience. After all, "You must have the necessary experience to give any new information flesh and blood and life, otherwise it remains a superstition" (18). Drawing on William James, he explains that the information must be related to a learner's aspirations. A revised curriculum would be relevant to African students and the project of decolonization.

Taban lo Liyong reminisced about Oruka's participation in and contribution to this larger project of decolonizing the curriculum. When Oruka came back from Sweden, he became a member of the decolonizing group. Lo Liyong explained that he had his students collect stories from their rural home areas, and that soon Oruka was also doing this.[15]

Donders remembered three activities happening roughly concurrently: the creation of the Philosophical Association of Kenya, the creation of the journal *Thought and Practice,* and the start of the sage philosophy project. During this time Oruka met and interacted with West African philosophers like Kwasi Wiredu and Peter Bodunrin when they came to UON as external examiners. The journal *Second Order* was being published in Nigeria and Oruka published an early article in it. Likewise, Kwasi Wiredu and other philosophers published articles in the Nairobi-based *Thought and Practice.* This pan-African exchange of ideas was an alternative to a Eurocentric dialogue. Oruka thrived in this atmosphere of mutual discussion and exchange. He had a forum in which to express his ideas on the need for social and economic reform. He was also reshaping his own ideas on African philosophy. He was attracted to the idea of philosophy rooted in the contemporary problems facing Africa. Oruka explained that the way he was taught Practical Philosophy in Uppsala meant that concepts and principles are "discussed an applied to the understanding and improvement of the conditions of human life" (1990c: 128).

Oruka founded the Philosophical Association of Kenya in 1973. Oruka was President, Donders was Secretary, and Jacob Ombonya (a student) was Treasurer. Oruka noted that "The majority of the members were students and staff from Departments outside ours" (1990c; 130). According to Donders, its beginnings were quite chaotic. He remembered the time period when Oruka was very active in the organization, the early 1970s, and chronicled the association's rough beginnings, learning "the hard way," by experience.

The first time Odera went to an international conference, I think it was in Bulgaria, and he went to the airport, arrives at the airport, and he was there without a passport. I had to go back in a hurry, with a taxi, to get his passport. He had made a whole list of things he needed, but he forgot to put the passport on the list. So I had to bring it to the airport. And he made his plane. Over the speakers it said "Dr. Henry Odera!!" I thought it would be better that he go than I. I could have gone. Then after that he organized the Philosophical Association of Kenya. And he was not a good organizer at all. And he had to organize, several times he organized conferences. But very often people did not turn up. But it started to work more or less.[16]

Oruka explained that at UON many people, including the theologians in his department (which combined philosophy and religious studies) didn't really understand the distinction between the two fields. Oruka was frustrated that the philosophy part of the department was kept small. He worked hard to finally get the Philosophy department separated from Religious Studies in 1980. On his way to Turkey for a conference, he was able to stop in Rome and interview Dismas Masolo, a Kenyan who was studying at the Gregorian and had completed a dissertation on African Philosophy. Oruka successfully recruited him to the department (1990c: 127, 156). Oruka was also frustrated that his colleagues back in the early 1970s had equated African philosophy with Tempels. His first talk and article addressing African philosophy, published in 1972, was intended as a criticism of Tempels and his own colleagues. "I gathered courage," Oruka wrote about the decision to publish the article, knowing that it would bring tension with his colleagues (1990c: 128).

Several philosophers in sub-Saharan Africa saw their role as encouraging Africans to renounce superstition, mythology, and dogmatism. Kwasi Wiredu was one of the first African philosophers to pioneer this effort to change religious beliefs. In fact, he insisted that change had to come to traditional Africa, because he felt that some old ideas were harmful. He outlined three major hindrances to African cultural regeneration: anachronism, authoritarianism, and supernaturalism. But he also insisted that Africa had very wise and philosophical persons from whom a lot could be learned, especially if one paid attention to the nuances of concepts in African languages. In a 1972 issue of *Second Order*, Wiredu wrote that "it is a particular (though not exclusive) responsibility of African philosophers to research into their traditional background of philosophical thought" (12). However, while traditional concepts and codes of conduct should be an area of study, they should not lead to anachronism—by which he meant, the attempt to turn back the hands of time or cling to the days of yesteryear.

Wiredu was the first to label "what 'our elders' said" as "folk philosophies." While attempts to construct from "the living wise men of the tribe" "the elaborate and argumentative reasons" behind the belief systems and moral guidelines of "our philosophers of old" is in itself sure to "provide exciting challenges to the dedicated researcher," the resulting material could not, he thought, help to tackle most modern problems in Africa (5). Along with interest in past traditions, there should also be attraction to scientific method and clear argumentation to guide African youths in the new moral dilemmas facing contemporary African society.

Three years later, in the same journal, Oruka (1975) explained that he and others at UON were already engaged in a project along the lines of Wiredu's description. He said, "We are seeking to unsheath, through constant contacts and discussions with those concerned, the elaborate philosophical views and reasons from the living traditional Kenyan thinkers and sages" (54n6). He follows Wiredu's words and ideas closely enough to repeat the descriptors "elaborate" and "reasons." In his subsequent book he adopted the descriptors "folk philosophies" and "folk sage," but clarified that, in addition to elders who are examples of folk sagacity, there are some who are philosophic sages able to scrutinize prevailing beliefs and give sustained arguments for their positions. The elders, he asserted, are more than just depositories of outdated folk wisdom.

Donders said that he helped Henry Odera come up with the project of interviewing sages. In early articles Oruka acknowledged that the project began between him and Donders, and he also mentions Jesse Mugambi's participation (54n6; Oruka 1991b: 17–18). After the project got started, Odera continued it and Donders dropped out to pursue other interests. Even before the project was called "sage philosophy," Donders experimented with getting his students involved in interviewing elder members of their family. As Donders explains, he was asked to write an article on African celebrations for a Dutch journal. At the time he was teaching a class of 110 students. He got the idea of asking them to go home over break and interview someone from their family about celebrations. He then reflected on their interviews in his article. He had been pleased with the results. So it was with that experience in the background that he and Oruka thought up the idea of asking students first to identify and then later to interview wise sages from their rural home communities.

As Donders explains, identifying sages was the first part. Donders thinks that he and Oruka looked at the names put forward by students from different ethnic communities and language groups. If certain names were repeated often, then the best students in that language group were asked to go and interview those individuals. Donders insisted that students had been told to go talk to the sages without asking leading questions. He explained that a student should not go up to a sage and ask, "What happens after death?" Such a question presumes there is something after death. Students were told to ask something more open-ended, like "What about death?"

Donders remembered going with Oruka to interview Oruka's own father, Oruka Rang'inya.[17] Mostly the interviews were assignments for undergraduate students. Donders said it was intended to be that way since Oruka wanted to have a collection of interviews from a variety of language and ethnic groups. They collected about sixty or so interviews, but Donders admits that at first they didn't know what to do with the interviews. The transcripts of the cassettes were in the department for months. Donders explained that there needed to be a sorting process, because some of the interviews were not very serious. But he left that sorting process up to Oruka.

In a letter to Hedenius about Donders dated July 3, 1974, Oruka stated that Donders had taken Neill's place as acting chair of the department. "He is younger and much more liberal and modern than the Bishop. But he is of course a priest and this puts a limit on his philosophical free argument. However I like him much more than the Bishop and we have much to do together."[18] Among other news of recent publications, Oruka also mentioned that just then the university was closed due to clashes between students and police. Students wanted the removal of a Danish architecture professor, saying that he was anti-African.

In the 11th Inaugural Lecture given by Donders on March 10, 1977, and entitled "Don't Fence Us In: The Liberating Role of Philosophy," Donders discusses the project he and Oruka had been engaged in. He explains, "Together with Dr. Henry Odera, a Senior Lecturer in our Department, we have been trying in cooperation with our first generation of philosophy students in the Department, to find out about that wisdom and about the wise men and women in this Republic of Kenya. . . . Thanks to a grant from the Dean's Committee of this University, these wise people were visited. They were asked not to answer questions but to air their views" (Donders 1977: 11). Donders notes that one sage, Paul Mbuya, said that he knew that people in his community considered him to be wise, but that he himself was hesitant to say he was wise, because there were many things that he knew he did not know. Donders then compared Mbuya's humility to the wisdom of Socrates (11–13). Donders went on to say that this epistemic humility is what makes philosophy different than imperialism, colonialism, totalitarianism, and dictatorship, all of which presume that they have the answers (13). Donders also referred to "another Kenyan sage, William Ayodo from Kabondo," who said that humans, unlike animals, were capable of liberating themselves (14). Donders then suggested that the contemporary world unthinkingly props up a "myth" that science can explain our whole world materialistically, a belief he thought denied that many aspects of our life are still mysteries (15). Thus Donders reasserted the importance of religious reflection on life and questioning the wisdom of equating philosophy with scientific thinking.

On June 29, 1976, Oruka wrote Hedenius to say that his book on punishment was published. He also wrote that he would be visiting Sweden with his wife Millicent and oldest son Owiso and staying with his friend Tommie Zaine. He hoped to see Hedenius in person, and he did.

Oruka's only novel, *In the Mother Africa (The Family Broke Down)*, a thinly veiled autobiography, is the main source for learning about his adventures and perspectives during a year's sabbatical in Nigeria, where he was Visiting Senior Lecturer at the University of Ibadan from 1976 to 1977. The trip to Nigeria was preceded by one month each in Sweden and England. Oruka submitted the novel to publishers, but it had been rejected.[19] It seems he did not continue his attempts to publish the work. Oruka gave the manuscript to Tommie Zaine for safekeeping, and Zaine shared it with me in 2011. There are characters intended to portray Oruka himself ("Omolo Jangaga"), his wife Millicent ("Akello"), and son Owiso ("Osino"); Oruka's Swedish girlfriend Gunilla ("Ulla"); Hedenius ("Gunnar Johansson") and his wife Astrid ("Brit"); Oruka's friend from graduate school Tommie Zaine ("Erick"); and Tommie's wife Lotte. Zaine thinks that the events closely follow what really happened to Oruka and his family during that year, although of course we can't be sure if certain details weren't added or changed.

The novel serves as a good setting for Oruka to express his views on a variety of subjects, usually through his main character Omolo. In fact, many of "Omolo's" arguments resurface in academic articles written by Oruka. But his main theme is how Africans should stay loyal to Africa, not participate in a brain drain, and take pride in Africa. Early in the book Omolo says he'd accept a job in Nigeria over one in the United States. As it turns out, this mirrors Oruka's life, insofar as he had had a job offer at Florida State University which he turned down in order to get a faculty position at University of Nairobi.[20] Omolo asserts that all African universities should exchange scholars among themselves (Oruka 1978: 13). Part of this anti-Americanism is based on Oruka's experience in Detroit. Omolo tells a fellow Kenyan longing to go to America, "I lived on a block infested by rats." (12) This is not the only reason to not go there. Rather, one should want to stay in Africa. This assertion is not coupled with a glamorous portrayal of Africa. Oruka shows both Kenya and Nigeria with their flaws. But those flaws just further convince him of the need to have more people dedicated to making Africa better. In the novel Africans in Sweden and London are shown in a very unflattering light to suggest that Africans who stay abroad rather than returning are ruining their lives by chasing after inessential things, abandoning their kin in need, and lowering their virtuous character.

As an example of some of the problems rampant in Kenya, he mentions the problem of "banana" scholars, by which he means someone who is not serious. But "not serious" does not mean not concerned about their career in a bourgeois sense. He puts into the mouth of another character, Mr. Wanyama, a dear position of his own when Wanyama says a scholar should be committed to societal improvement and solving problems. (7–8) Omolo admits that not everyone who wants a job, and is qualified for one, can find one in Kenya. (19) Oruka also refers to corruption in Kenya when his character Omolo reminisces about how he was pressured to admit an unqualified student (21). He also describes being harassed by police at a check-point, presumably for a bribe (15–16).

Omolo is filled with admiration for certain aspects of Sweden, such as their efficient bus system, automation, and the level of safety and cleanliness (39). He attributes Sweden's low crime rate to fair distribution of wealth (52). But he shows Gunnar (Hedenius) and himself disagreeing about the degree to which this economic factor was decisive. He has Gunnar say that the Marxist point that the "economic factor is the primary force behind the formation of ideas and social transformation" is an exaggeration, while Omolo claims that it is not an exaggeration. (57)

There is perhaps some vanity in Oruka's portrayal of Omolo's meeting with Ulla, his former Swedish girlfriend. She had been "hypnotized" by his personality, he explains. (43–44) Omolo tells her that his relatives had impressed upon him the importance of marrying a Kenyan woman, and so he had done so. "To live for oneself and not for others is impossible; one must strike a balance," he says, implying that marrying Ulla would have been living for himself (45). And yet in another passage of the book Omolo flirted with a Swedish woman bank teller, letting her know that in Africa one is allowed to have more than one wife, and she could be his second wife (29). Omolo also flirts with Gunnar's wife "Brit," whom he describes as seventy years old and still shapely. Hedenius' character Gunnar quips to Omolo's wife Akello (Millicent) that his wife and Omolo have been secretly in love (54). Still, Omolo is shocked by the Swedish practice of nude bathing, which he explains would never be tolerated in Africa ("turning the tables" on the usual European surprise and fascinated attraction to naked Africans) (55).

Omolo paints a sorry picture of Africans he visits who have been living in Sweden. There is "Miss Mamba" who had sexual relations with many Swedish men (as well as with Omolo himself), and never graduated from college. Omolo describes a man who claims to be a prince descended from African royalty and asserts that the man's father sells sweets and toilet paper back in Africa. Omolo clarifies that the reason he tells these stories is not to denigrate Africa; he does so because truth-telling is an important basis for any real foundation of self-worth. He explains, "Man cannot perpetually live on lies and self-deception without ruining himself and those who believe him." (67) He advises that Africans should become neither beggars nor robbers, but learn from the world in order to make the most of their potential. (79)

Oruka's portrayal of the Britons is not at all as flattering as that of the Swedes. He portrays the first couple Omolo visits as being stingy and miserly toward their African guests, and he describes the second couple as lacking intellectual grounding. (83) In Nigeria he runs into more "bogus" specialists, such as a scholar who had been taught anthropology and theology in Britain who says Africans do not have or give reasons for their actions or beliefs. Omolo disagrees with these views. (99–100)

Oruka's descriptions of Nigeria are filled with small and large problems that constantly beset Omolo and others in a similar predicament. He has continual problems with the organization of the university and the banking system. Constantly frustrated at the bank, where seemingly simple transactions become impossible or are drawn out for months, Omolo explains that, while this inefficiency is not due to being black, if Africans don't change their institutions, whites will insist that this is an inborn trait. (109) He witnesses an old man in a bank being cheated out of his life savings—$1,200. The poor man gets so frustrated he has to be rushed to the hospital. Omolo worries that Africans are creating conditions for a high suicide rate. (111–12)

While other faculty members find ways to sidestep many institutional problems, he does not favor this approach, since it leaves the problems intact. The faculty members aren't dedicated to making their own society run well. (115–16) Included in the long list of problems he saw in Nigeria were two professors of philosophy who died in a car crash. Another philosophy professor had actually killed two people, but bribed his way out of jail (138). Omolo grows critical of what he saw happening to those in the academic profession, and at the same time he notes that Nigerian academics liked to tell him that academic standards were higher in Nigeria than in Kenya. (117–18). Omolo's most tragic experience happens when he sees a man accused of witchcraft beaten to death. At this point he breaks down and expresses his frustration with people remaining silent in the face of tyranny. He says,

> And I wept...I cursed Africa. I cursed inefficiency, I cursed bureaucracy and red tape. "The man dies," not only "in all who keep silent in the face of tyranny" (Soyinka). The man dies also every time we acquiesce in inefficiency and senseless bureaucracy. The man dies as well, every time we reject rationality as being alien and instead believe in superstitions, myths and magics. How many men have died in Uganda because of Amin's superstitions and magical dreams?
>
> 128

Faced with all of these problems, Omolo explains what he thinks will restore dignity and self-worth to Africans so that they will be able to reform their own societies and make their lives better. He is concerned that the international economic and political situation in Africa is having deleterious effects on African self-pride. Foreign aid is a form of foreign begging, and begging is detrimental to one's self-worth. Without a moral reason to beg, a person loses dignity. In accepting foreign aid, "the receiver wears the rags of a beggar and the donor the mantle of a benevolent King." (153) Drawing upon both Frantz Fanon and Walter Rodney, Omolo explains that Africans are now only asking for ill-gotten goods to be given back by the colonial powers that had earlier destroyed Africa. But he clarifies that he thinks that this justification is only good for the immediate post-colonial situation, and it can't be used forever. At a certain point independent African countries have to take responsibility for their own inefficiency and callousness in bureaucracy and public services. (154) Those who have read Oruka's academic articles will recognize Omolo's words here are a paraphrase of Oruka's conclusions in "The Philosophy of Foreign Aid" (in Oruka 1997; see esp. 83) and other articles.

Witnessing FESTAC[21] celebrations in Nigeria, Omolo comments that he sees "negritude" as better than colonial mentality but still imperfect, in that it presumes Africa's contribution will not be manifested in rationality and logic but rather in rhythms and dances. He thinks that FESTAC celebrations are meant for whites to see thereby and recognize Black Africa's economic contribution.[22] If Africans are so interested in making a good impression economically, he wonders, why don't they reform the banking industry in Nigeria? (156–57). This gives Omolo the occasion to reassert his advice: don't always turn toward the Occident. Take care of African problems. He suggests that the Chinese did this by ignoring the West and coming up with their own development projects.

The concluding episode of the book (although Oruka made notes that suggest he thought of continuing the book further) involves a reference to the book's title, *In the Mother Africa (The Family Broke Down)*. After a big scene at the airport regarding Osino's yellow fever certificate, Omolo and his family are let go for a 15 naira bribe. After the ordeal, Omolo says with obvious sarcasm, "It'll be o.k. After all, this country is the Mother of Africa" (Oruka 1978: 170). Oruka clearly expresses his frustration with the gap between his hopes for the future of Africa and its current state.

Oruka's year in Nigeria resulted in more than just headaches over corruption and mismanagement. A Nigerian professor from University of Ife, M. Akin Makinde, claimed to be the originator of the term "philosophic sagacity" in the context of African philosophy (drawing upon concepts in Bombastus Paracelsus' essay "Philosophia Sagax"). He presented his paper in June, 1978, at University of Ife (Makinde, 1978; 1989: 107). Makinde claimed that Oruka used the term and concept "wrongly" but admitted that Oruka's usage became the more widespread (Makinde, 1988: 9, 122, 137). Oruka used "philosophic" in his Four Trends article, first presented at a conference on Dr. William Amo in Accra, Ghana, in July, 1978 (Oruka, 1991c: 21n1; also see Ochieng'-Odhaimbo, 2009). While I don't want to adjudicate the dispute over whether Oruka got the idea from Makinde, this may more generally be a sign that ideas were percolating in West Africa and Oruka was able to imbibe some of those ideas as well as share his own ideas during his year's sabbatical there.

Part Three

Sage Philosophy and Culture Philosophy

5

Myths, Traditions, Anthropology, and Philosophy

I mentioned in Chapter Two that even as an undergraduate at Uppsala, before he studied African philosophy but during his informal studies of African literature, Oruka mentioned the important work of evaluation Africans must undertake by "embracing selectively all the traditions that have affected our society" (Oruka 1968: 8). A recurring theme through his work on punishment at WSU and his book on liberty is this subjection of African tradition to rational evaluation, with an eye to embracing whatever will help Africa best cope with its present and future. Nuanced presentations like these led Kai Kresse to remark of Oruka, "He tried to bridge the gap between traditionalists and modernists" (Graness and Kresse 1997: 11–18, quote p. 13), and find a third alternative between the polarized views of ethnophilosophy and academic philosophy. Kresse muses that Oruka, "more than any other African thinker so far, constantly and in a systematic way sought to combine these competing aspects" (Graness and Kresse 1997: 11–18, quote p. 13). At his best moments, that is what Oruka did—he balanced the competing values, and embraced traditions or new ways (even sometimes foreign ways) if reason dictated, avoiding romanticizing the African past or worshiping and internalizing foreign culture and science. But at other moments, he championed the one at the expense of the other and did not hold them in balance. Over his long career, one could argue, the balance was achieved, but at any given moment, he may have been too harsh a critic in one direction or the other. With the benefit of hindsight, Oruka judged his early 1972 article, "Mythologies as African Philosophy," as being "too simplistic and unnecessarily offensive" (quoted in Graness and Kresse 1997: 12), and noted in his 1990 autobiographical essay that he dreaded reading it (Oruka 1997: 285). Over the years, his practice changed as he became more interested in the traditions, even the spirituality, of various Kenyan ethnic groups in addition to his own ethnic group, the Luo. But that was not his starting point.

The previous chapter already mentioned how Oruka found people who helped him develop the idea of interviewing sages. In this chapter, I will delve more specifically into why he thought such a procedure was called for, given the state of development of African philosophy at the time.

As mentioned in Chapter Four, Oruka wasted no time, publishing his article "The Meaning of Liberty" in the first issue of *African Philosophy Journal* of Zaire (January–June 1972). Perhaps he received a free copy of this journal, which included his article as well as articles by Paulin Hountondji and W. A. Hart, authors to whom Oruka responds in his first article about African philosophy, entitled "Mythologies as African Philosophy" (Oruka 1972b: 5–11). One will remember from Chapter Four that Oruka mentioned to Hedenius that he delivered this paper at the Goethe Institute in Nairobi on June 22, 1972, and that the priests in his department did not like it.[1] Who were the other influences on and immediate precursors to the article? He cites an article by Bethwell A. Ogot (1971), his colleague at the University of Nairobi, that had just come out in June 1971. He also cites a talk by another UON colleague, Okot p'Bitek, presented at UON in February 1972.[2] He cites an article Ali Mazrui wrote in May of 1972. His own talk was delivered a month later, and the article was in print within four months, in October 1972. Remembering that Oruka himself had mentioned that he had not studied anything of African philosophy during his formal education, the sudden influence of his new surroundings and the academic movements of the times had greatly shaped his ideas. Influences from his earlier studies that are named in this early paper are Marx and Fanon. The unnamed are clearly Hedenius and Russell. Those who Oruka criticizes are W. E. Abraham, Placide Tempels, and John Mbiti (whom Bishop Neill had tried to hire), and a Norwegian who studied in Sweden and Sudan, Tore Nordenstam.

Nordenstam's name hints at a source even earlier than Oruka's famous 1972 "Mythologies" article. In *East Africa Journal*'s June 1971 issue, Oruka published a book review of Tore Nordenstam's (1968) *Sudanese Ethics*. Nordenstam held degrees in philosophy and spent his career as a philosophy professor, but he himself professed to have "moved from the analytical philosophy of language into ethics, aesthetics and the philosophy of the humanities" (Nordenstam n.d.). Oruka noticed Nordenstam's departure from the usual interests and practices of analytic philosophy in this book but seemed to be annoyed by this departure. Oruka (1971) begins by quoting G. E. Moore's (1991: 54) definition of ethics as "the general inquiry into what is good." Since the philosophical search for ethics is universal, Nordenstam's attempt to describe "Sudanese" ethics is particularistic in a way that shows he has other than a philosophical intent. Nordenstam is the first to admit that he is using the word "ethics" not as academics use it, but rather in the sense of a system of norms, values, and ideals. Oruka (1971: 37–38.) seems to think that Nordenstam, so clearly departing from the usual meaning of "ethics," should instead say he is studying "virtues."

Nordenstam describes why he is proceeding with his study by using what he calls the careful anthropological methods of sociological data collection: he wants to avoid philosophical oversimplification. Oruka counterattacks, suggesting that anthropological methods in general, and Nordenstam's in particular, do not result in a study that's better than philosophy—rather, it's worse. Oruka wonders if Nordenstam realizes that there is hostility in Africa toward European anthropologists. Oruka alludes to his UON colleague Okot p'Bitek's criticisms of anthropologists as colonizers of African people. Oruka (1971: 37–38) says Nordenstam is a philosopher who "deviated from philosophy" to become a social anthropologist and is "guilty" of trying to explain Sudanese mentality to foreigners. Nordenstam has overgeneralized, Oruka argues, because he only interviewed three students from Northern Sudan, yet called his book *Sudanese Ethics* instead of *Northern Sudanese Virtues*. Oruka (1971: 37–38) points out that Nordenstam should not have interviewed his own students because they could have been influenced by their exposure to Western philosophy, and he cites as a specific example one student who refers to Aristotle (Nordenstam 1968: 82).[3] Oruka (1971: 37–38) also notices that Nordenstam and his students discussed only eight virtues commonly attributed to men: "No attempt was made to discuss the virtues that are primarily attributed to women." Oruka also notes that due to the repressive political situation in Sudan, which was ruled by military junta, the students declined to discuss politics. For Oruka this means that we can't really know or understand their ethical views, because political views are an essential part of ethics. He concludes by saying that, while the book has some scholarly merit, it will mostly be of use to "sociologists, anthropologists, psychologists, theologians, and historians." In other words, he himself is dismissive of the book.

In our attempt to understand Oruka's development as an African philosopher in general and his development of the sage philosophy methodology in particular, we have plenty of good reasons to study this passage. Here we see Oruka's hostility to anthropology and the roots of his later assertion that a philosopher can do a better job of interviewing people about their philosophies than can an anthropologist. We see early evidence of his idea that one must look for interviewees who have not had formal schooling in order to find a description of a philosophy truly indigenous to the area. And we have an emphasis on specificity—not to the point of individual specificity, but nevertheless against sweeping generalizations such as those found in a book that claims to illustrate "Sudanese" philosophy.

Before I go further I want to say something about the parts of Nordenstam's book that Oruka neglects to mention altogether. Nordenstam is a critic of certain popular procedures and methods in philosophy. In this book, his critique is meta-ethical and very philosophical, not anthropological. Nordenstam is critical of the philosophical traditions in which he was schooled: Utilitarianism and analytic philosophy. Oruka mentions nothing of this critique because, at this point in his life (and arguably for his whole life), he was not self-critical about the philosophical tools he was given at Uppsala. Nordenstam (1968) rejects what he calls the "deductive ideal" or "subsumption model" in ethics. According to this model, ethics uses syllogistic reasoning. Facts are subsumed under appropriate norms, such as utilitarian norms, and the conclusion follows automatically. Once one has identified the basic norms through ethical theory, the rest of an ethical system, ethical practice is known through entailment or logical implication. Ethical systems are presumed to be like mathematical systems, and in any system, Sudanese, Navajo, or otherwise, "the basic norms play the role of axioms and the derived rules the role of theorems" (29). But Nordenstam thinks that it is not good to compare ethics to mathematics. He thinks a more fruitful analogy is to law. Axiomatic systems are not open, but ethical systems need to be open. Law also needs discretion in application. The moral agent is like a judge in court; "his decisions make the rules more determinate." To apply a rule means to give it more determination, and this involves good judgment necessary for ethical decision making (30). This is a different model than deductive, "mechanical" ethics and formalism. Because of this character of ethics, Nordenstam explains, "knowledge about the general principles of somebody's ethics does not make it superfluous to assemble knowledge about his particular moral judgments" (29). Just as lawyers study cases as well as statutes, he as a philosopher intends to study people's applications of moral rules. He turns to social anthropologists because he finds them to be more sensitive to how moral systems and other systems interrelate (40). That was the source of Nordenstam's assertion, to which Oruka objected, that anthropologists may do a better job at understanding ethics than would utilitarian philosophers wedded to their deductive ideal.

But if we look at how Oruka has used moral reasoning in his Master's degree and Fil.Lic. thesis, he has indeed used the deductive model. There are several pages of his works where he uses symbolic logic to argue his position. The departments at both WSU and Uppsala emphasized mathematical logic in their approach to philosophical topics. Oruka does not mention in his coverage of Nordenstam's book that Nordenstam questioned that approach. But he does nuance his position in an article written in 1974, where he says that "Russell exaggerated the importance of logic to philosophy" (40). But later, through his practice of interviewing individuals, and coming to know their views and their decisions, Oruka perhaps comes a bit close to what Nordenstam was describing.[4]

So why did Oruka dislike anthropologists so much? Let's go back to his colleague, Okot p'Bitek. Here I will draw upon p'Bitek's own writings as well as those by Samuel Oluoch Imbo (2002) and Lubwa p'Chong (1986). Born in Gulu, Uganda, in 1931, to a father who learned to read from Christian missionaries, p'Bitek sang in St. Philip's Church and eventually attended King's College in Kampala. From this point onward he was involved in creating cultural activities based on Luo and Acholi heritage. He went on to attend teacher's training college, the University of Bristol, the University of Wales, and Oxford. It was in Bristol that he studied Christianity as a discipline, and due to that study, he ceased being a Christian. He studied law but decided to follow his interests in studying more about Africa by taking a degree in Social Anthropology. However, p'Bitek had a rude awakening at Oxford University, where he was admitted to a program headed by E. E. Evans-Pritchard, a specialist on Nilotic peoples in Sudan and East Africa. P'Bitek was greatly irritated by the descriptions of Africans as "primitives" and "uncivilized." Nevertheless, he earned a certificate in anthropology and a bachelor's degree in letters,[5] writing his thesis on the Acholi and Lango oral traditions. He then taught social anthropology at Makerere University in Uganda. Active in the arts, p'Bitek became director of the Uganda National Cultural Centre in 1966. In 1968 he left Uganda for an eleven-year exile, from which he returned in 1979. He died in 1982 (p'Chong 1986).

During his exile p'Bitek taught at the University of Nairobi and organized many artistic events. In his writings and artwork he castigated Christian missionaries as well as social anthropologists. He explained,

> Social anthropology has been the study of non-western societies by western scholars to serve western interests. Social anthropology has not only been the handmaiden of colonialism in that it analysed and provided important information about the social institutions of colonized peoples to ensure efficient and effective control and exploitation, it has also furnished and elaborated the myth of the 'primitive' which justified the colonial enterprise.
>
> p'Bitek 1979: 1–2; quoted in Imbo 2002: 3

This same bias against Africans was internalized by Africans who studied Africa, such as John Mbiti and Léopold Senghor. P'Bitek was concerned that African cultures were depicted as lagging behind European cultures, a scenario that justified racism.

P'Bitek sarcastically described Western scholars and their African apologists who dissect and, in the process, distort and kill the living meaning of a culture (Imbo 2002: 121, cites p'Bitek 1974: ix). Either songs, proverbs, and oral literature are "left to wilt" by being under-appreciated by the newly dominant settler community (Imbo 2002: 60), or they experience death by extraction from their context of meaning, like so many African art displays in Western museums (54). P'Bitek also thought outsiders couldn't understand

African culture. Anthropologists and missionaries didn't realize that their own conceptual frameworks made it impossible for them to recognize and understand African cultures, religion, and philosophy (44).

P'Bitek clearly had some valid criticisms of the colonial thinking that continued to plague Africa and academia after African countries won their independence. In his book on p'Bitek, Samuel Oluoch Imbo gives p'Bitek great praise. Imbo also criticizes him: p'Bitek generalized. He painted with too broad a brush. He essentialized African identity. He championed an African tradition that was too static and idealized. He did not engage in the fine distinctions we do now, critically evaluating the past and jettisoning some traditions while accepting some aspects of modernization. And Imbo, a twenty-first-century feminist multiculturalist, both praised and disagreed with p'Bitek. Imbo was not the first; he introduces us to a host of p'Bitek commentators who have proceeded just as gingerly, including Taban Lo Liyong, Kenyans Ngugi wa Thiong'o and Ali Mazrui, anthropologist Peter Rigby (1971), and others.

P'Bitek could be accused of being among those cultural nationalists who did not want to criticize any aspect of their tradition. Imbo notes that p'Bitek's heroine of Acholi culture, Lawino, uncritically accepts her group's traditions even when they harm her. Lawino's insight into the way colonizers have emasculated her husband is quite keen, but she is blind to the ways in which her own culture constrains her and other women (Rigby 1971: 75–77). Imbo notes that he can't find a criticism of a harmful practice anywhere in p'Bitek's account of Acholi traditions. In this way, Imbo suggests, p'Bitek indulges in one of the great shortcomings of the ethnophilosophers: uncritical description of traditions. p'Bitek must admit that "traditions may contain toxins" and so must be changed (Imbo 2002: 16). By painting Ocol, a whole-hearted convert to ways Western who looks at his own Acholi roots with disdain, as unattractive, a mere shadow of a man without cultural moorings, p'Bitek has portrayed a stark either-or in which Lawino easily seems to be in the right (12, 63). One should rather accept the best of tradition while discarding what is harmful and embracing helpful Western conceptions (64). Imbo also cites Ngugi wa Thiong'o and E. S. Atieno Odhiambo as two contemporary Kenyan scholars who found p'Bitek's single-minded emphasis on promoting past cultural traditions unhelpful in dealing with the pressing problems facing African communities (14–15).[6]

P'Bitek thought that one could not "pigeonhole" African knowledge into distinct religious, philosophical, and spiritual categories. Philosophy is embedded in many cultural practices and expressions. They were all together, and they could only really be understood by experiencing them, not observing or recording them (Imbo 2002: 44). Oruka did not appreciate this aspect of p'Bitek's message, and he criticized it in his 1972 article. What Oruka does take from p'Bitek is the wholesale condemnation of social anthropology.

Oruka's October 1972 essay "Mythologies as African Philosophy" draws upon Fanon's criticisms of African writers who champion African traditions but write for the white world and cater to a white audience's appetite for exoticism (Fanon 1967: 179; quoted by Oruka in Graness and Kresse 1997: 23). He agrees with Fanon, who says Africans should be future-oriented and shape their own future through their own free actions. Oruka says, "If the past and present can offer him wisdom to attain that future, well and good. But if they cannot, then to hell with the past and present" (Graness and Kresse 1997: 24). He insists that even if one takes away the "colonial degradation of the African past," there will still be much to criticize, and much of past tradition will have to be sacrificed "for the sake of the future" (24). This radical change from both the colonial and pre-colonial past is necessary because "The African present is disappointing" (24). In his estimation, there are good (or "beautiful") people in Africa, but they are not yet in power; in fact, many of them are in prison (24–25). In this article he definitely stresses the need for change, which will involve jettisoning much of the past.

Oruka then criticizes both Placide Tempels' book *Bantu Philosophy* and John Mbiti's book *African Religions and Philosophy* as backward-looking champions of absolutely unphilosophical African traditions. Oruka argues that these traditions are all mythical and unscientific because they draw upon ideas of supernatural powers. Mbiti's book goes directly against Oruka's focus on the future; according to Mbiti, Africans, Swahili speakers in particular, have no concept of the future because they have no word for the future beyond two years hence. Oruka then says he does not mean to challenge Mbiti's characterization of Africans, but instead wants to say that if they do indeed neglect the future, it is not because they are Africans or black, but because they are rural agriculturalists, and the same mindset is found among agriculturalists from other continents. As a reason for this particular conception of time Oruka draws upon Marx's insight that people's consciousness is shaped by their material conditions. He then notes that times have changed in Kenya, and there are plenty people who live a non-agricultural life and plan for a much longer future (25). He then goes on to criticize Mbiti's methodological presumption that a person whose language has no word for a certain concept cannot conceive of it (26).

Oruka goes on to criticize myth, which he insists is neither scientific, nor philosophical, nor historically true. Here he discusses not only African myths, but also Judaism and Christianity, which are also religions based on myth. While he admits that myths can be useful to society because they explain its collective beliefs about morals, historical destiny, and world view, Oruka wants nevertheless to insist that useful ideas can be false. Here we see that Oruka is so preoccupied with the literal falsity of a myth or story that he can barely acknowledge that it could contain any kind of truth or convey any deep insight about life. He notes that myths claim to be "imperishable truths" (28) and concludes that they are therefore static. He states that accepting myths involves suppressing critical thinking, and shaping one's moral views based on listening to traditional tales results in a static reproduction of unchanging habits and conventions. He fears that such a society will call its freethinkers "madmen" (26). Here again we see the influence of Ingemar Hedenius and Bertrand Russell. Religion equals mythology, error, and close-minded intolerance, and it should be swept away for philosophy, which equals science, future-orientation, and open-mindedness. It's important to note that Oruka sees that science advocates changing, not unchanging, truths. Covering the history of science in a 1974 article, he explains, "the objectivity of science is very much dependent on its assumptions and postulates," and he notes that "all scientists have to keep on examining and questioning these assumptions" (41).

Here Oruka interjects a claim for which he has little evidence: he presumes that those who listen to traditions are involved in the static reproduction of those traditions. Those who study oral traditions or ritual practices will note that traditions are always changing, even when people think they are merely reproducing them. People are often modifying their traditions in little ways. In his study of proverbs, Kwesi Yankah noted that a proverb is changed each time it is used in a new situation, even if the words used are the same.[7] This is a similar insight to Nordenstam's: an ethical ideal is modified and refined each time it is instantiated in a particular act. Religions have their commentaries, as in Judaism, where the Talmud adds to and refines the tradition spoken of in the Torah. Christianity has its gospels, its epistles, and a historical flow of church documents that come after them. Even if each new text claims only to reproduce or more clearly articulate something that was present from the beginning, there is nevertheless a change. This is one of many times where Oruka sets up this fallacious "straw man"—the static, unthinking person, society, or institution—to attack by contrasting it with his ideal, dynamic thinker.

Even his criticism of the mythical thinker, or the person influenced by listening to myth, is based on an unrealistic idea of the thought process of people who listen to myths. While a small child may believe that there is a Santa Claus or that animals are talking, adults who hear or convey these stories are focusing on the meanings behind the stories. Commenting directly on Oruka's article, Campbell Shittu Momoh (1981: 17) charges Oruka with ignoring "what is positively philosophical in an African philosopher's works." Momoh insists that there is no one in Africa who views myths in the simplistic way that Oruka is presenting them. Momoh claims that if "one actually holds discussions with an elder" then one will "be confronted with myth-in-use, and find that myths are used only as a ladder to climb to the higher realms of philosophy" (17; see also Kelbessa, 2002; 2009: 135–52).

While this section of Oruka's essay may seem like it is still criticizing Mbiti, it actually includes a criticism applicable to Okot p'Bitek. Oruka criticizes those who think that everyone is a philosopher. P'Bitek said philosophy is a part of daily life that everyone engages in through their everyday actions as well as their artistic, cultural expressions. Oruka (at this early stage) thinks this is a "debased" use of the word philosophy and suggests that it means everyone has opinions, and opinions are philosophy (Graness and Kresse 1997: 27–28). Here I think Oruka is too dismissive of p'Bitek's insights. Surely, it is the case that the word "philosophy" is sometimes used broadly and casually. However, p'Bitek is right to note that philosophy is embodied in daily life and cultural expressions. Kwasi Wiredu (2011: xx) makes a similar point in a recently written introduction to a reissued book by Okot p'Bitek, and he goes so far as to say, "customs can be a veritable philosophical text." It may be that philosophy as practiced in Euro-American institutions nowadays is not very interested in looking for philosophy in such places. Academic philosophers may think it a low priority, or they may think that such projects can best be done by people in other fields. But philosophies are expressed in cultures, not just in African cultures, but in European and American ones as well. Those engaged in cultural studies find the meanings embedded in cultural practices. But the fact remains that such philosophical studies are sidelined in mainstream contemporary philosophy, particularly analytic philosophy, although even there a focus on finding philosophy embedded in language continues, and language is part of culture. Oruka is not interested in this side stream at this point in his life; he wants to engage in mainstream philosophy in Africa because he has been trained in it and because he considers it prestigious.

Oruka goes on to say that he wants to use philosophy in the "exact" sense, and he defines that sense as "a rational and critical reflection on man, society, and nature" (Graness and Kresse 1997: 28). He goes on to say that philosophy uses reason as a "weapon" (28). Here an anthropologist of philosophy could note that Euro-Americans, especially those who have studied formal philosophy, have been taught that reason is a weapon. Contemporary feminist philosophers have criticized this characterization of philosophy and said that it has alienated women and people of color from the field of philosophy (Rooney 2010).

The point that Oruka makes regarding Tempels is that Tempels states that Bantu-speaking people all agree that "vital force" is an "imperishable truth" (Graness and Kresse 1997: 28). Any idea that is accepted as imperishably true is not philosophy as Oruka understands it. "At best it can be a religion," Oruka says (28). Finally, he refers to Paulin Hountondji's article, "The myth of spontaneous philosophy," which appeared in the same issue of *Cahiers philosophiques africains* as Oruka's article, "The Meaning of Liberty." Hountondji drew a similar distinction between myth and philosophy. Oruka agrees with Hountondji that philosophy is allied with science and that Africa needs "exact philosophical expositions," not descriptions of communal beliefs (29).

In this early 1972 article, Oruka begins to articulate his emphasis on the need to acknowledge individual thinkers. By anonymizing everyone and providing only group consensus, Tempels, Mbiti, and W. E. Abraham (author of *The Mind of Africa*) give us "philosophy without philosophers." He suggests already, "We can as well start afresh by interviewing sage Africans and eliciting philosophical expositions from them" (30). While individuals' thinking is influenced by their community and material conditions, they are not determined by them, and in fact individuals can also influence groups (31). Oruka also points out that a philosopher's role is not just to describe how people think and act, but to make suggestions as to how they ought to think and act (31). He relies on an article by W. A. Hart (1972) in the same journal issue as the Hountondji article and his own article. From Hart he gets the idea that the anthropologist's role is just to describe the case carefully. Hart says he has not seen a philosophical treatment of African concepts or thought yet, only anthropological ones (Graness and Kresse 1997: 31–32).

Three years later Oruka published another article in which he railed against the "debased" sense of the term "African philosophy." In the interim, however, *Cahiers philosophiques africains / African Philosophical Journal* published another article by Hountondji, "Philosophy and Its Revolutions," which Oruka references in his 1975 article, "The Fundamental Principles in the Question of 'African Philosophy'" (54n5). More importantly, Hountondji (1996: 71) mentions giving a talk related to "Philosophy and Its Revolutions" at the University of Nairobi on November 6, 1973, at the invitation of the Philosophical Association of Kenya, which Oruka founded. Hountondji's article has material relevant to the conception of the sage philosophy project. The piece was later incorporated into Hountondji's book, *African Philosophy: Myth and Reality*, as chapter three (71–108). Oruka and the Philosophical Association of Kenya were in the midst of launching a new philosophy journal called *Thought and Practice*, and in volume 1, issue 2 (1974), they published Hountondji's article, "African Philosophy: Myth and Reality,"[8] In "Myth and Reality" we have evidence that Hountondji read Oruka's essay, because Hountondji (1996: 65) says that Oruka's "Mythologies" article was excellent.

What did Hountondji (1973) say in "Philosophy and Its Revolutions" that was so important?

Hountondji's "Revolution" talk and article, which Oruka and other Kenyans heard in person in 1973, criticizes Tempels' use of anthropology but appreciates the works of two European anthropologists, Paul Radin and Marcel Griaule, suggesting that their approach was much more careful than Tempels'. In fact, Hountondji (1996: 76) said, Tempels' study was "behind the anthropology of the time." Twenty years earlier than Tempels, Radin wrote *Primitive Man as Philosopher*, a study of philosophy in Africa that focused on original thinkers who were members of an intellectual class in their communities. Hountondji explained that Radin denounced the prejudice that African individuals are submerged in unitary group-think and took it upon himself to transcribe faithfully what members of this intellectual class told him (76). Hountondji stated that "Radin's work is still, to the best of my knowledge, the most lucid ethnological critique of the theoretical assumptions of ethnophilosophy" (79). He praised Radin for showing the level of variations in the recounting of any particular myth and how each narrator influenced the myth in their own way, showing the "profound individualism" among African intellectuals (79). Radin emphasized that myths and proverbs were the result of individual thinkers' creativity, debunking conceptions of the timeless repetition of anonymous stories. Hountondji was struck by how, unlike other Western anthropologists, Radin conveyed Africa as a place of plural views as are Western societies (82). Hountondji still faulted Radin for use of the word "primitive" which was insulting (79).[9] But no doubt this procedure of Radin's had a role in the impetus to create Oruka's project of interviewing sages. Not that Radin was the originator of the idea—Oruka had mentioned interviewing of sages in his 1972 article, and Hountondji presented "Philosophy and its Revolutions" in 1973—but insofar as Hountondji's talk precedes the announcement of the project of interviewing sages begun in 1974, it may have played a role in the way the sage philosophy project was conceived.

The relationship and consistency between Radin's approach and that of Oruka's sage philosophy project has been alluded to by Kai Kresse (2007: 27–28), Lucius Outlaw (in Oruka 1990b: 244n27), Campbell S. Momoh (1989), and Godwin Azenabor (2009: 73). Oruka himself did not credit Radin as the source of his methodological preference. However, knowing that Hountondji described and lauded Radin's study in a talk at the University of Nairobi makes me confident that Radin's ideas played some role in shaping the project. Although he adopts a methodology close to the one used by the anthropologist Radin, for the rest of his career Oruka repeatedly asserts that anthropology itself is not helpful to the study of African philosophy, and the interviews he wants to undertake must be done by a philosopher, not an anthropologist.

Hountondji's 1973 talk and 1974 article not only mention Radin, but also include Marcel Griaule as examples of anthropologists who did not use Tempels' method.

Griaule had interviewed Ogotemmeli, a Dogon elder, at length. The book was published after Tempels' book, and Hountondji makes it clear that he can't fairly "upbraid" Tempels for not taking note of Griaule's methodology. But Hountondji wishes that Griaule's book would have been received as enthusiastically as Tempels' book was. Hountondji (1996: 77–78) was disappointed that certain political factions inside and outside of Africa preferred Tempels' style of massive definitive synthesis of all Bantu views to capturing the plurality and disorderliness of individual thought by direct interview. But Hountondji goes on to introduce a couple of problems with Griaule's study. First, although Ogotemmeli was an individual thinker, Griaule represents him in the preface of his book not as an individual but as a spokesperson for his ethnic group's cosmology (78). In the preface to the first edition of Hountondji's book (also later included in the second edition), Abiola Irele explains that Griaule came from a school of French Africanists based at the Musée de l'Homme in Paris, a school which emphasized the systematic reconstruction of collective world views and thought systems of Africa (in Hountondji 1996: 15).[10]

Later, in the preface to the second edition of his book, which included "Philosophy and Its Revolutions," Hountondji again reiterated his 1974 opinion of Griaule as such an important trend-setter.

> The French anthropologist had chosen to transcribe the words of *one* sage among many. He showed the possibility of a long-term project which would consist of a systematic transcription of such speeches, at least as a starting point of a critical discussion—what my Kenyan colleague the late Odera Oruka would later call "philosophical sagacity"— rather than as reconstruction of implicit philosophy behind the habits and customs of the host society through a lot of non-verifiable hypotheses which always amount to over-interpreting the facts.
>
> Hountondji 1996: ix, italics in the original

Hountondji sees Griaule's project as an earlier version of Oruka's project. Now, did Oruka ever agree that Griaule's method had served as a model for himself and his project?

In his 1983 article in *International Philosophical Quarterly*, later included in *Sage Philosophy*, Oruka argues that Ogotemmeli is at best a "folk sage" and not a philosophical sage, because he does not transcend his group's views. Therefore, Griaule was not engaged in sage philosophy, but only in "culture philosophy."

Now we have to clarify that in the 1974 article, Hountondji does not say that Ogotemmeli is a philosopher. He argues against this position. Hountondji (1996: 81–82) says that Ogotemmeli recounted myths and cosmogony, and not all creative thinking is philosophical. Also, he thought that Ogotemmeli conveyed a closed system considered to be eternally true and "admitting of no discussion" (84). In contrast, philosophy is more like the sciences, not the arts. A philosophical argument must always refer to its antecedents in the debate; literary or artistic works like fables and legends need not do so (82–83). Hountondji does claim that Ogotemmeli is an individual creative thinker, and he holds this position even against Griaule, who said in his preface that Ogotemmeli merely conveyed his society's beliefs.

Hountondji and Oruka both missed research published by other anthropologists ten years earlier, that cast doubt on whether Griaule really followed his professed method of interviewing one person and transcribing what that person said. Masolo (1994: 69, 77, 260) makes a thorough review of the anthropological literature on Griaule, most but not all of it in French, in which the authors question whether the conversation was recorded verbatim on the series of days that Griaule recounts. They suspect Griaule of reconstructing the conversation. For example, Jack Goody's book review discusses the painstaking detail an interview must have in order to meet standards of even a "soft" science like anthropology. The words of the person interviewed should be clearly demarcated from those that are the author's commentary. Field notes should be identified as such and distinguished from the words of the on-site translator. Original language transcriptions should be available, and the difficulty of translating esoteric words should be discussed by the author. Griaule's book did not meet these standards. Goody (1967: 240) finds particularly suspicious Griaule's intention, stated near the beginning of the book, "to prove that black Africans have as much claim to a philosophy, a cosmology, as the pre-Socratics or any later Europeans." Oruka's own study of sage philosophy could be said to exhibit similar methodological flaws, which suggests that Oruka's method was less, not more, careful than reigning standards in anthropology. While perhaps Oruka is blameless regarding his neglect of anthropology journals from a decade before, especially if half of them are in French, a language he didn't know, the fact that he continued to hold these views on Ogotemmeli for the rest of his life, even after having read the detailed exposé of Griaule in Masolo's dissertation, is more problematic.

This point came up in a debate at the Smithsonian Institution in Washington, D.C., in 1989. Oruka and Ivan Karp were both presenting papers at a seminar, "Anthropology and Philosophy in Africa." Karp mentioned that Oruka considered *Conversations with Ogotemmeli* to be an example of cultural philosophy since Ogotemmeli did not question his group's views or values. But Karp clarified that Griaule had little ground for his claim that Ogotemmeli had described the conventional world view held by most Dogon people. Ogotemmeli's may have been a view held primarily by ritual specialists.

In Karp's (1989: 2) estimation, Griaule's book is most likely "a synthetic work, one that combines elements of Dogon cultural philosophy, the sagacity of Ogotemmeli and the speculative thinking of the anthropologist Griaule."

The main thrust of Karp's critique of Oruka's claims regarding Ogotemmeli is that Oruka's distinction between "culture philosophy" and philosophic sagacity is unsound. According to Karp, Oruka collapses various categories together—he equates cultural philosophy with mythos and religion. But not all cultural philosophies are religious. They may have moral and ethical concepts that are not related to the eternal and sacred. Karp wants to distinguish "idioms of everyday life," which emerge in practice and are related to conduct, from the more specific "consciously elaborated world views" which may be better known by specialists in the society—whether that society is African or American. As an anthropologist, Karp has an interest in the moral judgments of people in their everyday life, and he goes on to share the results of his study of the Iteso, who live along the Kenya-Uganda border in Busia district. Karp then describes his own study, which was much in the footsteps of Tore Nordenstam's discussion of Sudanese ethics.

It is a little hard to understand the position on anthropologists Oruka (1989b) held when he delivered his paper at the Smithsonian in 1989[11] because several of his sentences use slang or casual lingo. He begins his paper, "Once upon a time there was no real distinction between philosophy and anthropology in the researches about the origin and nature of African thoughts." In the twentieth century, he says, "it is anthropology which gave birth to written African philosophy," and he names both Tempels and Mbiti. He does not mention Radin or Griaule. He says that anthropologists began to be sensitized to the philosophical aspect of their studies and argues that Robin Horton and V. Y. Mudimbe were "both anthropologists and philosophers" (1). He says that in the 1970s and 1980s the trend of combining anthropology (with its vices "plucked off") and philosophy ("deprived of its arm-chair arrogance") continues (1). Here he mentions Tore Nordenstam, A. B. C. Ocholla-Ayayo (1976), and Ivan Karp himself.

But then comes a confusing paragraph, where Oruka (1989b: 2) says there has been "an anthropological *hang over*" in some recent philosophical texts (italics in original). Some have tried to denounce the "hang over"—among them Hountondji, Bodunrin, and "some parts" of his own works—and others have enjoyed the "hang over" and "strive to philosophicate anthropology"—he counts Hallen, Sodipo, and Ruch in this group. Oruka suggests that his own approach is neither of the above because he will "go through the fogs of anthropology," unlike the ethnophilosophers who rested contented within the fogs (2).[12] He explains that his research on "Sage-philosophy in Africa (1974)" was linked with his conviction that it was necessary to pass through the anthropological fogs (3). What could this strange phrase about passing through the fogs of anthropology mean? As far as I can tell, it is just a poetic way of admitting that his sage philosophy project depends on the prior work of anthropologists, to which Oruka will then add "an evaluation, analysis and reflection" (3). He assigns the descriptive project to anthropologists and calls it "first order thought," and says that philosophizing about those descriptions is "second order thought" (3). He then reiterates that this is what he means by going through the fogs of anthropology (3).

Oruka had the opportunity to present this paper in the United States in 1989 because at the time he was already in the U.S. as a visiting professor at Earlham College, which his oldest son Owiso was attending. At this point, Oruka had a chance to read the criticisms of sage philosophy that were in D. A. Masolo's dissertation (1981), which would serve as the basis for Masolo's book, *African Philosophy in Search of Identity* (1994). He noted that Masolo said that the sages in Oruka's study might not be philosophers because not every witty or non-mediocre saying is philosophy. Oruka (1989b: 4) then asserts that the claims of his philosophical sages are philosophy because they address fundamental issues regarding human nature, society, and life, and they articulate their rationale for their views. "And if this is not philosophy then only God or some Masolonian Ideal Being can be a philosopher." How does Oruka reconcile his earlier statement that sage philosophy depends on reflecting on first-order thought, if the sages are already philosophers? (3). Wouldn't the project then be involved in philosophizing on philosophical thought, not anthropological thought? And how do either of these procedures fit in with the philosophical challenge as articulated by Hountondji when he says, drawing upon Edmund Husserl's ideas, that "The impulse to research must proceed not from philosophies but from things and the problems connected with them" (Hountondji 1996: 86n32)?[13]

When writing the preface to the second edition to his book, Hountondji explained that he was against the study of ethnology because it was considered apart from sociology, separated from mainstream sociology by the kind of societies it studied, that is, "simple" or "primitive" societies, in other words, a kind of "Bantustanization" of social science (xvii). But he is not against studying Africa in all its plurality. He also admitted, in 1996, that in his earlier works "I tended to dismiss African anthropology as a whole" because its works were destined for a Western audience, and was thus a case of "extroversion." But he said, "I would admit today that I probably overstated my case" (xviii). He also explains that his statement about African philosophy being done only by Africans had not been meant as a "Definition" of African philosophy, as some took it, but rather as a polemical counter-assertion, an attempt to free African thought from one hundred years of "Africanism," that is, Euro-American domination of African studies (ix–xi). He wants African studies to continue in a different way than that created by Euro-Americans, focusing instead on finding solutions to African problems (xix–xx).

In his 1975 article about African philosophy Oruka still refers to many works on African philosophy as using a "debased" rather than "exact" concept of "philosophy." He complains that Dr. J. O. Sodipo (1973) from Nigeria is trying to pass off African superstitions regarding the agency of the Yoruba gods as an African understanding of cause and hence philosophical (Oruka 1975: 48). Oruka argues that equating "folk philosophy" with pre-scientific philosophy, as Wiredu does in an article published in *Second Order,* debases philosophy. What ought to be the standard for exact philosophy? Oruka mentions that the form of arguments "would generally be granted in reputable philosophical circles to constitute the necessary conditions for any valid answer to our problem" (52). In other words, he is referring somewhat sociologically to what is accepted as good form in academia. He adds some specificity to what he would consider reputable, mentioning that the "methodology of its inquiry conform to the conception that philosophy is a logical argument, a critical inquiry, a rational speculation or else a synthesis based on a rigorously reasoned-out investigation" (53). He then quotes a definition of Wiredu's and agrees with it: "The free investigation of the first principles of human life" (Wiredu 1980: 100, quoted in Oruka 1975: 53). Measuring against exact criteria for philosophy shows that not everything that claims to be philosophy is philosophy. He thus thinks that Hountondji's recent definition of African philosophy, which includes writings that the author him- or herself thinks are philosophical, is not in itself strict enough.

Right after giving his exact definition, Oruka deals with an objection posed to him by a philosopher from Yugoslavia who spoke at the fifteenth World Congress of Philosophy. Miodrag Cekic (1973: 44) claimed that philosophical knowledge "is gained not only in rational but also in irrational ways (by intuition, specific insight, introspection etc.)," and that "we can hardly find any total rationalists in the history of philosophy."

Significantly, Oruka's 1975 paper announces that he is beginning a project to interview African sages. In the article, he responds to Wiredu's characterization of folk philosophies as "what 'our elders' are said to have said" (Wiredu 1972: 5; Oruka 1975: 50–51). To get at the substance of these folk philosophies is difficult, Wiredu says, because we have to rely "on the reconstructions of the living wise men of the tribe." But after all the effort of recording discussions with wise men, Wiredu still doubts that the results of such interviews could be incorporated into a "modern course in philosophy" (Wiredu 1972: 5; Oruka 1975: 50–51). If we look at Wiredu's article we see his argument as to why the insights of the elders cannot be modern. Traditional codes of conduct and practices of education were context-dependent, and African societies are changing. The youth of Africa desperately need a new philosophy, since traditions are outdated, and imported fundamentalist Christianity is so unthinking and unscientific. To try to reinvigorate past ideas as the nationalists do results in anachronism, which will not suffice for a younger generation that has to take into account the forward march of science (Wiredu 1972: 6–7). He explains later in his paper that he does not disagree that debunking false ideas and prejudices in African thought is an important task. But he sees the design of a curriculum for the youth of Africa that focuses on scientific thought and reflects on contemporary African experience as the more pressing and the more future-oriented project for philosophy (Wiredu 1972: 12–13).

Oruka takes up this challenge. He suggests that instead of trying to reconstruct the ideas of deceased elders, one should interview the living to get the thoughts of the living sages. Oruka says in 1975 (51),

> Sages (some of whom must turn out to be philosophers) have their own 'elaborate' and argumentative reasons for their "doctrines" and views. And such reasons can, given the patience and dedication of a trained philosopher-inquirer, be extracted from the sages and be made into written philosophical literature. There is nothing impossible or debased about such a task, for Plato had carried out a similar operation as regards Socrates.

He thinks that extracts from these interviews of "living sages" or "living traditional Africans" combined with writings of "modern African scholars of exact philosophy" can be incorporated into a "modern" course on African philosophy (51). In other words, he wants to treat the sages as contributors to the contemporary philosophical scene, not as relics of the past. In the midst of this description he notes that he and his colleague Joseph Donders have already embarked upon this project (54n6). Oruka clearly came up with the project in response to something Wiredu said, but came to different conclusions as to how to go about it and what status it should have in the emerging field of African philosophy.

Oruka carefully crafted his project to avoid several dangers of the approaches of African philosophers who came before him. First, he did not want to construct another ethnophilosophy that would be subject to Hountondji's criticisms. But he equally wanted to avoid being charged, as Hountondji was, with being Westernized and not African in his approach (Oruka 1991b: 42–47).

Oruka explained that his approach to these topics was different than that of the social anthropologist or the oral historian, both of whom had as their main goal the reconstruction of "facts" through the search for consensus among a number of informants. In contrast, Oruka intended to find select wise persons who could provide detailed explanations and reasonable criticisms of certain beliefs and practices of the community. He also sought sages who possessed lesser-known background information about practices.

Oruka tried to distinguish sage philosophy's method from that of the social anthropologist by saying that his own interviews were intended to be free-flowing conversations, not dry questions and answers. Many of the transcripts show discussions that were more like cut-and-dried questions and answers because some assistant researchers were provided with a list of "philosophical questions," but the interviews were not intended to be so. In my own experience as a first-hand observer, Oruka's interviews were indeed free-flowing. But according to the anthropologist Clifford Geertz, this is indeed the method of the social anthropologist! In *Available Light: Anthropological Reflections on Philosophical Topics*, Geertz (2000: 93) explains that what anthropologists do best is talk to men and women of the community in a "largely free form, in a one thing leads to another and everything leads to everything else manner, in the vernacular and for extended periods of time, all the while observing, from very close up, how they behave." He calls the approach holistic, humanistic, qualitative, and personal, like an improvising artisan. Certainly there is a lot of overlap between what the sage philosophy interviewers do and this particular description of social-anthropological method.

Oruka goes one step further in trying to distinguish his method from social anthropology. He notes that not only should the conversation be aimed at finding out what the sage thinks, but the researcher should also feel free to raise objections to what the sages say, in that way challenging the sage either to explain him- or herself better or to change his or her view. In this way the dialogues are based on a Socratic model, where interlocutors challenge each other. The point is not that the sage has the answers, but that the sage can explain his or her views and either defend them under attack or agree to modify them. This is part of the core description of philosophical practice. Many social anthropologists think that their role is to observe and not disturb what they are trying to observe; in this way their goals differ from philosophy's.

In fact, this point regarding philosophy's distinction from anthropological method was made by W. A. Hart in an article that Oruka read and referenced in his 1972 article. Hart argued that anthropologists were supposed merely to describe how people think, and the relationship between peoples' thoughts, actions, practices, and institutions. In contrast, the philosopher's role is to discern how one ought to think. The philosopher is allowed to, and in fact should, criticize, but even then, the philosopher should only do so after taking time to understand the context, initially suspending incredulity (Hart 1972:

50). Despite the clear separation of these roles, anthropologists do sometimes make judgments. Hart mentions E. E. Evans-Pritchard's comment that the Azande are mistaken in their beliefs about causality (50). When Evans-Pritchard remarks that witchcraft was a means used by the Azande (in Hart's words) "to compensate for their limited knowledge of natural causes, thus enabling them to feel themselves in control of their situation," Hart does not characterize Evans-Pritchard's thought a judgment or speculation but calls it instead a description of the role witchcraft plays in the life of a society (46). This description is presumptuous and belittling. It is similar to the claim that Napoleon conquered vast territories to make up for feelings of inadequacy caused by being short. Not only is this claim a speculation with little ground in evidence, but it also belittles significant accomplishments. Likewise, the Azande system of witchcraft is complex and extensive, as Evans-Pritchard himself (1937) documents. To attribute it to an effort to cover up human weakness is to give it an uncharitable interpretation.

Not only philosophers but also many missionaries converse with rural elders in order to challenge traditional beliefs. When done sensitively, the results can be philosophical, as are Michael Kirwen's dialogues in *The Missionary and the Diviner*. When done insensitively, the "dialogue" degenerates into a contest of wills or, in many cases, the attempted or successful destruction of traditional African beliefs or practices and the power play of the Christian missionary or colonial administrator. For example, a Christian preacher in Mukogodo recently chopped down a sacred tree used in peace rituals among Maasai and Dorobo members of the community. He argued that it was his duty to stop Africans from worshiping "things."[14]

Researchers pursuing philosophical studies in Africa can benefit from careful use of anthropological methods and studies. In the past, anthropologists have held dismissive and paternalistic attitudes toward Africans and under-recorded African philosophical contributions. They also, as Okot p'Bitek argued, misunderstood Africans and came to hasty conclusions by projecting their own understanding on a new context.

In an essay, Kwasi Wiredu (2011) encourages African philosophers to do careful particularist research into African cultures, customs, and traditional philosophical concepts. He advocates "intensive studies of those elements of culture that play significant roles in the constitution of meanings in the various African world views" (xvi). He specifically encourages them to seek out "individual indigenous philosophers" and insists that Oruka's sage philosophy project needs "urgent continuation" (xx).

Studies on the early development of sage philosophy would do well to delve more deeply into certain issues such as the importance of the sages' oral philosophizing (Presbey, 1996); questions on the definition and role of "wisdom" in contemporary philosophy, and how those concerns (or even skepticism) about wisdom impacts other philosopher's estimation of the sage philosophy project's viability (Presbey, 1999); and Oruka's provocative use of the Socratic metaphor of "midwife" in describing the role of the interviewer of the sages (Presbey, 2002a). Oruka has had a series of critics of his goals and choice of method in sage philosophy—even among those who champion the study and growth of African philosophy and even a revised sage philosophy project. Bruce Janz (1998: 58–60) is worried that Western philosophical ideals were being imported into Oruka's attempts at creating African philosophy. He worried that Oruka treated the sages as objects of study, using them to prove a point he wanted to make about African rationality. Janz suggested that Oruka depended too much on the idea of philosophizing as critique and divergence from communally accepted beliefs. Why not look for other signs of wisdom, such as creative thinking? (Janz 2009: 107, 109) Other critics were unconvinced that African philosophy needs the emphasis on individual sages. W. J. Ndaba thought that the ideal of philosophy as "an individual, explicit, critical and self-critical ratiocinative consciousness" was a Western notion, since such emphasis was "counterproductive for the emergence of a genuinely rooted African philosophy" (Ndaba, 1996: 17). My earlier research critiqued sage philosophy's marginalization of women sages (Presbey, 1997, 2012).

With these and other voices of caution, it is important to note that none of the above wanted sage philosophy research to end. Their only wish was to modify its goals and methods. All agreed that the sages' wisdom needed to be taken seriously and better incorporated into the history of philosophy. And as Ochieng'-Odhiambo noted, the trajectory of Oruka's interests in the sages showed that over time, the issue of proving anything to outsiders diminished in importance, as the question of how sage wisdom and reflection could help Kenya and Africa took center stage (Ochieng'-Odhiambo, 2006: 21; 2002a: 29; and 1997: 78; see also Presbey, 2007, 2014). For example, sages addressed issues of jealousy and disharmony, marital strife and superstition in rural communities (Presbey, 2004). Sages also addressed political issues and ethnic strife (Presbey, 2002b). Sage philosophy has continued to be a popular project, albeit with methodological changes, as attested to by the recent collection by Kresse and Nyarwath, *Rethinking Sage Philosophy* (2002). In these revised ways, Oruka's sage philosophy project lives on.

6

Exploring H. Odera Oruka's Position on Luo Practices of Burial and Widow Guardianship

1. How is the Sage Philosophy Project Related to Oruka's Testimony at the S.M. Otieno Burial Trial?

The book that Oruka edited, *Sage Philosophy: Indigenous Thinkers and Modern Debate on African Philosophy* (1991b), contains three distinct parts. As he explains, Part One "give[s] the rationale for treating sage philosophy as a fully-fledged trend in the development of African philosophy" (Oruka 1991b: ix). The second part contains interviews with sages, and the third part contains papers about the Sage Philosophy Project written by other scholars. However, in Part One, there is a section unlike all the others, that is, Chapter Five which contains Oruka's testimony at the S.M. Otieno burial trial. While there is a brief preface to the excerpts, there is little mention by Oruka of how his testimony at the trial is related to sage philosophy. Is it an example of sage philosophy? Is it an application of the fruits of wisdom gleaned from sage philosophy? Is Oruka a sage, being questioned, not by a philosophical interviewer but by a lawyer? The latter seems to not be the case, for it does not appear alongside the interviews with sages in Part Two of the book, none of whom are interviewed by lawyers. While Oruka does not come out and directly state the purpose of including the trial, let me suggest that he intends it as an application of the fruits of wisdom gained by sage philosophy.

But how is being an expert witness on Luo customs, and telling a judge all about the longstanding, rarely changing values, customs, and practices of a particular ethnic group related to the project of finding individual critical thinkers interested in philosophical topics among elders of multiple ethnic groups of Kenya? The latter description is what sage philosophy is most known for, as Oruka championed the abilities of rural elders to be sagacious evaluators and critics of their own groups' beliefs. A focus on named individuals as sages was intended to be an alternative to both ethnophilosophy and anthropological methods that anonymized African philosophical views, attributing them to a group rather than to an individual. Oruka also envisioned the project as one that would help build national culture, as Kenyans of various ethnic backgrounds learned from the wisdom of sages of their own as well as other ethnic groups (Presbey 2014: 5). This aspect of the project is illustrated in Part Two of his book, since it contains interviews of sages from a variety of ethnic groups.

A series of subtle clues throughout the early parts of the book show how Oruka's testimony fits in to the Sage Philosophy Project. The first round of interviews with sages, conducted by both Oruka and his colleague Joseph Donders in 1974 (Oruka 1975: 54n6; 1991b: 17–18), was financed by grant money from the Dean's Committee. In that early 1970s project, the goal was to interview sages who were identified as such by their students (Donders 1977: 11n16). The next set of interviews, as Oruka mentions in his chapter 4 of the 1991 edition of *Sage Philosophy*, were financed as part of a project sponsored by the Institute of African Studies (IAS). The goal of the IAS project was to study "socio-cultural factors in change and development." (Oruka 1991b: 60). Oruka argued that the best way to understand ethnic cultures was not to survey people in general, as he presumed anthropologists did, but rather to seek out the wisest and most reflective individuals, who could both recount and evaluate the widespread beliefs of their communities. He calls this description of widely held beliefs and longstanding practices "culture philosophy" and insists that it is more reliable and insightful than accounts of group views attained by other means (58–60).

Oruka explains that his Sage Philosophy Project enabled him to construct a description of the Luo belief system and their philosophies of life. (He does not mention whether the project led to similar descriptions of other ethnic groups' beliefs or philosophies of life.) The IAS was interested in these findings insofar as it could help them to discern how better to approach topics like development in a culturally sensitive way. Oruka explains that the IAS was most interested in the communal viewpoint, and so for their purposes he highlighted commonalities and downplayed differences (Oruka 1991b: 60). Oruka also explains (65n4) that he provides only the summary report, rather than individual interviews, because some sages did not want their names associated with the study. He specifically notes that Barry Hallen and J. O. Sodipo's study is similar, because the sages they consulted were also left anonymous. In the earlier 1983 article (1991b: 50), Oruka clarifies that the Hallen-Sodipo project is not philosophy in the second-order sense, that is, strict philosophy, but only culture philosophy. So certainly, Oruka's own report of Luo beliefs and philosophies of life (1991b: 60–63) is also an example of culture philosophy, but this culture philosophy is one of the "fruits" of the Sage Philosophy Project.

So, is "culture philosophy" actually philosophy? In *Sage Philosophy* (1991b: 48–49) he explains that culture philosophy is philosophy in the broad or loose sense of the term, since "first order" philosophy, which he calls the "mythos" of a culture, is full of prejudices, dominated by communal conformity and anachronism, and is absolutist and ideological. In contrast second-order philosophy, which he calls "philosophy proper," is tentative and ratiocinative. While every individual in a culture has some familiarity with its mythos, sages are experts in their society's mythos (48). From his description one senses that he might not be very interested in the mythos; his interest seems to be directed toward the second-order analysis of first-order culture philosophy.

As it turns out, in the Kenyan context there may have been even more interest in this culture philosophy than there was in the rarer "philosophic sagacity." While the international philosophy scene may have been more impressed by the existence of individually named philosophical sages, Oruka was in demand in Kenya because he had completed this study of Luo beliefs, customs, and philosophies of life. As he explains, due to this report he was asked to be an expert witness at the S.M. Otieno trial. He asserts that his account was more authoritative than the other elder women and men who were witnesses at the trial, because the others were only "folk sages," whereas his testimony was based on the account of "philosophical sages," that is, the intellectuals and experts in the Luo community. He thought that the other witnesses became mired in "contradictions" while his testimony contained no contradictions (Oruka 1991b: 43n2). This assertion is an interesting one, since Cohen and Otieno Adhiambo in their in-depth analysis of the S.M. Otieno burial trial noted that Oruka's testimony was met with skepticism due to his youth, while the words of the elders who testified were more easily believed by Kenyans who were socialized to revere wisdom and authority in the elderly (Cohen and Atieno Odhiambo 1992: 49–51).

Oruka also explains in *Sage Philosophy* that due to his role as expert witness at the trial, he was invited by various Provincial Commissioners to give a series of seminars to District Officers and District Commissioners, explaining Luo beliefs and philosophies of life, and he did so extensively in 1987–88. He summarizes these talks (1991b: 60–65, esp. 65n1), which included discussion of witchcraft, religion, health, burial, and related customs, and the impact of modernization and development (58). It is interesting to note as well as presenting his insights into group-held beliefs, he also shared his study of wise individuals and their individual beliefs and rational arguments in defense of their positions. For example, he explains that traditionally many Luos believed in witchcraft and the need for expert protection from "evils and devils," but he puts that in historical context and explains that some contemporary Luos appear to be "indifferent" to witchcraft (61). He claims that "a large number" of Luos in Siaya are still "extremely superstitious" (62), but then quotes Njeru wa

Kanyenje from Central Embu, who regarded witchcraft as a "deceit" or "bluff" and said that witchdoctors were "clever manipulators of the weakness of human minds ..." (65). While the emphasis in Luo society is upon marriage and robust procreation (62), Oruka references a sage named Mbote Koria from East Ugenya in Siaya who notes that past practices of warring with neighbors to seize their lands are no longer practical, and given this change, parents should attempt to regulate the size of their families according to the ability of their land to support them (65). (Neither of these sages are included in section two of the book, which is one of several clues that Oruka engaged in many interviews that have not yet been published.)

Given these examples, does Oruka value the traditions he has learned so much about? He follows descriptions of two deeply and widely held beliefs and values among the Luo, witchcraft, and prolific procreation, with the testimony of a sage who criticizes and / or problematizes these views, thus showing that the respective societies already critique these practices. Rural areas are NOT a place of unquestioning, unthinking allegiance to past values. They are also the birthplace of critical thinkers. As Oruka travels among Kenyan institutions he educates people not only on the traditions but also on their contemporary critique.

Soon after the trial, and around the same time he was speaking to District Officers, he received funds from USAID to participate in a study organized by the National Council for Population and Development, which involved studying the beliefs and attitudes of rural Kenyans regarding family planning. Oruka oversaw sage interviews in five districts in five provinces (Siaya, Bungoma, Nyeri, Nandi, and Machakos). Again, he relied on his method of finding wise sages who could shed light on beliefs and attitudes in their own communities that could be overlooked by usual demographic methods. Some of the ideas included were the emphasis on having a male heir in a patriarchal society; the preservation of names of the dead by naming the living after them, which requires having children to name; the belief that one must have many children to ward against witchcraft practices such as "footprint picking"; and taboos against counting children, which make family planning difficult. Dorothy Munyakho wrote that she warned Oruka "that he was likely to be torn apart by demographers" who may not have appreciated his unique approach to the study (Munyakho 1990: 21). Still, the study shows that Oruka was confident that his sages could do a better job than outside observers at analyzing their own society. Also, the fact that the study involved five provinces shows that this study had the same inter-ethnic character as his Sage Philosophy Project for IAS of several years earlier.

Oruka's account of Luo practices in *Sage Philosophy* also includes ways in which traditions have eroded, sometimes due to foreign influence. Not all change is good. He complains that foreign influence on Luo society has led to promiscuity among wives and young unmarried people (62–63). He also complains that colonial regimes, which had been ignorant of African cultures, marginalized the wisdom of the Kenyan elders (63). He appreciates that the contemporary Kenyan government of his time is trying to rectify some of the past Eurocentrism by handing over land cases to be decided by local elders (63). In Oruka's work over the years one can find a tension between setting aside anachronistic practices in favor of progressive change and championing neglected traditions in the hope that Kenyans would abandon recent developments. In an article Oruka reflected on the deeper philosophical meanings of the S.M. Otieno burial trial, explaining that in contemporary times one must avoid the twin evils of attempting to continue everything traditional, on the one hand, and advocating the adoption of everything new and/or foreign, on the other hand (Oruka 1989c: 85). He discusses defending African traditions against anti-African bias and prejudice and championing reform when traditions need it. We'll see if this same tension or balance is present in his testimony during the S.M. Otieno burial trial, as well as articles that he wrote on related topics within the next few years after the trial.

2. Oruka's Testimony During the Trial: Harmful to Women?

There is a longstanding debate among scholars, including many feminist lawyers in Kenya, about whether or not the provision for customary law in the Kenyan constitution is harmful to women. While that dispute can't be revisited here (although I have done so in print elsewhere[1]), we can turn to Oruka's testimony in court and see if we can discern his motives as well as the effects of his testimony.

Oruka's description of Luo customs during his testimony to the court included the following remarks: "A woman is knowledgeable on matters involving the house. A man runs the home ... Daughters are not expected as permanent residents of the home ... A girl belongs to where she is married" (Oruka 1991b: 70). Oruka also explained that although customs do change with time, some Luo customs have been around for a long time, and will not change easily. For example, "in marriage, the husband is the head of the family, and home and also among the Luos, a man needs to have a son to build a home, and before marriage, dowry is paid" (Oruka 1991b: 78).

Now in the bulk of his testimony, Oruka was not necessarily stating what his own beliefs were, although he himself is also a Luo. Rather, he was recounting the traditional beliefs of his community. So one could argue that, although these Luo practices could be seen as based on the notion of women's inferiority, or as having the result of disadvantaging women, it was not necessarily Oruka's own view. If the courtroom was not the proper venue to describe his personal views (since from a professional ethics point of view, his role was to describe Luo ethics, not his own personal ethical positions), then we would expect him to clarify his position outside of the courtroom. The introduction to the excerpts of his testimony which he included in *Sage Philosophy* explains that Oruka didn't mean to appear as a supporter of the clan, but since he was ridiculed by the lawyer on the widow's side, he got defensive, and in the end his testimony was used by the clan to help win their case. It's not made clear in *Sage Philosophy* who the author of this introductory text is (Oruka 1991b: 68). We can wonder if Oruka's male Luo identity and the fact that he was invited by the clan's defense team, meant that in some way he had, perhaps, a pre-disposition to side with the clan rather than to be completely neutral regarding the outcome of the trial. Oruka never wrote anything autobiographical enough to comment on the trial's subject matter in relation to his own identity, and in fact he clearly takes offense when the widow's lawyer, Khaminwa, wants to personalize the issues at stake by drawing attention to Oruka's own status as an educated Luo man. But no doubt the first affront was at the very beginning of Khaminwa's cross-examination, when Khaminwa suggested that the issues at hand regard religion, while Oruka's field is philosophy, not religion (Oruka 1991b: 72).

However, there is one place, early in his testimony, where Oruka clearly takes sides with the clan and against the widow. He states that he rejects the argument that S.M. Otieno, having moved to Nairobi and embraced other modern customs, was exempt from the duty to carry out Luo customs. In Oruka's words, "We have no rationale to show that the man had a religion or an explicit philosophy of conscience which justifiably exempts him from being subjected to the Luo customs" (Oruka 1991b: 74). This is clearly a response to the earlier *ex parte* order given by Justice Shields to the widow, Wambui Otieno, allowing her to bury her husband's body in Karen (a suburb of Nairobi), on the grounds that S.M. Otieno was a metropolitan lawyer who had opted out of customary law (Twining 2010: 491). The Court of Appeal that heard the trial thought that it was not possible for individuals to opt out of Luo customs, as they explained: "At present there is no way in which an African citizen of Kenya can divest himself of the association with the tribe of his father if those customs are patrilineal" (quoted in Wanjala 1989: 111; Nation Newspapers, 1986: 1).

In other words this would mean that according to Oruka and those who share his view, that every Luo individual has the right and the liberty to opt out of following Luo customs if they can demonstrate to the community that their request for release is due to a carefully thought out and clearly articulated principled position. Here the stipulation would be that S.M. Otieno's problem is that he did not clarify the extent of his divergence from their beliefs and practices or his reasons for noncompliance. It may be that he presumed he had the liberty to depart from customary law without such formalities or express opinions.

But as the testimony stands, while Oruka concedes that customs do change, he said there was no ground for being "flexible" in the S.M. Otieno case, for "while they [customs] are in force, it would be absurd to suggest that we should not follow them" (Oruka 1991b: 82). With these words, Oruka is seen to embrace the argument of the clan, and the verdict of the court, that "there is no way in which an African citizen of Kenya can divest himself of the association with the tribe of his father" (Nation Newspapers, 1986: 1). This position is considered unrealistic by M.D. Okech-Owiti, who says that the preceding claim of the court is an "unsustainable assertion," since it suggests that a person can't show by their actions, conduct, or lifestyle that they reject certain customs (Okech-Owiti 1989: 20–23).

In fact, when Oruka testified, Wambui Otieno's lawyer, Khaminwa, asked him whether in traditional society there may be people opposed to customs, who want to depart from those customs and do things their own way. Oruka replied that "in a traditional communal society there were very few rebels." (*Daily Nation* 1987: 4). But Oruka doesn't add how in his Sage Philosophy Project, he especially likes the rebels, those who don't conform to customs. He doesn't mention that he and other philosophers, like Kwame Gyekye for example, or earlier anthropologists like Paul Radin, insisted that there were always individual free thinkers in "traditional," that is, rural and unschooled African contexts. Nor did he say that, while there are few rebels, those who are rebels are special, and should be lauded and appreciated by their communities, known by all Kenyans as philosophical sages (rather than folk sages). He did tell Khaminwa that during his study of sages he found there to be two types of sages, those who were flexible and recommended changes, and those who were rigid (*Daily Nation* 1987: 4). But he doesn't say that his study portrayed the flexible sages as great role models. In fact, those who heard his testimony were worried that he was repeating (what they thought were) outdated Luo practices as if they were timeless and unchanging. As Judge Cotran explained, customary law should be revised often, based on new oral evidence from experts (Cotran 1989: 155).

Wim van Binsbergen (2003) has written critically about this tendency to presume that cultures are reified and clearly bounded. In a provocative chapter entitled "Cultures do not exist," (459–524) he criticizes the widespread understanding of culture as something that all humans have (and have just one), and "in that 'culture' they live their entire lives as if they have no option" (461). He thinks an idea of "cultural orientations" in the plural, that co-exist and intersect in persons, and are not "natural" or inborn but are learned and practiced through performativity is closer to the lived truth of culture in human life (ibid.). Such perspectives could have been helpful in the context of this court case.

Khaminwa asked Oruka directly whether or not he was a traditional Luo, and Oruka replied: "I am a Luo, although I organize my life according to values some of which are not traditional Luo" (Oruka 1991b: 75).

From a philosophical point of view, the conversation between Oruka and Wambui's lawyer, Khaminwa, is interesting, because Oruka was drawn into a discussion where he astounded the lawyer by suggesting that no matter how "modern" of a "professor" he was, he still thought that Luo customs should be followed (Oruka 1991b: 74, 78). He admitted to having ingested a *manyasi* (elixir) created by an herbal specialist. In a passage that needs close scrutiny, it sounds as if Oruka said he held many of the Luo traditional beliefs, such as belief in the existence of spirits. However if one looks more closely, it is apparent that he was only expressing a more nuanced position that claimed one could not definitively prove that there were not spirits. Oruka did not say he believed in spirits, but rather, he turned each question around, answering a question with another question, asking the widow's lawyer about his own criteria for proving there were no spirits (Oruka 1991b: 77–78). It seems Oruka was attempting to defend indigenous culture from a modernist view which was ready to dismiss it wholesale as backward and primitive.

In the chapter in *Sage Philosophy* preceding this testimony, Oruka claimed that most Luos were superstitious, and he had, in the context of discussing how to recognize wise assertions, quoted a sage who claimed that witchcraft was bluff and deception (1991b: 65). But earlier in his description of Luo beliefs and practices Oruka said, when referring to witchdoctors (or "medicine men" called *ajuoke* in Dhuluo), that some of them were "bogus; others are genuine and seem to have power of fulfilling their mission" (1991b: 62). What would it mean to say some of these *ajuoke* are genuine? Oruka does not explain exactly what he means. Does that mean that some succeed in driving away evil spirits? This would imply that there actually were such spirits. Oruka had explained that such persons use two methods. Some use a combination of herbs as well as psychological drama. Others use only drama. When he says they are able to help people, does that mean that from a pragmatic perspective, they help their clients by making them feel better? If he actually believes there are such spirits and that some medicine men successfully drive away evil spirits from their clients, he has been a bit indirect in making this claim.

Oruka does not have a chance during the trial to explain under what circumstances in his own life he ingested the *manyasi* (elixir). Did he do it as an experiment? Did he do it because he was being haunted and hoped the elixir would help him? Is his assertion in *Sage Philosophy* that some medicine men are efficacious based on his first-hand experience, or on his research findings? We don't know.

Oruka also explains in chapter 4 of *Sage Philosophy* that Luos are careful and respectful regarding how they bury their dead because they believe the dead are intermediaries between the living and God, and that the dead are in a special position to help the living (1991b: 62). During his testimony at the trial he explained that many Luos think that if they do not follow the burial customs correctly, they will be haunted by the spirits of the dead (1991b: 80–81). Oruka does not himself comment on whether he thinks this is true or not.

Wambui Waiyaki Otieno described her own reaction to Oruka's testimony. In her memoirs she reflects upon how Oruka described a father and his son deciding where to build the son's house in the family compound by observing the behavior of a cock: "Surely the business of being shown where to build a home by a cock cannot be anything else but primitive! I could not envisage that our modern courts and judges could hail such a custom" (Otieno 1998: 188–89). Much of the ire of the clan and Luos in general against Wambui has to do with her using the word "primitive" to describe Luo actions and beliefs.

Customary law specialist Cotran explained two aspects of the S.M. Otieno trial that deeply disturbed him. The first was that S.M. Otieno's own wishes for his burial were considered irrelevant to the case. How, Cotran ponders, can it be possible for a person to write a will, thereby disposing of their property as they wish, and yet be unable to express any wishes regarding the "disposal" of their own corpse? (Cotran 1989: 161–62). Cotran was also disturbed that the widow's wishes were wholly ignored (162–63).

The funeral service in the Anglican cathedral in Kisumu and the burial in Siaya attracted large crowds, and gave occasion for many in attendance to express Luo nationalism. Men were warned to think twice before trying to marry a woman from another ethnic group. Another irony about Oruka's testimony helping the clan and hurting the widow's case is that a man he greatly admired, Oginga Odinga, was busy speaking out at funerals in Siaya District, arguing against the parochialism of the Umira Kager clan, and promoting inter-ethnic marriage and Luo-Kikuyu alliances (Stamp 1991: 839–40).[2] Oruka had envisaged the Sage Philosophy Project as interviews of sages from a multiplicity of ethnic groups which would herald their wisdom as the common heritage of Kenyans on a national level. This goal of national unity would be sidelined. Instead, the emphasis on Luo customs and their application in favor of the clan's case can be seen as an instance when the project of building national culture and intercultural harmony is temporarily neglected.

D. A. Masolo shared his interpretation that Oruka intended his testimony to defend "the ordinary person's dignity" because the ordinary person in Kenya is under threat from elitist academia (including philosophy), the law, and government (Masolo 2018: 183). Supposedly, Wambui's living in Kenya and being a Christian who criticized superstitions made her an elitist in this scenario. But we have to keep in mind, Wambui grew up in a rural area and spent her childhood working on a farm. She ran away to Nairobi, to work for the Mau Mau undercover, where she risked her life smuggling arms (Otieno 1998: 19, 37). While she was raised Christian by her parents, she said in her autobiography, "As a Kikuyu and a Christian, I was brought up to be a part of both cultures, yet I rejected many of the restrictions imposed by each" (25), thus portraying herself as a person who made her own independent decisions. To portray her as an elitist or duped by the West would be unfair to her, I suggest.

Completely missing from Oruka's account of his experience as expert witness on customary law is any criticism of the continued incorporation of customary law into the constitution of Kenya. One would think that his commitment to anti-colonialism would have led him to be familiar with post-colonial studies which speak of customary law as historically an arm of the colonial state (Ranger 1983: 250–51; Stamp 1991: 810–12; Mamdani 1996: 109–17). And yet he never makes reference to such literature, and does not show any self-critical awareness of the moral ambiguity of participating in the courts of customary law. Rather, he seems flattered to have a venue in which his knowledge of Luo customs can be of use. In fact, he cites and agrees with Ali Mazrui, who claimed that the African judiciary was dominated by European models, laws and constitutions in English, and even by expatriate judges (Oruka 1994a; see Mazrui n.d.).

With a history so influenced and distorted by colonialism, how could Oruka's participation in a contemporary system of customary law be unproblematic? But it did not seem this way to him and other Luos of the time, who saw instead the decision of the lower court and Justice Shields in favor of the widow as the decisions of white foreigners enforcing colonial law, in contrast to the decision by Justice Bosire in favor of the clan and local African law (Twining 2010: 492).

However, there is another side to the issue of customary law. Later in this article I will explain how customary law may sometimes do a better job at defending women's rights and liberties than civil law.

3. Oruka's Proposed Procedure of Evaluation

Without a clear statement by Oruka during the trial that he believed women in Kenya need rights equal to men's, the clan could argue that the status quo was justified, and a famous precedent-setting case, supported by feminists, in which a Kenyan woman tried to assert her rights was lost. If Oruka were able to explain his own view as a more nuanced version of acceptance as well as rejection of various aspects of Luo tradition, his expert testimony would not have seemed so clearly to side with the clan against the widow. I consider this one of Oruka's missed opportunities to support women's equality in Kenya.

As it turns out, one year after his February 5, 1987 testimony during the S.M. Otieno burial trial, Oruka finally took the opportunity to distinguish his own views about the role of men and women from the traditional Luo practices he had described at the trial. In 1988, Oruka gave a presentation at a seminar run by the National Council of Women in Kenya (and a few months later he presented the same paper at a conference on Philosophy and Traditions).[3] He began by complaining that in Kenya, too many people too quickly associated the modern with the foreign, Western, and progressive. On the other hand, they associated the traditional with the African and backwardness. While emphasizing that reason appeals to a universal standard, he clearly wants to detach the idea of reason and justice from being linked to the model of European thought and practice, as he states:

> There is no doubt that any reasonable person in Kenya or anywhere would support a change from backwardness to progress, from economic stagnation to economic independence, for male domination to gender equality and from superstitious beliefs to scientific beliefs. What is not true, however, is a belief or claim that Europe is the custodian of progress while Africa is a die-hard defender of backwardness.
>
> Oruka *Ethics* 1990a: 102

Oruka points out that such views are the residue of colonialist thinking. Such simplistic dichotomies also encourage people to believe that in Africa women are dominated, and in the West, women are liberated. But Oruka notes that some European practices affect women negatively. He notes that the European custom of a woman changing her last name to that of her husband is a sexist practice, since men do not change their names to their wives' last names (although as we know, hyphenated names that combine the two are becoming more common). He also disapproved of European practices of taking young women as mistresses while in effect blocking their chances at marriage. The point of his examples was to caution Kenyans from approving of everything European.

Oruka goes on to clarify that in a healthy, normal society, tradition and modernity are inseparable. Colonialism seriously disturbed African societies, and due to that disturbance, "the imposed foreign values pose as modernity while the indigenous values are labeled backward and primitive" (Oruka 1990a: 103). The disturbance also created a "sharp clash" between tradition and modernity, while more normal times would have assured a smoother transition. In healthy societies, values and practices change by adapting traditional values. His example is how in the West, homosexual practices which were once considered wrong are now gaining acceptance, not because old values are discarded, but because there is an application of the traditional value of liberty.[4] In contrast, a colonial way of thinking questions the helpfulness of the African past, and encourages Africans to give up old ways to take on new, foreign ideals.[5] Oruka clarifies that he is not in support of change just for the sake of change, or change for the sake of fitting a Western norm of progress. Each case should be analysed to see if the change is actually for the better (Oruka 1990a: 108).

Moving to specific examples of traditions that impact the issue of women's equality, Oruka notes that in Kenyan tradition (as he has mentioned in court in the case of the Luo), the husband provides the home for the couple and is considered head of the household. He is quick to mention that such is also the case in many parts of the West. Oruka predicts that this aspect of tradition, as in the West, will change as women gain more economic equality. Oruka notes that African women, following the lead of Western practice, have adopted the last names of their husbands, even though it was not their tradition to do so. But, as this trend is changing in the West, he predicts it will also change in Kenya. Oruka notes that in Kenya the wife is expected to adopt the customs of her husband's ethnic group. He notes that what made the Wambui Otieno case so unusual was her insistence that her marriage to S.M Otieno had nothing to do with tradition, and so she did not adopt his customs. Oruka's praise or blame of Wambui regarding her independence in this matter is muted, because Oruka quickly shifts topic to suggest that in Western, Christian practices, the wife also adopts her husband's customs. It is still hard to read whether Oruka supports Wambui or not; if so, his support is muted. Chances are, he sees her as someone who has unthinkingly and in a wholesale fashion jettisoned all traditions, without stopping to evaluate them one by one.

Regarding the customary practices surrounding remarriage of a widow to a brother or cousin of her deceased husband (often called wife inheritance, while it should instead be called widow guardianship), Oruka claims that he is not sure whether he is in favor of it or not. But, his support of the idea comes through in his following words, and he is popularly seen as having supported the practice by his colleagues in the philosophy department, and by his own widow (who said she followed the custom, at least on a symbolic level, out of respect for her husband's position on the issue). Oruka notes that the practice is everywhere on the decline, due to both Western influence, and the reluctance of educated wives to be married to relatives of their husband (who often do not share the deceased husband's level of education and social status). Yet he suggests that the practice was an important way in which wives honored the memories of their deceased husbands. He clarifies that in the Luo context, marriage is not considered to be "until death do us part," but continues beyond the grave. The relative of the deceased husband does not become a "new" husband, but is considered a surrogate for the deceased man, and any children borne to the wife will still be considered the progeny of the deceased. Giving up the practice, therefore, entails taking on a foreign idea of marriage as limited by death. Is the foreign idea better or worse? Oruka's limited point here is that we should not prejudge that there is no merit in the tradition (Oruka 1990a: 107–8).

When it comes to issues of inheritance, Oruka clearly states that women should be able to inherit property. As he explains, it used to be the case that society could not imagine single or divorced women. It therefore did not need to provide for women outside of marriage, and husbands' property was seen to be sufficient for their (indirect) support. But Oruka explains that he considers there to be good reasons for women to choose to remain single or to leave their marriages. Therefore, there needs to be a way for women to have and inherit property (Oruka 1990a: 108).

Also in 1989, Oruka published a book chapter entitled "Traditionalism and Modernisation in Kenya: Customs, Spirits and Christianity," in which he revisited some of these themes (Oruka 1989c). He again reiterated his point that "modern" should not be equated with "Western," and Kenyan traditions should not be equated with backwardness, since there may be some customs that are more humane and helpful than imported Western traditions. To presume this erroneous dichotomy to be true is to engage in racism, be it conscious or unconscious (1989c: 84). He emphasized a popular theme at the time of the S.M. Otieno burial, that is, the claim that African traditional ideas of spirits and Christian ideas of spirits are not that different from each other, and so one should not be dismissed as "backward" while the other is considered progressive (Oruka 1989c: 82–83; see also Stamp 1991: 834–35).

He insists that his goal is not to fend off all foreign influence, but to evaluate and select from both foreign influence and African traditions. He says he knows of different people who each err too much in one direction or another, either championing all African traditions and accusing all harmful trends as being results of foreign influence, or on the other hand, those who worship everything foreign. He explains that his own approach is a careful middle road that "utilizes the best of their traditions and harmonises them with the liberating values borrowed from contact with foreigners" (Oruka 1989c: 85). He advocates subjecting the practices of others to careful evaluation before borrowing them. He then quotes his position, stated ten years earlier in his book *Punishment and Terrorism in Africa*: "When something traditional is negative and stagnating to Africans, it cannot be reasonable for Africa to adopt it simply because it happens to be traditional." (quoted in 1989c: 85).

While this part of the article emphasizes that traditions should not be held rigidly and regarded as sacrosanct, he ends this article emphasizing the caution from the other end of the continuum, that is, he warns against too eager a rush to "modernization." He says, "We must season our modernization by seriously cleansing its evils and sins with the *manyasi* of traditions" (1989c: 87). "Manyasi" refers to the medicine one must take to ward off the effects of *chira*, that is, (according to Oruka's testimony in court), "a misfortune which befalls someone because of a bad action done in the past ... you must be cleansed by experts with *manyasi*." (Muhoho and Gicheru 1987: 4). While his use of manyasi here can only be as a metaphor, his use of the traditional metaphors could be taken as a demonstration that he does not want to distance himself from the ideas of *chira* and *manyasi* by indulging in prejudices against such thinking and practices (when, for example, Christians may accomplish a similar cleansing through practices that include prayers, asking for the intervention of saints, or going to confession). In other words, Oruka is suggesting that only by deep reflection and by holding onto the valuable aspects of traditions can we safely and confidently open ourselves up to new ways.

Here I want to briefly explore Oruka's point that there may be some African traditions that protect women's rights more adequately than Euro-American models. Wangari Maathai has often insisted that some African traditions gave women more rights than they received under British colonial administrations. Traditionally, land was held by a family; it was only during colonial times that there would be a title deed for property that would only be given to men (Maathai 2009: 227).[6] Maathai explained that in the case of her own divorce, British-inspired Kenyan civil law had insisted that the only grounds for divorce from an otherwise permanent marriage bond would be in cases of cruelty, mental torture, adultery, or insanity. These rigid laws put her husband at the time (who filed for divorce in 1979) into a situation where the wish for divorce due to simple incompatibility had to be described in harsher terms to reach the British-inspired threshold for dissolution. When she wrote her memoirs in 2007 she expressed gratitude that such divorce criteria were no longer upheld in Kenya (Maathai 2007: 140, 148).

In other African countries, where customary marriage laws are jettisoned in favor of civil marriage, it could work against women (Barker 2011: 449–52; Griffiths 1997: 54–56).

Oruka did not mention Barker's, Griffiths's, or Maathai's examples, but they fit into his overall argument that one should not presume that traditions are bad for women and that European-inspired laws are always better. Barker explicitly says that while she admits some marriage customs were not favorable to women, she wants to "avoid the common tendency to posit African (polygamous) customs as inherently oppositional to gender equality, whilst (monogamous) civil law is tacitly assumed to embrace it" (Barker 2011: 452). She thinks it is fairer to state that all forms of marriage currently legal in South Africa have aspects that are unequal and result in gender oppression. She agrees with Suzanne Lenon that to insist that there is a "European 'tradition' of anti-homophobic and anti-sexist 'core values' is less a reflection of progressive gender relations than of regressive race relations" (Barker: 458). In other words, it is a case of Europeans trumpeting their racial superiority based on their "enlightened" ideals in comparison to the presumed backwardness of Africans, while being in denial about the European tradition's long history of oppressing women and condemning relationships outside of the heterosexist norm. And so, Barker shares Oruka's suspicion that behind some criticism of African traditions lies racism and Eurocentrism.

Kenyan philosophy professor John Murungi, in his analysis of the S.M. Otieno trial, also mentions the role of Eurocentrism. He says that Justice Shields of the lower court, who originally passed judgment in favor of Wambui Otieno did so because he made his decision based on Eurocentric notions of justice. Shields could not help but understand the situation from a Western-oriented nuclear family perspective which made it seem clear to him that a wife should have the right to decide the burial place of her husband. He says that Wambui should have realized that when she married a Luo man, she married a community (Murungi 2013: 187, 193). Some of Murungi's stated goals sound similar to Oruka's, in that he explains that he doesn't advocate going back to an African "golden age," but rather only wants to look for what is "salvageable" in African indigenous practices (193). Murungi himself admits that the current Kenyan status quo is patriarchal and that the court's final decision was conservative, not only echoing what the "elders" said but going further to state that what the elders said was considered "reasonable" from the perspective of any Kenyan man (184–86). Grasping the philosophical import of the judgment, Murungi states that the court holds the position that the ontological relationship between men and women is such that "it is through African men that African women will receive their being" (185). He argues that Kenyan women and men have the challenge to decide what dignity in marriage means, and that they must tackle that question without being dependent on Western individualist conceptions of marriage. Murungi explains, "They have to find a way of ensuring that spouses do not become each other's hostage, and that neither of them should be a hostage to the community" (193). But the community will nevertheless have an important role, because no marriage can have meaning without its community context.

4. Later Continuing Debates Regarding
ter / Widow Guardianship

Part of the context of the S.M. Otieno trial included the clan spokesman Siranga's attempts to stop Wambui Otieno from being the executor of the estate of her husband. He tried to force Wambui to engage in levirate marriage practices, known as *ter,* although neither the brother nor Wambui wanted to participate. This leads Patricia Stamp to conclude that the clan had only won a "Pyrrhic victory" when they were able to bury the body in Siaya, since they had lost a wife, children, and an estate (Stamp 1991: 838, 844).

It was in January 1994 that Oruka had an opportunity to clarify that he supported a contemporary practice of *ter*. He held this position in contrast to Dr. Maria Nzomo, who argued that *ter* practices inhibited widows' liberty to choose how to live their lives. Both professors exchanged their views in newspaper stories. Oruka explained that he agreed with Ali Mazrui that translating "ter" as wife inheritance was a misnomer, intended by the British to make the practice seem morally intolerable. The new guardian of the widow does not "inherit" her or any property, but rather is present to give guidance, security, and financial assistance. If the widow does not like the guardian she is free to leave him and remarry any brother or cousin of her deceased husband. Oruka successfully rebutted the uncharitable understandings of the practice. He advocated a revised practice in the new context of the AIDS epidemic, which he called "honorific" widow guardianship, that does not involve a sexual relationship with the widow. He insisted that such practices were needed to care for tens of thousands of orphans in Nyanza. He was already sensitive to feminist critique of his innovation, which he had announced at a press conference on January 11, 1994, as he insisted that "I was sincerely being progressive in my view" (Oruka 1994a). Nzomo (1994a) argued that even Oruka's revised practice was unacceptable because it inhibited women's free choice of a new mate.

Maria Nzomo's point, made in her response to Oruka back in the news columns of 1994, was that women need more economic independence overall, so that they would not need to be so dependent on men to raise their children (Nzomo 1994a). In general Oruka himself was an advocate of the idea that people need adequate economic support so as to reach their larger life goals. But he was convinced that the practice of *ter* could already meet the challenge of supporting women and their children adequately. While in his other books, such as the *Philosophy of Liberty* (1996), he emphasizes the human need for a host of liberties, in his written response to Nzomo he is callously insensitive to concrete examples of particular women's expressions of their liberty. For example, he is hostile toward Jacqueline Kennedy-Onassis's decision as a widow to marry "the hairy old Greek Millionaire," relinquishing her late first husband's relationship to the United States (Oruka 1994a: 7). In this case, Oruka's tone and position are quite different than the one he expressed in 1988 to the National Council of Women in Kenya, when he said that he understood that there could be good reasons for women to choose to remain single or to leave their marriages, and so there needs to be a way for women to have and inherit property (Oruka 1990a: 108).

Discussion of *ter* in the new century continued with papers authored by Pamela Abuya (2002) and Humphrey Ojwang (2005). The question was often whether current abuses of the practice could be ended, and whether reforming rather than jettisoning *ter* would be helpful to women. Abuya suggested that the practice was abused by men who would gain a woman to support them, feed and house them, and cater to their needs. Ojwang, on the other hand, clarified that such kinds of abuse were not part of the tradition. Additionally, there is testimony from widows who were grateful to have been inherited (Auma 1998). Still, to this day newspapers report stories of women who were ostracized for not participating in *ter*, and public health advocates continue to blame the practice for high HIV/AIDS rates in Luo areas (Wanja 2013). One account says that a business in professional "cleansers" or *joter* have sprung up, that is, men who especially seek out widows and suggest to their families that they will "cleanse" the widow of bad spirits in a traditional Luo ceremony, for pay (Makoye 2013). Those who refuse to be inherited are dispossessed of property and livestock, which they never owned but belonged instead to the husband (Makoye 2013; 2014). In Migori, a Baptist church is funding a house for widows. It will accommodate 400 widows, and is intended to be an alternative to "wife inheritance" (Odeny 2013).

A recent contribution to the debate regarding Oruka's position on Luo practices of caring for widows ("*lako*") has been written by Oriare Nyarwath (Nyarwath 2012). Nyarwath takes into account the concrete examples of current abuses of the tradition, but asserts that with proper guidelines the tradition can still be practiced in a way that upholds the dignity and freedom of the widow. He explains that the tradition respects a woman's free choice and consent, and he quotes Paul Mbuya's 1938 *Luo Kit Gi Timbegi* (the translation here is Nyarwath's): "A widow should never be forced to live with any man except the one she chooses" (Nyarwath 2012: 104). He notes that this emphasis on a woman's choice has been neglected in recent years. Therefore, to emphasize women's free choice and consent would not be to change the tradition but rather to uphold it more faithfully. He is therefore proceeding in the careful way advocated by Oruka, Gyekye and others. While Nyarwath does well to rescue the practice from many forms of contemporary distortion, he does not challenge some of the presuppositions upholding the tradition. For example, drawing upon writings by Humphrey Ojwang (and he could have as well drawn upon Oruka's portrait of Luo values in Oruka 1991b: 62) he asserts that for Luo women, choosing not to marry is not an option since not having children is "self-annihilation, and hence an abdication of the sacred duty of partaking in and perpetuating life" (Nyarwath 2012: 103). While this may or may not be an accurate description of values held by a majority of contemporary Luo women, whether life without child-bearing is or is not meaningful and valuable for a contemporary woman is a subject for debate. Perhaps presuming that a woman's life must entail child-bearing is still an imposition on her freedom of choice. It's also important to note that such positions on the relation of women and motherhood are not limited to Africa.

Nyarwath notes that autonomy is currently valued more now than it was in earlier eras, and due to this new emphasis, he is willing to concede that a widow could prefer to refrain from practicing *lako* and remain by herself. But he shows his measured support of the tradition when he urges widows, if considering remarriage, to choose a guardian from her late husband's clan for the sake of the children (Nyarwath 2012: 105). This is a case of championing a tradition due to belief that it possesses value relevant to contemporary society. While willing to defer in some instances to current pressures regarding the value of autonomy (such as regarding practicing guardianship at all), Nyarwath is reluctant to let autonomy trump all other values, and is willing to curtail women's autonomy in regard to the value of continuity for the younger generation.

It remains to be seen whether contemporary Kenyan women could be satisfied with this sort of revived tradition. Testimonies from Kenyan women show the diverse views on marriage held by Kenyan women today, ranging from acceptance of arranged marriage as best, to those who refuse marriage altogether. Their reasons for their differing positions are also widely diverse, as they draw different conclusions from their experiences and observations (Halperin 2005: 41–74).

Conclusion

Oruka's own position was that universal, equal human dignity and worth was important for all, including Africans. However, as a caution against its possible misuse and co-optation for Eurocentric purposes, a careful analysis of African practices regarding men and women should be undertaken, with care to ensure that there are no presumptions that the African practices are backward. Only after careful and fair scrutiny should African practices that are found to disadvantage women be discarded.

And so now we see how having an accurate "culture philosophy" is an important preliminary step in the project of evaluating traditions, so that we can fairly and with sensitivity decide which aspects of past beliefs and practices should continue as before. Oruka asserted that the philosophical sages were keen evaluators of these traditions as well as innovators. Oruka, being someone who learned from them, also engages in this process of evaluation. He also sought out social roles—such as being an expert witness in customary law cases—where he could put what he learned from the philosophical sages to good use.

In this way Oruka's project parallels that of Kwame Gyekye of Ghana, who argues in his book *Tradition and Modernity* that we need to practice a critical *Sankofaism,* by which he means we must look back to learn from traditions, but always in a spirit of critical discernment. As Gyekye explains: "A realistic normative assessment of the cultural past or cultural traditions of a people must proceed by examining the experiences of the practice of specific aspects or areas of the tradition" (Gyekye 1997: 241). Which values of the past should be embraced by the present and future?

We have seen in this chapter that Oruka has defended traditions, stating that one must have a carefully thought out and clearly articulated principled position before one attempts to exempt oneself from the customs of one's own ethnic group. He criticized certain European practices of marriage and sexual behavior, and he implied that a concept of marriage like that held by the Luos, that suggests that marriage does not end in death, may be better than Western conceptions.

On the other hand, he also suggested (or foresaw) changes to traditions. He suggested that more economic equality for women might change the idea of husbands as head of households. He also foresaw both European and Kenyan women being less likely to take their husband's last name as their own. He suggested that women should inherit property, since they may, after all, choose to be single or to leave their marriages. But he also advocated a changed tradition: honorary *ter,* a form of widow guardianship that would provide security, guidance, and assistance for a widow and her children, without involving sexual relations.

Is the new Kenyan Constitution able to reach this proposed middle ground, of respecting traditions when they are helpful but discarding them when they are unjust? Certainly the new Constitution is closer to that goal than the former. Muna Ndulo cites an example of a land case where reference to Kamba customary law was used to argue against a woman being able to inherit land from her deceased father's estate. The court decided in this case that the Kamba customary law was discriminatory toward women, and that this particular customary law was in conflict with section 40(1) of the Succession Act, which uses gender-neutral language to describe inheritance in the case of polygamous marriages. The court therefore decided that the Kamba woman could inherit the land from her father. This is not necessarily a "defeat" for African customs, but is better understood as an example of how African customs can grow and adapt to a changing world. As Ndulo explained, "Respect for the law can only be achieved if the law furthers the needs and conforms to the circumstances of society subject to the law. Failure to use the law to achieve just social solutions to issues confronting society and to reform society effectively thwarts development and advancement in customary law and consequently also reduces respect for it" (Ndulo 2011: 109). If I understand her correctly, she is challenging advocates of customary law to adapt it to the changing times and values, lest it become irrelevant.

The persistence of a dual system of law in which issues of marriage, divorce, burial and inheritance are decided by a reference to customs seemingly frozen in time will have to be swept away in order for Oruka's progressive humanism, including more equality for women, to be realized. Women need their legal rights. Which of the customs will be compatible with such equality? This needs to be determined case by case. Maybe in this way, Oruka and his fellow practitioners of African philosophy can forge an egalitarianism that does not just mimic Western versions but is filled with the rich details and insights of African practices.

Part Four

Global Justice: Addressing Poverty, Neo-Colonialism, and Environmental Destruction

Ecological Ethics Modeled on the Family: The Intertwined Issues of Environmental Preservation, Poverty Reduction, Land Ownership, and Women's Status

That Odera Oruka was deeply concerned about environmental crises is of no doubt. He put forward two very different arguments in favor of concern for the environment. Both arguments were intended as direct contrasts to the individualism dramatized by Garrett Hardin's lifeboat ethics. While one argument was filled with examples of cultural practices and beliefs, and the other argument was an abstract argument models on Rawls' *Theory of Justice*, Oruka wrote about them seamlessly, without commenting on their different approaches.

This chapter has four parts. In the first section, I'll look at two of Oruka's articles where he outlines ecocentric and human-centered moral arguments for caring for the environment by drawing upon African and Hawaiian cosmology, with a special focus on discerning Oruka's position. Second, I will look at Oruka's abstract "parental earth ethics" principles, focusing on his use of the term *family* in the context of environmental ethics. The first part of this analysis will highlight the extent to which his model of philosophizing draws upon John Rawls. The use of the term *family* is very abstract and yet is open to feminist critique. In the second part I will ask whether he intends his insight regarding "family" to be a spiritual or biological claim. In the third part of this chapter, I will survey questions neglected in his own account regarding power relations within families, in Kenya and in Africa generally. His own position will be compared with that of another Kenyan, Wangari Maathai, a Nobel Prize winner, author of several books, and member of a matrilineal Kikuyu community who is noted for her environmental activism. The chapter explores how Maathai's notion of family, women's roles, and human's relationship to nature is similar to, or different from, Oruka's approach. In general, eco-feminists insist that the change in relationship to the environment that we envisage is necessary to avert disaster can't be done without also critiquing cultural masculinity. In the fourth part I will address continuing struggles regarding women's ability to own land and Oruka's comments on land ownership in "Parental Earth Ethics" (in Oruka 1997: 146–51). How can we resist the colonial model of land use (cash crop monoculture) and go back to living off and in harmony with the land? The proposals of Oruka and Maathai are relevant for Africa's environmental crisis of today. I will then conclude, arguing that Oruka's insights and his concerns for the environment, combined with Maathai's critique, may provide guidance for the current land reform movement in Kenya. Their messages are also relevant regarding contemporary relations between men and women in the continent. A final summary will look to the future to see the application of Oruka's message regarding the looming climate emergency.

1. Background and Overview

How much did Odera Oruka care about environmental ethics? More than a quick look at his publications is needed to divulge the answer. His publications addressing poverty and misgovernance are many. While he has only three articles that address environmental issues as a major topic,[1] he is well-known for having organized an international conference in 1991 and having edited and published a book on the topic (based on the conference) in 1994. Indeed, he attempted to found an educational organization devoted to environmental issues. The idea of the center was a resolution of the 1991 Nairobi conference (Oruka 1994b: xv), although it was difficult to realize the idea.

A discussion with environmental ethicist Robin Attfield reveals just how long Odera Oruka was concerned with environmental issues. Attfield, now well-known as a leading expert on environmental philosophy, taught for one term in 1975 at the University of Nairobi. He and his wife and children were there for four months. During this time, Oruka looked up Attfield (his colleague) and wanted to share with him a paper that he had received in the Proceedings of the World Congress of Philosophy in Bulgaria in 1973. Oruka was particularly interested in Richard Routley's (1973) article, "Is There a Need for a New, an Environmental, Ethic?" They discussed Routley's "last man" example. Is there anything wrong with the last surviving person on earth chopping down the last tree? They both thought so, and so did Routley. But to explain why it was wrong meant going beyond traditional Western ethics, with what Routley regarded as its human species chauvinism. There must be some value in the tree. At the time the university library was in disarray, but Oruka gave Attfield a copy of the article. Attfield (2021) admits that this discussion with Oruka put him on a new path, of deciding to devote himself to environmental ethics as a field.

It was sixteen years later when Attfield returned to Nairobi to chair a session and present a paper titled "Development and Environmentalism." Attfield thought that Oruka valued environmental philosophy a lot more than the general philosophical community did at the time. He was about ten years ahead of his time, Attfield surmised, since the wave of interest in environmental philosophy only came later. Attfield returned to Nairobi to attend another conference organized by Oruka—this time it was the World Future Studies Federation conference in 1995. Michael van Hulten of the Netherlands had especially helped with raising the funds to hold the conference, Oruka himself explained (in Ogutu et al., eds., 1997). Van Hulten's paper (in Ogutu et al., eds., 1997) presented at that conference clearly stated that global warming is caused by human activity and that activity must be severely curtailed to avoid calamity. Some of the calamities would impact small island states as well as the coastal areas of Africa and India.[2]

The extent to which environmental issues concerned him is shown in his dedication written for the book he was working on right up to the time of his death, published posthumously. It says: "To futures: to future African philosophers and all future thinkers; and workers for human justice and a better environment" (Oruka 1997: dedication page).

In his two main environmental articles, he addresses eco-philosophy's challenge to environmental ethics. As he explains, before considering moral issues, one must settle on an accurate ontology, that is, what is. He insists that science shows that all of life is interrelated and depends upon other organisms to survive. This, Oruka asserts, is not just spiritual jargon preached from a pulpit. It is not mere moralization. It is the truth, proven by science (Oruka and Juma 1994: 127). However, since all life is interrelated, one can use this fact to argue for a moral philosophy built upon that fact. Here, let me note, an "ought" is following from an "is." Since the environment is interrelated, and therefore the effects of environmental destruction are felt elsewhere, including across national boundaries, what follows is that there should be international effort to mitigate environmental damage (Oruka and Juma 1994: 127).

I have no doubt that the conclusion is prudent (in the long-term interest of humans) and is moral as well (in the sense of recognizing that nature has the right to exist and be spared harm if possible), but the argument is not yet constructed in a way to convince people that an "is" (the scientific facts) should lead to an "ought." The moral skeptic (in particular, the skeptic of natural law) may think there is no reason that humans should value what nature values. An egoist may think the damages of nature can have their bad consequences aimed at people other than the egoist, while the egoist reaps the benefits of resource harnessing. While egoism looks like an amoral position rather than a moral one, we all know authors who have argued that selfishness is a prerogative of individuals. I do think that Oruka is right in that the study of climate shows that the effects of climate destruction may impact all of humanity and so can't be controlled as the egoist presumes.

Oruka explains in several articles that there are two rationales for protecting the environment. One is that, as humans, we depend on the environment for our own health and well-being. If the environment is destroyed, humans will not flourish. This is the anthropocentric version of environmental ethics. He also calls it the animal and plant welfarist model (Oruka 1997: 248). While Oruka will soon argue for the superiority of the ecocentric model, he does not condemn the anthropocentric model. Followed carefully, the anthropocentric model will also defend the environment because any careful anthropocentrist will realize that human flourishing is so caught up with the need for a healthy environment that they will defend the environment similarly to an ecocentrist. In fact, he points out that his coauthor, Calestous Juma, and his environmental center, the African Center for Technology Studies, engage in many environmental projects, all of which express an anthropocentrist rationale (249–50). Those projects have good consequences for humans as well as the nonhuman environment.

But, as a philosopher he is dissatisfied with the anthropocentric view, for reasons related to the Routley example. He gives his own example. If humans were able, someday, to ensure their nutrition and overall survival without the use of nature, would it then be perfectly fine to destroy all of nature? Would the only loss, under those circumstances, be some diminished amusement to humans who would no longer have nature to occupy their interest? Or would there still be something wrong with nature's frivolous destruction? He thinks it would be wrong (248–49). This conviction, then, is his reason for choosing ecocentrism. Here he imagines it would result in a similarly good program of environmental defense, but for the reason of holding the right view, of properly valuing nature for its own sake, regardless of its role in saving human lives. He bluntly states that his position differs from the one supposedly in the Bible, which says that nature exists for the sake of humans (1994b: 116).

He also reviews the philosophies of several African communities, Hawaiian cosmology, and other sources, saying that these sources, along with his already asserted scientific basis for the insight of interdependence, provide evidence for ecocentrism. He says that studying the cosmologies of Hawaii and Africa (the Dogon, in particular) "lend us some solid scientific and philosophical ground on which to postulate pan-organism as the basic truth underlying all nature" (1994b: 122). He thinks the same texts also provide evidence for treating the earth as a common good for all of humanity, a view that he thinks is correct, and is the opposite of Garrett Hardin's (which we will explore in the next section) (123). I would like to examine his claim briefly. He earlier thought the evidence of interdependence just from science was enough to argue for a global response to the environmental crisis. Then he added brief mention of three cosmological views and said that the scientific insights plus these three views lend "scientific and philosophical ground" (122). He actually spent only two paragraphs each describing the world views of Indian dharma, Hawaiian cosmology, and Dogon cosmology, with just one source referenced for each. He says they postulate "pan-organism" underlying all of nature. It was the Dogon section that came close to describing "pan-organism" (although the earlier sections don't use the exact phrase, so Oruka seems to have coined a new term). He draws on Anyanwu, who says the Dogon have "a unitary and an organic view of reality in which humans, nature and society are continuous with the universal creative process" (122). Oruka seems convinced that the Dogon and others have expressed philosophically what science has shown to be the case. He then wants to say that the "principle of the earth as a common good to all mankind and to all creatures" is made plausible by this postulation of pan-organism. The argument on pages 122–23 could be a bit circular. Is the philosophical pan-organism proven by the science, or does the philosophical pan-organism lend credence to the science? He briefly suggests both. But it is hard to take Oruka to task for putting forward a moral imperative that is so vital today for earth's and humankind's survival.

Oruka also notes that, according to some African practices, certain animals or insects might be given more respect than humans, to the point that humans are restricted from killing, or sometimes even touching them (Oruka 1997: 252–53). He also refers (without a specific reference) to Kwasi Wiredu's insistence that for Africans, land belongs to not only the living but also the ancestors who have passed away, and the future generations. Oruka makes a challenging statement in which he asserts that African communalism is not just a matter of reciprocal relations among the living; it is extended to communion with invisible ancestors, and that "the invisible part of ecology has the knowledge and power to control man's irresponsible behavior on earth" (253). He doesn't comment on these beliefs individually but takes them all as evidence for the close interconnection of parts of nature, which extend to what he calls the "invisible world" as well.

Oruka also thinks that, since many African philosophies and value systems are ecocentric, the current African public can be educated about the need to preserve the environment by drawing upon traditional African knowledge, of which they might already be familiar. From this perspective, humans are members of the natural community, with possibly some privileges, but that would not justify hubris. Humans must not cause damage to the environment (unless they can offset this by repairing and improving it), and they must not engage in any species extinction (252–53).

While he advocated these views in academic circles, it is important to note that Oruka was a busy public intellectual. For example, he reiterated these insights about the need for environmental preservation when he spoke in 1992 to the Kenya Consumers Organization at their conference in Nairobi. While he reiterated to this audience the need to feed the hungry, he also cautioned them about the over-consumer and the companies who encouraged individuals to over-consume in an unhealthy way (265). He suggested that the deep ecology of ecocentrism would do better than anthropocentric ethics when it comes to putting constraints on "superconsumers," as he calls them, since ecocentrism is concerned for all members of the biotic community, not just humans (266–68). He also notes that he spoke about ecocentric ideas at a conference on the environment in Belém, Brazil, that was organized by UNESCO in April 1992 (268).

2. Parental Earth Ethics

Oruka on Hardin and Rawls

Odera Oruka's own major contribution to the topic of environmental ethics discussed humans' relationship with nature using the model of human family members. In his "Parental Earth Ethics," he stated that "the world is a kin or family unit in which the members have kith and kin relationship with one another" (Oruka 1997: 150). He argued that the use of this family metaphor (clearly intended to help us care about nature) was not an exaggeration but instead a recognition that there will be a "common fate of all creatures"—in other words, we either all survive or none of us survive. Oruka was also insistent that saving the planet's environment would necessarily involve a "global redistribution of the wealth of nations," and Oruka offered his analysis as an alternative to Garrett Hardin's lifeboat ethics.

For Oruka, ecological ethics and global justice were interrelated. He began one of his publications outlining a challenge from Hardin, who had the backing of a contingent of environmentalists who saw the world as a place of limited resources. They jumped to the conclusion that growing population would overtax the planet, and that for the survival of some, others would have to die. And so was born the scenario of "lifeboat ethics." Many philosophers love dramatic examples. Hardin, from his perspective as an affluent North American scientist, liked the safety net involved in a boat that was not overloaded. To allow more people in the boat would result in the whole boat sinking, and so he did not cringe at the thought of passing up opportunities to save people's lives. The Southern Poverty Law Center lists

Hardin as an "extremist" and notes that he cofounded the anti-immigrant group Californians for Population Stabilization and served on the board of directors of the Federation for American Immigration Reform. Hardin's environmental organization lobbied the U.S. Congress for anti-immigrant legislation (SPLC n.d.).

Ideas similar to Hardin's are still popular today (although, anti-immigrant sentiments might be connected more to wrong-headed ideas of what is good for the economy or security than an ecological pretext). For example, former U.S. President Donald Trump did not want the U.S. to be overrun with immigrants, and so he began to construct a border wall, more symbolic than practical, to reinforce the idea that he was saving Americans from being overwhelmed by foreigners—particularly black and brown foreigners. The idea that impoverished people harm "civilization" makes Hardin a contemporary version of Thomas Malthus. Back in the 1800s, Malthus had the British so worried about their own poor population's reproducing that the government came up with a plan to put poor family members in workhouses where they couldn't function as families and reproduce (Clark 1995: 180–91). Hardin's population and environmental fears have since been shown to be inaccurate understandings. First of all, people in the Global North consume so many resources compared to persons in the Global South that it would be erroneous to assume that persons in the Global South are creating the most pollution or using the most resources. Second, the Malthusian calculations of population growth have been shown to be wrong and alarmist. Many nations have much lower population growth, showing that it is not necessary to stand back and let people starve, as Hardin's lifeboat analogy suggested.

Oruka early on criticized Hardin's lifeboat ethics. He argued that all individuals have a right to a human minimum based on the commonweal of all humans. He pointed out that Hardin denied the connections and debts between the affluent and the poor of the world. He specifically pointed out that past plunder gave the rich nations the added wealth they needed in the past that led to today's greater disparities. He also argued that the continued wealth of the richer nations was dependent upon the cheap labor and products of the poor nations (Oruka 1997: 147–48). Oruka came up with an alternative to Hardin, coining the phrase *parental earth ethics*. His way of proceeding, with various abstract rules and principles, is (I suggest) clearly reminiscent of John Rawls in his *Theory of Justice*, a work that Oruka read and wrote about in several of his articles. Oruka talks about family in an abstract and ideal way, as did Rawls. It is obvious why Oruka would want to discuss humanity as a family. After all, Rawls (2009: 90) had explained that family was a place where "principles of maximizing the sum of advantages" is not practiced, as family members show concern for the interests of all their members. Rawls further explains that in a family "those better circumstanced are willing to have their greater advantages only under a scheme in which this works out for the benefit of the less fortunate" (90). Rawls asserted that friends, lovers, and family members would "take great chances to help each other" owing to their love for each other, and that "once we love we are vulnerable" (502). Despite his emphasis in this example on the role of affection and feeling, Rawls nevertheless asserts that a principle of fraternity is "perfectly feasible" for a society nationwide even if it is not based on feelings of affection (91). One therefore wonders why Oruka did not call his own view "fraternal earth ethics." After all, his own writings emphasize the need of siblings to help each other. The parents in his example (called the "parental debt rule") are more responsible for background conditions that aid or inhibit children's ability to flourish (Oruka 1997: 148–49).

Anke Graness in her book-length study (2011) of Odera Oruka as well as in her article (2015) on global justice noted as well the extent to which Oruka bounced ideas off Rawls' philosophical models, at times criticizing Rawls and at other times modifying him. While Oruka was influenced by Rawls, as Graness claims, Oruka goes further than Rawls. It is only reasonable that Oruka became part of a global philosophical conversation by joining other academics worldwide in using and critiquing Rawls. As she explains:

> This is in my opinion not a sign of dependency or that African philosophy is unable to offer an original alternative to European theory, an idea which is based on a kind of 'othering', namely the belief that every culture or region has to develop by default ideas essentially different from European theory to be worth consideration. Rather, it shows a critical discussion of prevailing theories from a deliberately and consciously chosen African perspective and demonstrates that, from this perspective, Rawls' claim of his theory's universality has to be seriously interrogated.
>
> Graness 2015: 131

Oruka's article draws on the family metaphor in two ways. One is to suggest that all people must live as family or all people will perish. He used this in many of his articles to address the rich-poor gap throughout the world. This metaphor was very popular. For example, Martin Luther King Jr.'s famous "Christmas Sermon on Peace" (1968: delivered 1967) stated famously, "We must either learn to live together as brothers or we are all going to perish together as fools." Such insights were popular in the 1960s during the Cold War when superpowers aimed their nuclear arsenals at each other. The possibility of all persons (and all nature, except maybe the cockroaches) perishing because of war was not just a far-off fantasy but a nightmare that might come true at any time. King reinforced his point with two arguments: one was a religious, saying that we are all children of God, and as siblings of each other, we should have the same care and mercy toward each other as we would our brothers and sisters. The other argument pointed out the many ways in which we are dependent on each other due to world trade. He asked people to recognize this dependency (68–75). Note that his metaphors hoped to reach people, even if they didn't believe in God. Atheists may still value family connections, and economic scientists could acknowledge that economic flourishing depends upon a delicate web of relations, regardless of whether people are Christians, atheist, or other.[3]

I don't have any evidence that Oruka got his idea from King, since he cited Rawls instead. But it is important to remind readers that Oruka came to Detroit, USA, for the years 1968–69 to complete his Master's degree at WSU. At that time in the U.S. the ideas of King were quite popular. But I could also note that King had a personal friendship with Thich Nhat Hahn, the Vietnamese monk who taught in the U.S. before going back to Vietnam to try to stop the war using nonviolent methods. King had nominated Thich Nhat Hahn for a Nobel Peace Prize. Thich Nhat Hahn had advocated the Buddhist metaphysical insight of interdependent origination—the idea that all of reality needs each other to exist and emerges simultaneously. He founded a religious order in 1966 at Plum Village in France, called the Order of Interbeing, where monks engaged in "direct experimentation on the nature of interdependent origination" through "the continuous practice of mindfulness, ethical behavior, and compassionate action in society" (Plum Village n.d.). So at the time of Oruka's writing, this emphasis on family metaphor and interrelatedness is in the air, and very much talked about as an alternative to cutthroat capitalism and survival of the fittest scenarios like Hardin's.

Discussions such as these were active in philosophical circles as well. While clearly Oruka has gone beyond Rawls and emphasized an absolute right to a minimum of resources for each person in the world, such a view was argued on moral grounds by James Sterba in a 1981 article, "The Welfare Rights of Distant Peoples and Future Generations." Oruka cited Sterba's article as the source of his conception of the right to a human minimum, in his article "The Philosophy of Foreign Aid" (see Oruka 1997: 93n12). Sterba (1981: 104) argues that the moral point of view that agrees that people have a right to life and a right to fair treatment would necessarily lead to accepting rights of distant peoples to welfare. He describes people as therefore entitled to having the requirements for their basic health and sanity provided by any who can do so. Their own societies are also obliged to do as much as they can to fill their own citizens' needs, but when they have done all they can, other distant persons and governments are obliged to do all they can to meet the rest of the unmet basic need. Since there exist enough goods, including food to fill the needs of all people, people and governments of the world have the moral obligation to modify their behavior (including limiting their nonbasic needs) to meet this moral requirement (113–14). Sterba realizes that the calculating of basic need is difficult, and that it is contextual, because in more wealthy nations such as the U.S., policies that would ensure that persons not be excluded socially would entail funds for education as well as food. But he nevertheless argues that the U.S. government implicitly agrees that people have a right to a "minimum of goods and resources," shown by the U.S. Department of Agriculture's calculation of the poverty index (111). Sterba considered his view to be an unnoticed conclusion of applying Rawls' ideas in *A Theory of Justice.*

The Earth Family: Spiritual or Biological?

While Oruka continued his "Parental Earth Ethics" with an example that directly relates to the issue of addressing and rectifying the global wealth gap, he then connected it to the issue of environmental ethics. He argued that the earth or world "is a kind of family unit in which the members have a kith and kin relationship with one another and the earth is a commonwealth to all humanity" (Oruka 1997: 150). But importantly, he explained, in another article cowritten with Kenyan environmentalist Calestous Juma and originally presented at the International Federation of Societies of Philosophy conference in Nairobi in 1991: he doesn't intend his use of family metaphors to harken to some spiritualistic sense of fellow-feeling or "moralization" but rather to a scientific understanding of how different aspects of our environment depend upon and influence other aspects, regardless of human-made borders (Oruka and Juma 1994: 127). He considers the principle of reciprocity to be based on the "organic constitution of all life," and he draws on the American philosophers F. E. Abbot and Creighton Peden (presented at the 1991 Nairobi conference by Peden), who insisted that narrow individualism should be replaced with universalism (Oruka and Juma 1994: 120–21; Peden 1994: 289). He refers to an important point, that Darwin is often misunderstood, since "a more detailed interpretation" of Darwin's *Origin of Species* notices how Darwin himself emphasized "that no particular species can exist independent of that web [of complex relations]" (Oruka and Juma 1994: 126–27). In other words, Oruka's main reason for using the family metaphor is to focus on interdependence in a materialist sense, not a moral or spiritual one. (However, he also discusses humans as having psychological and identity needs fulfilled in the family and in the nation, and he hasn't directly addressed how the same concerns would translate into the context of the human-nature relationship.) The family model might therefore be more complex than necessary because family can mean a lot more than just interdependence. There are inequalities and power relations in the family as well. While inequalities of power and ability do not have to translate into oppression—take, for a key example, the way in which loving parents devote themselves to care for less powerful and able children in their care, with the goal of children's growth and flourishing (Ruddick 1995)—in fact power differences have often led to oppression, even inside the family.

This quick reference of Oruka to American philosophy (as in Abbot and Peden) just scratches the surface. There have been many American critiques of Herbert Spencer's distortion of Darwin's "survival of the fittest," with Spencer misusing Darwin to advocate the cutthroat competition model of human relations. Erin McKenna and Scott Pratt (2015) go into great detail regarding Native American philosophical insights with social and environmental impact. However, they explain that Native American examples rest on spiritual insights and claims. For example, the Dakota physician and writer Ohiyesa, known as Charles Eastman, wrote *The Soul of the Indian*, published in 1911. Eastman and the Society of American Indians emphasized that all things are relational. Eastman asserted that "every creature possesses a soul in some degree," and knowing that the waterfall and creature have souls leads to reverence and acknowledgment of reciprocal relations (McKenna and Pratt 2015: 19–20). Oruka and Juma (1994: 121–22) also draw upon religious conceptions of this unity between humans as well as between humans and other aspects of nature (as in Hawaiian and Dogon cosmology and Indian dharma)—this despite Oruka's insistence that he wants to steer clear of such religious conceptions, even in the same 1994 article that reviewed those conceptions. For example, in reviewing possible objections to their position, Oruka and Juma clarify that their focus on kinship should not be considered a "quasi-religious exaggeration" or a "moralization" (127) but, rather, an "ecological truth" (meaning, a scientifically proven and materialist assertion) about how nature operates. They cite as proof of this assertion the fact that pollution in one place on earth affects other parts of the globe (127).

While Oruka and Juma say near the end of their article that "all sentient beings have an intrinsic value" (128), they caution against going overboard with the idea. That all are necessary and connected is not the same as saying they all have equal moral worth. The authors explain, perhaps with some humor, that the earthworm and a head of state are not morally equal. Nevertheless, Oruka and Juma assert, "Earthworms are a part of the biodiversity without which even a head of state would be non-existent" (128). It may seem just a humorous juxtaposition, but in fact environmentalists insist that without earthworms' constant efforts at soil engineering, for the most part unnoticed by humans, most human food sources would dwindle, making life on earth impossible. That's what makes earthworms "the number one most influential species in the history of the planet" (*Conversation* 2017). But note that Oruka has gone out of his way to insist that this central role of the earthworm should not be translated into moral terms—just taken as a matter of fact to prove a scientific understanding of interdependence.

Oruka explains in another article, "Eco-philosophy: Environmental Ethics," that he hopes to steer a middle course between anthropocentric arguments for environmental ethics and a broader eco-philosophy. He advocates the position of Frederick Ferré, who makes a distinction between moral agents (only humans) and moral patients (morally entitled to our ethical concern), with nonhuman aspects of nature being considered moral patients (in Oruka 1997: 251). He wants to sympathetically and accurately portray some African thinkers as possessing a world view or ontology that would support eco-philosophy, while explaining that he as a scholar would take a middle position, vigorously defending the environment but not depending on the same kind of ontology or spiritual insight. Examining the text, I discern Oruka's middle ground position insofar as he calls deep ecology on the one hand, and anthropocentrism on the other hand, "two extremes" (250), whereas Ferré's position "helps us avoid the problem of positions expressed by deep or holistic ecology" as well as the problems of anthropocentrism (which posits a different morality for humans and animals, when there should be only one morality) (251). In other words, he thinks nonhuman nature should be treated as moral patients and therefore the subject of concern of humans.

In the article on eco-philosophy, Oruka draws upon the wisdom of the African sages that he had been interviewing and studying. However, he does not mention any of the sages by name as individuals. Instead, he speaks of "traditional African wisdom" and its categorizing of the world or environment into two parts, the visible (with humans, plants, animals, waters, and mountains) and the invisible (including those humans who are yet unborn or are dead, and other spirits). Traditions have it that certain trees can never be cut down; others can be cut down only by special permission ("consultation with the members of the invisibles") (251–52). Even though Oruka quoted here a sage who was in fact his father, Oruka Rang'inya (see the original interview with Oruka Rang'inya that mentions this passage in Oruka 1991b: 128), he did not mention the name of the sage but quoted him as saying that when the leaves shake in the trees, due to wind, since the dead live in the wind, the dead are shaking the tree. This is a concrete example of the "traditional African" conception of the world having visible and invisible aspects. Oruka (1997: 254n20) went further to suggest, in an endnote connected to the passage, that the comment (of his father) implied that, because the dead live in the trees, the trees should not be cut down if it can be avoided, since you might be harming your ancestor who resides there. Referring again to the spirits of the invisible world, he says that "the invisible part of ecology has the knowledge and power to control man's irresponsible behavior on earth" (253). Realizing this, humanity should commit itself to wise and sparing use of the environment. One can only notice that, in his reference to traditional African wisdom, Oruka has drawn upon religious or spiritual understandings of the environment, despite his having argued elsewhere that one does not have to resort to a religious understanding to appreciate the interrelatedness of humans and nature. But perhaps he is here alluding to the idea that a spiritual or invisible aspect of nature can punish people for having harmed the environment. One could also try to ground an idea of punishment on scientific evidence. Nuclear waste will remain radioactive for many generations; harm to the environment in one place can harm another place, as in the case of acid rain.

While I think that it's clear that Rawls was the biggest influence on the concept and structure of Oruka's parental earth ethics, Oruka is not the only one to conceive of environmental relations as analogous to family relations. Oruka references Dusty Gruver (1994), whose article "The Earth as Family: A Traditional Hawaiian View with Current Applications" is included in Oruka's edited book on environmental philosophy, based on the 1991 conference he hosted in Nairobi. Gruver argues that Native Hawaiians see all of nature as a family, with the Earth Mother and the Sky Father as heads of this large family. Islands, animals, plants, mountains, and humans are also family members. The Earth Mother gives birth to islands, humans, and all of creation in a birth travail, further emphasizing the family relatedness of all of creation (Gruver 1994: 302). Recognition of this relatedness fostered an ethics of mutual support and prohibited harming nature (303–304). I think it's important to point out that this conception of nature as family specifies a role for both mother and father and asserts that both are important. This is different from Oruka's abstract principles derived from Rawls that just mention parents. Next, we will look at the question of whether it is important to think about both genders when exploring nature as family.

3. Womanist/Feminist Critique of Rawls and the Question of Power Relations in the Family

As analogies go, the relationship between the head of state and earthworms (as a whole) is a different form of interdependence than the relationship between family members. The latter is probably better categorized as a moral relationship, although customary morality may play a bigger role than philosophical ideas of ethics. One could also, possibly, project upon the family a context of social contract, although such a move is controversial despite its having been done by Hobbes, Locke, and Rousseau. A head of state could indeed ruin millions of earthworms, for example in construction of a presidential palace, while still not causing his or her own ruin if the species of worms overwhelmingly functioned on a global scale. In the human family context, while children may have a direct dependence on their parents for biological life, the ongoing physical and emotional thriving of family members has more to do with understandings of social obligation and certain expectations that make them prioritize each other's well-being, whether through a sense of duty or a conscious calculation that their own thriving depends on the unit's thriving. Indeed, it could be argued, as it was by J. P. Clark at the 1991 Nairobi conference, drawing upon the philosophy of Murray Bookchin, that what humans must essentially do is associate with each other in some way, as free social beings and for their mutual benefit, not necessarily according to biological family lines. Humans, using their intelligence and freedom, would realize that environmental preservation is a key goal (Clark 1995: 333). This is different from the mere materialistic dependence, for example, of one human on another for their genetic code and prenatal nourishment. Indeed, adoptive families flourish because members freely take on responsibilities for each other regardless of lack of biological ties. I suggest that the unique human dimensions of family life can't be ignored if the analogy is to be used.

While animals may also have families, too much of Oruka's definition of parental earth ethics is explicitly tied to humans, so it can't be considered species neutral. For example, he says the pride of any family member is affected by the decadence of any one family member. He refers to some siblings as destitute and others as rich, and he describes their morally prescribed relationship in that context. He says those who are injured will have a right to reprimand and/or punish family members to restore justice. These are cases drawn from human activity and social roles.[4] Additionally, Oruka (1997: 148–49) often slides into political (national and international) examples that show dependence of countries upon each other when trying to illustrate his principles of parental earth ethics. Whether this is just exuberance to illustrate his ideas, or he did not have any African or Christian "nuclear" family in mind, remains to be seen through further exploration.

Oriare Nyarwath understands the use of analogy in "Parental Earth Ethics" in an interesting way. Nyarwath (2018: 273) thinks that in the analogy, the earth or nature is considered the parent, and all "inhabitants of the earth" are understood as children of that parent. Perhaps this explains why there is gender-neutral language in the choice of "parent": nature is both mother and father. But if the earth is parent to all and the earth is a "common wealth," how in the analogy is it explained that of the six children of parent earth, one child is extremely rich, another moderately rich, one moderately poor, and three are extremely poor (Oruka 1997: 148)? Is this a reference to deserts compared to jungles or savannahs? Probably not. Nyarwath notes that there is evidence in the text to read these inequalities in two different ways, and I agree that there is great ambiguity in Oruka's subsequent explanations. Nyarwath notes that it could be that those who are rich are those who used the resources they were given, such as the education provided by the family during childhood. (The Bible story about the use of the "talents" could be relevant here, perhaps?) But the other interpretation could be that depending on which country one is born into there is a great chance that one will be rich or poor, due to these circumstances (Nyarwath 2018, 273). The problem with either example is that it shows that the analogy is packed with political meanings, and so is not really a description either of the relationship between humans and nature or the relationship between family members, as Oruka purports it to be.[5]

Oruka's use of the family metaphor, influenced by Rawls, is very abstract and never mentions different roles for mothers and fathers, or brothers or sisters. Rawls' (2009: 405–409) notion of family overlooks power relations, although he does address "parental" moral authority in the family, never mentioning roles for mothers or fathers. This neutrality regarding the gender of family members can be found in Oruka's parental earth ethics as well. Some may think it is a progressive move to refrain from reinforcing ideas that the male is the head of the family and the moral authority with regard to the children. After all, Ruddick (1995) stipulates in her book *Maternal Thinking* that she thinks "mothering" is an activity that could be engaged in by men or women. Nevertheless, she still calls it "mothering" because she thinks the virtues she is championing (care and protection relevant to the level of growth and maturity of the child, and cheerfulness, for example) are culturally expected of mothers but not fathers. Rawls' reference to "parents" does not address these nuances.

Some feminist critics of Rawls think that the emphasis in his view on impartiality, supposedly reached through the mental experiment of going behind the "veil of ignorance," is impossible as well as a false ideal. As Marilyn Friedman (2000: 400) describes Rawls' critics such as Susan Moller Okin, Seyla Benhabib, and others, "They have suspected that, under the guise of sexlessness, male bias reappears covertly, for example in Rawls's suggestion that all social contractors be considered 'heads of households,' a traditionally masculine role identity."

Iris Young (1990: 111–16) expresses her frustration with a Rawlsian indulgence in abstract reasoning about an ideal society and its ideal judges who transcend all partial and petty perspectives and are implied to have the power to make sweeping distributive decisions (see also Friedman 2000: 401). Such an approach was clearly widespread in the generation of scholars after Rawls. There were Rawls critics within Africa as well, such as Justin Ekennia (1996). While Oruka criticized Rawls' liberalism and wanted to modify Rawls' approach to be more consistent with communitarian rather than capitalist ethics, Oruka nevertheless embraced this abstract ideal and used it in creating his parental earth ethics.

Susan Moller Okin (1998: 454) criticized Rawls, saying that in a "gender-structured society" one would have to seek out and take into account "the distinct standpoint of women." While "genderless customs and institutions" might be a long-term goal, they could not be attained until men and women both have similar moral and psychological development and participate equally in parenting. In the meantime, one can't talk about the family without directly addressing women's position and their insights based on their experience. Indeed, even during the same time frame in which Oruka was writing "Parental Earth Ethics," a Kenyan woman, Elizabeth Akinyi Nzioki (1993) of the Public Law Institute was criticizing not Rawls per se but the Kenyan government for neglecting women's role in the family when deciding their land tenure policies. She asked the Kenyan government to "immediately stop treating the household as a collective unit represented by one individual. The gender, nature of socio-economic unit, decision-making and distribution of resources within the household must be reflected in policy in order to addresses different needs of women" (2).

There are other contexts where the financial and time burden of raising children was placed on the woman, and men felt free to use their own income for their discretionary needs. Chesaina Ciarunji (2005: 211–12) noted that in contemporary Kenya men often held onto the role of decision maker even in households where women's work supplied the family's basic needs, with women capitulating in order to "keep peace" in the home. In Kenya, families that grew tea were headed by men who made all the big decisions, while their wives provided labor.

Seth Agala currently runs workshops for Kenyan tea workers where gender issues are directly addressed. He reports that one man who attended the training said, "I have not been discussing or sharing with my wife information regarding the earnings obtained from tea although she is the one who works on the farm. From today, I shall not only share this information with her, but I will also give her the money she needs to cover her basic needs" (Agala 2015). This example of a man who transformed his views and practices gives us a window into the status quo situation where women are not privy to information, let alone having decision-making status in the family. While these changes were coming to Kenya in 2015, no doubt during Oruka's writing from the mid-1970s to the mid-1990s, such practices were rarer then.

Monica Awuor Ayieko's 1995 study of Njoro and Kikuyu in Kenya showed that on smallholder farms women spend more time in agriculture and household work than do men. Women self-consciously engaged in male-designated chores as a way of coping with male absence from the farm due to emigration. Given all the complexity of patriarchy and contested authority in the family, it is a wonder that both Rawls and Oruka could abstract away from these contexts to posit the family as the ideal scenario under which family members cared for each other's needs.

All these examples of coerced or unequal labor in the family complicate Rawls' and Oruka's uncomplicated description of the family as a place that has the welfare of each family member in mind. I have drawn the examples from Africa because I am particularly noting that Oruka avoided addressing these difficulties; but of course the critique could and should target Rawls and Western societies as well. Examples of unequal power and strained family dynamics could be found in England and elsewhere (Clark 1995).

Wangari Maathai had written about the current Kenyan context of rural women, and how it differed from African traditions. Traditionally, a family held land in common. She says it was only during colonial times that land title deeds were given exclusively to men (Maathai 2009: 227). This historical point is echoed by D. J. Chandler and Njoki Wane (2002). Wane interviewed an eighty-five-year-old Embu woman named Mami. Mami explained: "When I was growing up all the trees in our neighborhood belonged to the community. Children could eat fruits from the fruit trees and women could 'harvest' the branches for firewood. That changed with dividing of pieces of land between members of the same clan and men claiming ownership to the land through Title Deeds" (Wane's interview with Mami, August 1998, in Chandler and Wane 2002).

Elinami Swai in her book *Beyond Women's Empowerment in Africa* (2010) claims that there have been significant advances on farms since the 2000s. Women are being paid for their work on farms, and girls are demanding part of the inheritance. Women are now negotiating for shared power on their farms. Regardless, women are still widely considered to be "helping" their husbands when they work on farms (60–62). While there have been improvements since the 1970s and 1980s, she says, "The level of gender equality in terms of role sharing in the rural community is still not enough. Women are still excluded from major decision-making processes of the family and community. They are denied access to strategic resources, higher education, employment and are continually kept in agriculture and subsistence production" (57).

Wangari Maathai is of course better known for her environmental activism. Maathai was Oruka's colleague at the University of Nairobi, although she was in a different department and was removed from the faculty when she attempted to run for political office. She eventually became the assistant minister for the environment, natural resources, and wildlife. I have already in another work addressed her philosophy and legacy at great length (Presbey 2013). But in the context of the theme of this chapter, I wanted to revisit some important aspects of her work and her movement. Through her activism, Maathai fought deforestation that was happening on the fringes of Nairobi, owing to a corrupt Kenyan government giving land grants to private individuals as favors, thus destroying a forest needed to preserve the water and air quality around the city (see Cesar 2010: 128; Gorsevski 2012: 9; Nixon 2006–2007: 22). Her work to save public lands could clearly be seen as challenging colonial and post-colonial practices of giving individual title deeds to men, insisting instead that land should be a common heritage of all citizens through its preservation (similar to her earlier example of family ownership, rather than individual ownership of land). As Rob Nixon explained, Maathai exposed the "slow violence" that was eroding healthy living conditions for Kenyans through environmental degradation. Maathai also argued that the "cash crop" economy not only degraded the environment but also made women farmers' lives harder (Nixon 2006–2007: 25).

Maathai did share that, according to traditions she was told by her grandparents, there was a sacred relationship to the forest, and there were taboos against cutting down trees in the forest, and these restrictions preserved the environment. Brendon Nicholls (2005: 185), in his study of the Mau Mau (who came from Maathai's ethnic group, the Kikuyu) noted: "These elders invested the landscape with spiritual significance, in which the slightest human action (such as cutting down trees, killing animals needlessly or shooting towards mountains in which spirits dwelled) interacted with a network of taboos and portents and could invoke adversarial meteorological, military or even cosmological consequences." Maathai (2010: 167) expressed concern that Kenyan environmental knowledge and traditions were being forgotten.

The University of Nairobi is now home to the Wangari Maathai Institute for Peace and Environmental Studies, which helps rural people have access to environmental knowledge that will help them in their farming, and it also emphasizes values of reverence for the earth and labor for the common good of all.[6] But not everyone thinks that the Green Belt Movement has had the best approach to environmental issues. Chandler and Wane (2002) think that the Green Belt Movement did not consult women when it came to the choices of species of trees that they were planting. They approved instead of a project funded by CARE Kenya that consulted women regarding the best species of tree. CARE Kenya did not promote the planting of eucalyptus trees, since they drank up large amounts of water, and because their wood was not easy to use for household necessities (Chandler and Wane 2002).

Chandler and Wane also draw attention to how the motivation of many women to plant trees is primarily due to their increasing difficulty in collecting firewood for household cooking and other purposes. As forests dwindle, their search goes longer and farther. But Chandler and Wane warn us not to blame women for deforestation. Women usually collect only felled wood. In contrast, men often fell wood for timber or charcoal, or to clear pasture and grazing areas. Of course, for women to plant trees in order to replenish the supply of wood is definitely looking at the long-term effects of their actions rather than short-term gain. Many Embu women they interviewed explained in addition that they have a moral conviction that the earth should not be harmed.

Chandler and Wane also noted that a common way to blame African women for deforestation and environmental destruction was to fault them for overpopulation. This is a topic that Oruka addressed in one of his projects that he completed entitled "Ethics, Beliefs, and Attitudes Affecting Family Planning in Kenya Today." He wrote the proposal for funds in 1986 and completed his project in 1989. He proposed to interview both sages and non-sages for the project. He received funds from USAID as well as the International Development Research Center (see Oruka 1990b: xviii). Without these funds for a very practical project, he could not have been able to interview many of the sages that appear in *Sage Philosophy*. Oruka noted that Kenyan couples knew many natural family planning methods that in the past had helped to ensure that births were three years apart. He found through interviews that women experienced a lot of pressure from husbands, other family members, and peers to continue to keep having many children. One of the main sources of pressure was relatives who wanted to name a child after a deceased relative. Every time a relative died, the pressure would be on to have a child, a practice Oruka did not approve.

Clearly Oruka and Maathai share some common ground in their efforts to preserve the environment, critique capitalism and individualism, and work for equality and social justice (for her critique of capitalism, see Maathai 2007: 125). However, the two did not work with each other. The papers Oruka collected and published from the large 1991 conference in Nairobi on environmental ethics do not include or mention her or her Green Belt Movement, although she had founded the organization in 1977. I have not noticed Oruka citing her work in any of his articles, or even his newspaper articles.

Can issues of justice, whether human or environmental (including humans in a larger web of life), really be accomplished without attending to gender roles and power dynamics? Can Oruka really call his environmental philosophy "parental earth ethics" and then use gender-neutral language throughout, when other Kenyan women who are his contemporaries see gender and power analysis as central to the environmental justice movement?

4. Implications for Contemporary Land Reform and Sustainable Agriculture Movements

However, it is important to note that, at least in some communities, the land was considered to belong to men. Kavesta Adagala (1992) analysed a story from Kenyan oral literature that argued that, since the men centuries earlier had been the first to explore an area and settle the ethnic group on that land, clearing it of trees to practice agriculture, therefore the land belonged to men. I interviewed (in 1998) an elder sage in Bungoma named Saulo Namianya, who in the first years of Kenyan independence had as his job giving individual title deeds of land to families.[7] (During colonial times many families did not have any official deeds to land that had been farmed by their families for generations.) He always gave the title deeds to all the brothers in the family, and he described how he came up with a fair methodology based on the already existing example of how brothers share pieces of meat when a cow or other animal is slaughtered. He explained with special care to all the brothers so that they could be satisfied with their parcel and not quarrel with himself or each other. But no women of the family were given title deed. When I asked him why women were excluded, he explained that the women of the family would relocate to the land of their husbands, and so they did not need any land at their family's location. If exclusive male ownership of property was something against African traditions and due to colonial influence (as Maathai suggested), one would wonder why Kenyans upon receiving independence would not rectify the erroneous practice and revert to family or joint ownership. But of course, sometimes colonial changes become so deep-seated that they continue during independence.

In Nzioki's 1993 study of 150 households in Mumbuni location, Machakos District, Kenya, she found that none of the land was registered in the name of a daughter. Fifty-five percent of land deeds named the husband, and another twenty-seven percent named the son. Only twelve percent of women had their name on any land deed, meaning that most women farmed land that they did not own (46–48). Women were rarely the decision makers about what would be done with family land (49–50). In some cases where a woman's name is on the land registration documents, the woman (for example, Kiatu) is holding the land in trust for her sons (and not her daughters) (109). Nzioki thinks it is very important that daughters can inherit land. Despite legal guarantees that women can purchase land, for practical purposes, whether a woman has land depends upon her relationship to a husband or other males in a patrilineal inheritance system (115–17).

A little-known tradition, still practiced in Kenya, is "woman-woman marriage" among the Gikuyu, Nandi, and some other ethnic groups of Kenya. Researchers Wairimu Ngaruiya Njambi and William E. O'Brien (2005) explain that in Murang'a District, local *mbari* elders allocate land-use rights according to their customs. In this system, some women can end up owning land. Women who own land can decide to take a wife. They interviewed *muhikania* (landowning women who marry a wife) who explained that their motivations involved a wide range of factors, including "companionship to appease loneliness, to be remembered after death, to have children to increase the vibrancy of the household, to fulfill social obligations in accordance with indigenous spiritual beliefs, and not least to avoid direct domination by male partners in a strongly patriarchal society, including men's control of both the women's behavior and household finances" (153). As stated by Nduta, one of their informants, "We have no interest with a man who wants to stay in our home.... What for? To make me miserable? If I kept a man here who will then start asking me for money to buy alcohol, where would I find such money? No, I won't agree to live like that" (151).

These issues of women's land ownership should have been addressed by Oruka, but here, in the context of his environmental work, were not. But he does address, to a certain extent, the question of colonization. And so, there are implications of Oruka's philosophy for contemporary land reform and sustainable agriculture movements. Oruka's emphasis on the earth as a commonwealth could be an argument against national sovereignty and in favor of free migration (a possible anti-Hardin move), but he doesn't draw those conclusions. He realizes that his assertion that the earth belongs in some way to all humans argues against the claim by First Nations of the Americas ("American Indians" as Oruka calls them) that they have a right of first occupation. He similarly notes that his argument could not result in the expulsion of colonizers who invaded the Americas five hundred years ago, or Africa and India more recently. In "Parental Earth Ethics" he seems to accept all of that, perhaps purely due to the march of time and the feeling that colonization can't be undone. Oruka (1997: 150) states, "Concerning colonization, we, by this time, just lament the fact that we have no share in, or claim to, any of their current possessions." This critique is along the lines of his comment regarding Hardin, which explains that the current prosperity of the North is due to historical and contemporary dispossession and exploitation of the Global South. And in his article with Juma, he notes, "But given the organic constitution of life and the principles of parental earth ethics, the former colonies have a legitimate claim to such possessions" (Oruka and Juma 1994: 126). But I think that clearly a distinction can be drawn. One could say that of course colonizers can remain, but only on grounds of fairness and equality, and respect for all persons. They can't remain as colonizers but only as co-inhabitants. One could also argue that an apology for past wrongs and a serious attempt at restitution on the part of past colonizers should be undertaken. If lands can't practically be given back, there needs to be another way to show sincerity of remorse for past wrongs, like just compensation (reparations).

Olúfemi O. Táíwò's new book (2021b), as well as his talk at Harvard University (2021a), argue that colonization (as well as post-colonial economies of extraction) led to environmental degradation that scientists know now will hurt island and equatorial nations first and hardest. The BBC News called this "climate apartheid," meaning that the rich will "escape overheating, hunger and conflict" (Philip Alson, U.S. Special Rapporteur on Extreme Poverty, cited in Táíwò 2021a). Given that historical injustice, current reparations can and should be aimed at climate mitigation, climate adaptation, reparations for loss and damage, resettlement, and carbon removal. These costs should be paid by the Global North, which benefited from their colonialist and racist programs of action for centuries. Táíwò (2021a) uses the definition of racism provided by Ruth Wilson Gilmore (2006: 28): "The state-sanctioned and/or legal production and exploitation of group-differentiated vulnerabilities to premature death." Táíwò surveyed other competing ideas for reparations but chose to focus on climate reparations, even though he admits that in his version everyone will benefit, including the Global North. He likes other reparation schemes as well but prefers this one because it is forward-looking.

Likewise, in a recent book, Malcom Ferdinand (2022) wrote on decolonial ecology. He asks the question, what is a non-colonial way of being with each other? How can we meet with dignity and justice? As he explains, he writes from "the conceptual sea of the Caribbean" (2). Storms are raging, fueled by climate change, and they batter Caribbean islands. But problems in the Caribbean began earlier, with the practice of slavery. Only a decolonial ecology can result in freedom from the practices of slavery, social violence, and political injustice. He argues that some of the world's violence and injustice happens from within the environmental community, or at least shows itself in environmental policy. The problem being that, in both the U.S. and France, people of color are not in leadership positions in these organizations. Likewise the "pantheon" of environmental thinkers are mostly white males, who he says have ignored many ecological disasters created in the colonial and post-colonial context. For example, Great Britain and France have exploited mines in Africa, even extracting uranium and other dangerous metals in Gabon, Niger, South Africa, and Madagascar (6). He notes that Aimé Césaire in 1950, Frantz Fanon in 1961, and Thomas Sankara in 1986 each criticized how colonial powers changed the way that the land was used and the relationship between people and the land; they insisted that decolonization would usher in a new way to be related to the land (and even the sun, prefiguring our contemporary discussions of solar power) (15, 16). This is more evidence that decolonization and environmentalism belong together—it is an intellectual heritage that has been overlooked.

Ferdinand refers to Wangari Maathai as a theorist and activist who explained that both colonial and anti-colonial forces were against women. Colonial ways of inhabiting the earth amount to matricide, he charges. Who practices "matrigenesis"? The maroon communities. Colonial people were prevented from making the new land they arrived at into their Motherland. As he explains: "The urgency of the struggle against both global warming and the pollution of the Earth is intertwined with the urgency of political, epistemic, scientific, legal, and philosophical struggles to dismantle the colonial structures of living together and the ways of inhabiting the Earth that still maintain the domination of racialized people, particularly women, in modernity's hold" (14). For Ferdinand, of African descent and born in Martinique, it is not enough to embrace an eco-Marxist understanding of the world, like Jason Moore and other eco-Marxists, seeing the grave injustices as due to material conditions and economic forces. Ferdinand also critiques the rampant gender discrimination in our world and notes the parallels between harming women and harming the environment, including animals. Ferdinand wants the environmental movement to see that we humans must make free political decisions to change our relationship to nature. But can it happen? With the weight of economics against the movement—with fossil fuel companies pouring their billions into lobbying Congress? He turns to Hannah Arendt for her conception of the world as including earth, our bodies, nature, and so forth, but being made up of our relationships, all the encounters of the in-between, as she would say, and human deeds and words. Our challenge is to live with each other, understand each other, challenge each other, and act together to end injustice and save our environment (16–18). Or as Ferdinand puts it, we are challenged to answer this question: "How can a world be made on Earth between humans and with non-humans?" (20).

These recent theorists (Táíwò and Ferdinand) can tie together the topics of colonization and ecology at a greater length than does Oruka, but of course, they have the benefit of coming many years after him, when more work has been done in this area. Oruka was in the vanguard of this environmental movement, and then he died early, before he could comment further upon developments intended to address climate change. But there are certain passages in Oruka where it becomes unclear whether he has a principled stand against colonization. Let's explore these passages.

Oruka (1997) vigorously embraces a concept of property advocated earlier by John Locke and used to justify conquest of American Indian lands in the past—the idea that if a resource is not used, it can be taken away by those who will use it. Oruka stipulates that in his family model, if some members of the family aren't using what they are given, then their siblings can take it away and use it. He explains that his model "allows creative and hardworking members of the family to repossess undeveloped possessions of the idle relatives and develop them for use to posterity" (149). It is interesting how implications regarding women's ownership of land are not drawn from this argument. After all, it is women who work the land. Why can't they own it? Why must men (in the Luhyia case described by Adagala) get permanent ownership of the land for one act of clearing it, when it is women who will maintain the farm from then on?[8]

Ward Churchill (2003) explained how in the past, colonizers coming to the Americas considered Native people to be possessors of the land, so that they could negotiate and sell to colonizers; but if they wouldn't agree to sell, then the land could be taken by force. The rationale for taking the land by force was the idea that the current inhabitants weren't using it. The concept of use was tied to European ideas of farming, which involved tilling the soil with plows. Since Native American groups practiced agriculture by sowing and gathering without plowing, it looked to the Europeans like they weren't "using" the land; and yet, European colonizers themselves saw first-hand that their practices of cutting down forests led to erosion and the spread of disease (Churchill 2003; Ferdinand 2022: 30–31). This narrow concept of "use" of the land has had devastating effects in some areas, such as contemporary Brazil, where land speculators cut down the Amazonian forest to ensure their land claims, leading to erosion of a fragile topsoil (Mendes 1992: 65–67). In these circumstances it seems to be unfair and discriminatory to use these definitions of "use" to justify colonizers' taking away lands of indigenous communities. Environmentalists like Chico Mendes organized rubber tappers, many of whom relocated to the Amazon area in search of livelihoods. They augmented rubber tapping with Brazil nut harvesting and created a political union between themselves and indigenous communities, the latter of whom also wanted to preserve the forests from speculators (48–50). Mendes explained that rainforests provided important crops for humans only in the context of uncut forests, since Brazil nut trees would not flourish in agrobusiness-style monoculture forest plantings. And so, the issue here is not to keep foreigners out, per se, but for the non-indigenous (in this case, rubber tappers who generations ago were brought to the area in the nineteenth century as "virtual slaves in a system of debt bondage" [10]) to coordinate with indigenous people and work together to preserve the environment, finding ways to live in harmony with that environment.

We can also turn to Brazil for an example of communities struggling for equality and justice who uphold this same centuries-long argument that if someone has an asset like fallow land, while others are willing to work that land, then the landless can take that land and make it fruitful. This is in fact the tactic of the Landless Workers' Movement in Brazil. They target large landholdings of government or banks that have been neglected, and they occupy it, turning it into a working farm, and then petition the government for property rights. The movement is communitarian rather than capitalist, and their goal is to have a thriving community, not rich individuals (Almeida and Sanchez 2000). Farms that I had visited were also adamant about using farming practices that were sustainable, growing a variety of food and small crops instead of becoming large agribusiness farms. And so, we can see that the idea of land belonging to those who use it can be used for colonial or liberatory ends. There have been many cases of landless farmers in Central America occupying the unused lands of large multinational fruit corporations, so that as a group they can repossess it. In these cases, application of this principle of "use" can be helpful. But to make quick mention of "use" as Oruka does without describing the history seems inadequate and ripe for misunderstanding. Even as a principle of sibling relations within one family, it seems to me that it would be highly contested. Which sibling ever easily acquiesces to their land or property being taken by their more industrious siblings?

Notably, despite lip service to this idea that those willing to work the soil should be given title deed, it was in many nations enforced only according to racial guidelines. African American farmers who won freedom from slavery, established productive farms, and then were driven off their land by racist neighbors have been many. Since the 1920s, they were pushed off farms by racist application of loans and laws (Holloway 2021). Maroon communities and *quilombo* communities in Brazil who escaped slavery and went inland in Brazil, establishing farms and becoming self-supporting, were not given title deeds. They were pursued militarily and destroyed, as in, for example, the attack upon Palmares, as chronicled by colonial government documents (Anonymous 1999).

Kenya advocated a new National Land Policy in 2009, followed by three new land laws in 2012. There was a recognized need for land reform when it was realized that pressures due to scarce land were part of the heightened tensions around electoral violence in 2007. They recognize that land problems go back to colonial days, when colonists took land for their tea estates, displacing communities that lived in the region. During independence years, corruption led to abuse of public lands, which were parceled out to individuals in a manner that was not transparent. In Kenya eighty percent of people still make their living from agriculture, so the demand for land is high. Because implementation of land reforms was moving so slowly, owing to land cases being bogged down in courts, in 2014 the government's National Land Commission announced that it would use local village councils and headmen to decide the land cases. While Oruka may have been happy with such a development, others are worried that a move like this comes too late, when already the authority of the traditional elders is waning. For example, George Kimemia, an assistant chief from Kajiado North, said, "Old men of high integrity who resolved disputes with honesty and fairness are long gone, replaced by dishonest people at the land offices. . . . People pay a lot of money to have their cases heard and determined in their favour. There is no justice" (Gathu 2014).

It is hard to know at this time whether Kenyans will be satisfied with the land reform project of their government. Some researchers note that the devolution of powers in the new Kenyan Constitution gave some local politicians and administrators "veto power" that slowed or stopped the hoped-for land reform (Boone et al. 2019). In the meantime, private persons and companies have somehow found a way to get private land deeds to public lands that were intended to house public government buildings like schools, police stations, and hospitals. This is clearly "reverse" land reform—the "commons" being whittled away by private individuals with the help of corrupt public servants. The government is too weak to fill its own mandate of protecting the especially vulnerable, including women, subsistence farmers, pastoralists, and hunters and gatherers (Okowa 2020).

But if reforms are too slow, the Kenyan people might follow the example of the Landless Workers in Brazil, who have occupied unused lands and turned them into fertile farms. Oruka's comments about property rights, and the earth belonging to all as a commonwealth, would serve as a philosophical justification for such nonviolent occupations of the land. Maathai had already enacted several high-profile nonviolent actions in her time. Not only did she protect the Karura Forest through nonviolent actions, but she also saved Uhuru Park, a large green space considered the "lungs" of downtown Nairobi, from being encroached upon by President Moi's plan to build a large hotel and conference center (Nixon 2006–2007: 2011). A redistribution of wealth through a concrete redistribution of land in a society heavily dependent on agriculture could lead to a more just society.

Conclusion

Oruka certainly did well to draw our attention to a host of important ethical issues with both theoretical and practical implications. He was ahead of his time in his concern for environmental preservation. While he did not fully embrace ecocentrism, he was convinced that nature had worth and should be protected because it is so essentially interconnected. He saw issues of the environment linked with development and poverty reduction. While his Rawls-inspired philosophical solution of parental earth ethics may be vulnerable to some of the same feminist critiques that could be aimed at Rawls himself, he nevertheless put forward some unique and compelling ideas. A decolonial history of environmental thought, as Ferdinand requested, would have to include Oruka. It is up to Kenyans today to decide, through careful weighing, how they will determine their future. The new 2010 Constitution of Kenya gives women many civil rights and defends their right to own property. Philosophers should turn their attention to these developments and challenge themselves to give helpful and unbiased interpretations of events, so that Oruka's goal of carefully weighing past practices, jettisoning harmful ones, and encouraging the good of tradition while accepting helpful innovation can be carried out.

As I mentioned before, Oruka was at a disadvantage, with his life being cut short before he could continue with decades of intellectual environmental activism. Robin Attfield wrote a paper in 2012 in which he mused, what if Odera Oruka had lived to see the various climate agreements engaged in today? What would be his position? Attfield noted that Oruka was a committed empiricist. Based on the environmental facts and the need for workable solutions, he thought that Oruka would propose strategies of contraction and convergence. As Aubrey Meyer of the Global Commons Institute recommended in 2005, all persons should receive egalitarian emissions entitlements based on the population of countries at a certain point in time, and all should have this entitlement equally reduced over time to meet climate goals. Oruka would want to study global remedies, he insists, and this proposal is global in scale. He thought Oruka would reject geo-engineering ideas as risky or too expensive. He thinks Oruka would agree with Henry Shue's argument for technology transfer from the north to countries of the south that could not otherwise afford them (Attfield 2012). He also thinks that Oruka would agree with himself and other coauthors regarding their joint article in 2004 expressing the need for land reform. There, Attfield and his coauthors note that we have obligations toward fellow humans and the environment, and we can't meet those obligations without a just land reform (Attfield 2012; Attfield et al. 2004). While one can wonder whether Attfield's reconstruction of the environmental positions of Oruka, had he lived, sounds a bit too much like Attfield's own views (and thus, maybe not that different from Plato putting his own philosophy into the mouth of Socrates), this convergence might just be the result of two thinkers and friends who shared, from those early days in the mid-1970s, a similar moral conviction that the environment must be preserved.

Oruka on Political Philosophy—Domestic and International—and his Ongoing Legacy

While Oruka often mentioned the philosophers who inspired him from the start—Bertrand Russell, and Voltaire, for example—he also mentioned Leo Tolstoy. In his autobiographical essay that focuses on his university years, he admits that he was "mesmerized" by the story of Tolstoy's life, and says, "In him I saw the soul of positive humanity and I thought I should be like him" (1997: 282). This explains Oruka's commitment to the public good, not in the role of a politician but as a thinker and social reformer. According to his friend from graduate school at WSU, David Felder, around that time (1968–69), Oruka had told him that he went into philosophy because he thought that in that way he could be a greater influence for social change in Kenya than if he went into politics directly (Felder interview, 2015). I can't help but note that this conviction mirrors Socrates' comments about his own decision (to philosophize rather than pursue politics) spoken in Plato's *Apology*. There were two facets to Socrates' decision. He thought he could be more effective if he approached people one by one, asking them to reflect more deeply about their thoughts and actions, and to be more consistent between their professed values and their actions. And perhaps the second part of Socrates' motivation mirrors a concern of Oruka's too. Socrates states that if he had engaged in "public business" then "I should have perished long ago and done no good either to you or to myself" (Plato, Apology 32a). Felder says that he thought, given the fact that intellectuals and others were often rounded up in Kenya and treated badly, that it might save Oruka's life if he were to make it to the U.S. For those reasons, in 1983 he tried to get Oruka a job at Florida A and M, in their huge department of Visual Arts, Humanities, and Theatre. But Oruka declined (Felder interview, 2015).

As a public intellectual, Odera Oruka would sometimes write articles for the newspapers, or even appear on television. He addressed a range of topics that were on the minds of the general public and not just of concern to academics. It is important to note that Oruka's academic career and his role as a public intellectual happened, for the most part, while Daniel arap Moi was President of Kenya, and Kenya was a single-party state. This impacted, to a certain extent, what Oruka could say about politics. Moi was known to use both the "carrot" and the "stick" approach. Moi would give small (or large) tokens of appreciation to his loyal followers (funded by the taxpayers, of course), while those who challenged his authority could find themselves detained and tortured. As D. A. Masolo noted, he and Oruka were once invited to an audience of President Moi at his home and farm near Nakuru, and witnessed about 200 of their colleagues also invited there receiving gifts of 10,000 Kenyan shillings from the President, which Masolo interpreted as a form of bribe (2018: 193). At the same time, Masolo notes that Oruka was not free to speak his mind during a Kenyan television show, during which Oruka was asked by the moderator whether Oruka could give concrete examples of the miscarriages of justice he was discussing generically. Oruka did not give an example. Masolo opined that the question could even be considered a trap, because if Oruka dared to give any of the well-known contemporary Kenyan examples, he could have been targeted for judicial or extra-judicial bad treatment by the President (210).

In this chapter's first section, I'll look at how Oruka addressed Kenyans on contemporary issues of interest to them. We'll take special note of Oruka's interview with Kenyan politician Oginga Odinga, and how Oruka describes his work on Odinga in the context of sage philosophy. In the second section I will look at some of Oruka's writings (which always started off as public lectures) addressing politics in general from a political point of view, as well as some of his more pointed critiques of some African governments. In the third section I'll explore how Oruka was involved with African American philosophers in a philosophy of struggle, as well as in the Afro-Asian Philosophical Association, creating bonds with philosophers from Turkey, the Middle East, and India. Oruka was even engaging in South-South dialogues when his life was cut short in 1995. The fourth section shows how he addressed international issues and was active in international organizations like FISP, addressing universal human rights. I'll also look at his activities hosting the World Futures Studies Federation conference in 1995. The final section looks at the last months and days of his life.

1. Addressing Kenyan Issues

On November 4, 1979, one week before the general elections for Kenya's Parliament seats were to be held, Odera Oruka wrote a news article that took up half a page in the *Sunday Nation*. In this article, Oruka (1979) exhorted both voters and candidates to keep in mind the most important aspect of the election: the people must elect candidates who are committed to upholding the common good. All the candidates, being very patriotic, describe to the public what the public good consists of, and they can describe it as involving material goods such as adequate education, health, employment, food, housing, and transportation for everyone, as well as safeguarding freedoms such as freedom of religion. But Oruka goes on to suggest that some of the candidates, despite their rhetoric, actually run for office because they hope to achieve their private good. In Kenya, that usually means not only material goods like "individual ownership of estates, a fleet of vehicles (both for commercial and private use) and large farms" but also social goods like "one's power to secure employment and scholarships for relatives and friends" (5). To achieve these goals, the successful candidate might find him- or herself in need of helping political friends and being deferential to the more powerful politicians.

How can the Kenyan public know whether a candidate truly cares for the common good? Here Oruka aims gentle criticism at the voting public. Candidates love to spend money on some of their constituents. If they are doing so, that should be a signal to voters that the candidate perhaps is not safeguarding funds for the public good. And yet, too often voters are only too happy to be the beneficiaries of the largess of a particular candidate. Oruka does not use euphemisms here. He says that in these conditions, participants, both candidate and electors, are treating a democratic exercise like "a commercial venture in which the candidate *buys* the electors in order to be elected to Parliament" (5, italics in the original). Once there, this candidate will then pursue his or her own private good, until it is time for the next election.

Oruka notes that some candidates on the campaign trail have suggested to voters that the candidate's current economic success ensures that they will not steal when they are elected, since they already have enough for themselves. They tell the public that, clearly, their running for office is an altruistic ambition to help society. The same well-off candidates will warn voters that they should not vote for less materially well-off candidates because those will be greedy to fulfill their own needs first. Oruka thinks this kind of campaign talk is disingenuous. He suggests that it is never the case that a person will feel they have enough money or power. He concludes that the only candidates that should be elected are those who realize that their own private good can only flourish if the common good is well taken care of. They should therefore focus on the common good, and their own private good "will take care of itself" (5). And in this way, without naming Aristotle or Jacques Maritain (1994), Oruka has put forward philosophical ideas well known to be theirs, but with a modification. He agreed with Aristotle that the best government is one in which the public servant serves the common good (neglecting their personal fortunes), whether that person be a monarch or a citizen in a democracy. However, Aristotle imagined that only one who was well-off could spare the time to engage in politics (and to somewhat ignore their personal household). The requirement of being well-off is one that Oruka (1979) particularly rejected. He did not want politics to be "elitist."

Oruka continued his interest in politics by writing about Jaramogi Oginga Odinga. Odinga firmly believed that politics should be a moral activity, engaged in to promote the common good of society; and so, one can see why Oruka would be so interested in interviewing Odinga. If you will remember from chapter 1, Oruka first contacted the former Kenyan vice president in 1979 (the same year he wrote the news article mentioned). Oruka explains in the foreword to the 1992 book that he engaged in the first set of interviews in early 1982. Because there was an attempted coup against the president in 1982, Oruka feared he would be targeted, and he hid his transcripts of the interviews with one friend and the cassette recordings with another. While the transcripts were saved, the cassettes were inadvertently ruined because his friend had dug a hole in the floor of a small shop and hid the cassettes in the hole. He remarked that it was a good thing that he hid the evidence of the interviews because later that year police came and searched his home for four hours, and then arrested him (Oruka 1992: viii–ix).

Oruka writes his assessment of Odinga in the first two chapters of the book, before presenting the interviews. It is important to remember that Oruka considered this book to be an important work of sage philosophy (19; also see Kai Kresse's interview with Oruka, in Graness and Kresse 1997: 252). And a key point in sage philosophy was that interviews of sages would provide text to be analysed, evaluated, and debated by other philosophers, just as they debated the works of Plato or Kant (Oruka 1992: 19). Oruka thought that the world of politics and journalism had not paid attention to the core of Odinga's message. They had unfairly pigeon-holed him into categories like "communist" or "pawn of the East" but had overlooked his "uncompromising African nationalism and his strong attachment to the wisdom of his native culture" (20). In fact, Odinga embodied Luo wisdom.

Oruka then explained that Odinga embodied many leadership traits valued by the Luo. He was a *jahulo* or prophet, warning people about crises on the horizon, and an *ogaye* or "dignified, prosperous and generous individual" (22). He was also a *japaro* or thinker, whom people often sought out for help with difficult problems. This term is related to *jang'ad rieko*, a "professional advisor" (23). He was a *ruoth*, that is, a leader. It is a more recent category than *ker*. But Odinga is also a *ker*, that is, "the ultimate moral or spiritual leader" (23). While the *ruoth* holds political position and is backed by the power of the army, the *ker* is a thinker, a *japaro* who has been promoted to leadership by his or her people. The reason Odinga was called "Jaramogi" is that the honorific means a follower (or descendant) of Ramogi. Ramogi was the "Moses" of the Luo, Oruka explains (24).

Odinga is also a *thuon* or a fighter. He takes risks and is a hero (24). Earlier, he had fought for Kenyatta to be the new leader of Kenya, even while Kenya was still ruled by the British. Later, he quit the ruling party in 1966, disappointed that Kenyatta was not choosing the path of African socialism (8–9). Odinga would be jailed for ten years for opposing independent Kenya's rules for one-party government. After his release, he dared in February 1991 to insist on starting his own party, despite Kenya's outlawing of other parties. Luckily, by December 1992, Kenya became a multiparty state. It was during this enthusiastic time that Oruka was able to interview Odinga a second time, and during which he dared to publish his writings on Odinga.

But Oruka's enthusiasm was tinged with caution because, as he noted, while multiparty democracy was legalized, it would be an uphill battle to be able to truly practice it. Also, he feared that many politicians still had their own power and self-gain as goals (29–30).

Oruka admired Odinga for his three important political virtues: courage, frankness, and perseverance. He used these qualities to solve problems at a certain point in history. While it is beyond the ability of humans, through politics, to achieve a perfect society, they can make society less evil, which is what Odinga was able to do (28). While Odinga, like any politician, fought for power, he did not want "naked power" but only "power with honour and wisdom—the moral power" (31). Just as Plato explained that a main motive to rule would be to prevent being ruled by the "incompetent," that was the extent of Odinga's ambition and the main impetus for his running for president (31–32).

Odinga disagreed with Plato on another point, however—the idea that the truth should be hidden from the masses, as in the "noble lie" mentioned in Plato's *Republic*. Oruka explains that Odinga served in politics to serve the masses. While Ali Mazrui noted that the masses did not always support Odinga, Oruka thinks that is because the masses can be (and in this case were) manipulated by others (14). Oruka claims that this love of truth is one of the great gifts Odinga bequeaths the Kenyan people. In addition, his hard work bore fruit in many areas, as he encouraged Kenyans to start businesses, and through his role in government he was able to build hospitals and find funding for overseas scholarships for Kenyan students (14–15). Odinga wanted to end racism and ethnic favoritism (112–13). He also says he holds a "moral-honour" conception of power (98). Oruka admires Odinga's commitment to the idea of politics as a "clean game" in which one should not engage in any underhanded pressure tactics or deceit. Oruka therefore characterizes Odinga as holding a political position that is the opposite of Niccolò Machiavelli (153).

Oruka's book on Oginga Odinga gives some hints, in the annotations at the end, of how far along Oruka's research went, including allusions to further unpublished works. For example, the annotations explain that Oruka's research into the Luo concept of *jotelo* ("leaders" who by their wisdom give direction to the community) included extensive "conversations" with two Luo sages, Oloo Agwambo Jarieko of East Ugenya, and the late (at the time of publication in 1992) Michael Were of North Ugenya (Oruka 1992: 24, 148–49). While Oruka "hoped that it [the interviews] will one day be published as a booklet," up to now the interviews have not yet been located by other scholars, let alone published (149). The annotations suggest to readers a host of publications by Luo scholars, and included in the impressive list is a work of Oruka's, "Sagacity: A Case Study of Siaya District," completed in 1986 for the Institute of African Studies, University of Nairobi (149).

Not everyone appreciated Oruka's book. When Oruka published his book calling Odinga a philosopher, not everyone agreed. One critic, Joseph Irungu Simon, in a letter that was published in the *Daily Nation* (August 24, 1992), said it was "blasphemy" to call Odinga a philosopher and to suggest that he is on par with Socrates or Aristotle, or contemporaries like Bertrand Russell. While conceding that in a broad sense anyone who asks a philosophical question is a philosopher, the author nevertheless charges that "there is a difference in asking a question about the logic of your culture and political system, and the systematically profound interrogation of the universe engaged in by a Kant or a Plato" (Simon 1992). The same article is skeptical of the sage philosophy concept, noting that similarly in oral philosophy, attention is paid to "any tale spun by a peasant grandmother" as if it were the equivalent of Wole Soyinka's or Leo Tolstoy's great masterpieces of literature. This author, however, says nothing about any of Odinga's ideas; he is simply annoyed that the tile of "philosopher" is given out too freely, in what the author calls "intellectual charity and philosophical alms-giving."

Criticisms like this miss what Oruka thought was so important about philosophizing. He really wanted philosophy to address the issues of the day. He thought that Odinga lived out the life of critical reflection and moral integrity that the world so needed.

Back in 1981, the newspapers in Kenya were covering the International Society of Metaphysics (ISM) conference, which was being held in Nairobi. Fr. George McLean, secretary/treasurer of ISM, along with other international scholars such as E. A. Ruch from the University of Lesotho, attended. There, Oruka is quoted as being concerned that some philosophers did not think issues facing society were important for scholars to address, since they were ideological and not academic. Oruka warned that such dismissive positions were "a greater danger to politics and mankind than the existence of Idi Amins and Adolf

Hitlers" (*Sunday Nation* 1981). He again warned about "stagnating traditions" and "unchecked foreign values," saying instead that people should think through and evaluate the ideologies, consulting "logic, ethics, and factuality (practice)." He wanted more cooperation between philosophers and politicians, he said. Politicians should make more use of the contributions of scholars. On the other hand, he wished and hoped that scholars in Africa would be more concerned about political issues and more critical of the current status quo.

What else can Oruka mean when he says that his book on Odinga is just going to be the first in a new series of books, part of the ongoing sage philosophy project? And could that project ever satisfy critics like Simon, who prefer to read Aristotle over any contemporary Kenyans? Oruka wanted to encourage reflection and debate among Kenyans, about the crises their society was facing. In 1992 when Oruka was interviewing Odinga (for the second time), Wanjiku Mukabi Kabira and Patricia Ngurukie were interviewing Kenyan women (in Lari Division of Kiambu District) who were also very much the thinkers and doers, just like Odinga. (However, their book was not published until 1997: after Oruka's passing.) The authors argue that the women they interviewed have "powerful analytical minds that are usually dismissed without much thought" (Kabira and Ngurukie 1997: iii). Rahab Wabici, for example, not only played a key role in the liberation of Kenya from colonialism, which she recounts for the sake of the historical record, but she also constantly witnesses and evaluates the many developments she sees in her society since independence—both good and worrisome trends (1–36). The authors don't refer to the sage philosophy project or claim that Wabici is a sage or a philosopher (this despite being scholars at the same university as Oruka). But as readers, we can see the commonalities between her narrative interview and that of Odinga. She did not rise to the same prominence as did Odinga; but then, many sages interviewed in Oruka's *Sage Philosophy* were not prominent.

More recently, Mary Njeri Kinyanjui (2019) has written on Kenyan women as embodying a philosophy that she calls feminine Utu. *Utu* is a Swahili word that means personality or sensibility, as well as humaneness and dignity. Kai Kresse has noted that utu has received a lot of philosophical reflection from the male sages he interviewed in Mombasa for his work, *Philosophising in Mombasa* (2007). The women she interviews, Kinyanjui asserts, have a philosophical ideology and method for managing everyday pain. They also strive for peace and harmony, and they connect humans in their communities through coping, dialogue, and negotiation. These are important sage skills. Works like these are great examples of furthering sage philosophy—even if they don't call themselves that explicitly.

But wouldn't they then be visited by the same scrutiny of the unhappy reader who did not want Odinga to be compared to Aristotle? But why should the whole world, for centuries, listen only to the ancient Greeks address and debate among themselves the various crises and tensions in their society? Why not listen to one's contemporaries and engage in discussion of one's own society? Why do some philosophers think it would only be a distraction to notice and try to grapple with today's problems? Luckily, there are hundreds of counter-examples of philosophers who are always trying to sum up and gain insight into the current crises of our world—too many to mention.

D. A. Masolo, in his 1994 book, suggested that while the sages in Oruka's *Sage Philosophy* book were intelligent and smart, he was not sure that every smart saying was a philosophical one. He thought that for something to be philosophy, it had to be more in-depth and systematic. He seemed to be looking for something more rarified and academic (234–40). But a few years later, he changed his tune. Soon he was also seeking out sages. Influenced by Ivan Karp, he began to write, not about interviews per se, but about discussions he witnessed as a participant observer. The scenarios he described would be fraught with intergenerational conflict, gender role challenges, and debates around the interpretation of culture and traditions (Masolo 1997). Later he would write a book related directly to key socio-political challenges of the modern world, centering around the values and practices of communitarianism (Masolo 2010).

2. About Politics in Africa

While the previous section focused on why Oruka thought that Odinga would be of special interest to philosophers, and his study was part of the sage philosophy project, most surely some of his interest in Odinga was as a politician who was, from Oruka's perspective, better than other politicians and country leaders in Africa. Oruka was well known for his "Four Trends" article, in which he put sage philosophy on the map, so to speak, by suggesting that sage philosophy is different from ethnophilosophy and escapes the shortcomings of the latter. But there he also outlines what he calls nationalist-ideological philosophy, that is, the study of political philosophy in Africa. He describes this branch of philosophy as involved in "the creation of a genuine humanist social order" (Oruka 1990c: 17). Oruka identifies the main articulators of this philosophy as Léopold Senghor, Kwame Nkrumah (especially in his *Consciencism*), and Julius Nyerere. The authors in this trend argue that contemporary African political philosophy should revive and build upon pre-colonial traditions of egalitarianism (18, 24–26). Interestingly enough, Oruka explained that he saw the need to develop nationalist-ideological philosophy even more than sage philosophy (1997: 238). And yet, this wish of his, and his own works on political philosophy, may be less well known than his sage philosophy project.

In his essay "What Is Justice?," which appears as chapter 14 in Oruka's *Ethics* (1990a), Oruka puts forward some of his own critique of African politics.[1] First he describes political categories in general, by referring to the works of Plato and Aristotle. Referring to Plato's *Republic*, he suggests that there are two types of rulers outlined in the text. One is the Thrasymachus-inspired "might makes right" ruler, while the other is the philosopher-king, who becomes a leader because his moral qualities and commitment to the common good are tested by the community. The philosopher-king does not rule with the same impunity as the "might makes right" ruler. But limits to his power don't come from a system of checks and balances—rather, it is only the conscience of the ruler, and his or her ability to foresee the consequences of his or her actions that place limits on their actions. These two very different rulers nevertheless have something in common. They both see society and its people as an organic whole in which individuals are necessarily members.

The first two governments are in contrast to the third kind of government he outlines, the voluntary society of individuals who associate with each other and form a contract. Everyone is an egoist who agrees to join society because they calculate it will best help their own survival. Only in this third kind of government is there a "rule of law," since in the first two versions, the ruler rules directly by their will (109–14). So far, however, it is unclear to me if Oruka advocates this social contract because he has, in his environmental philosophy and in his championing of African ideas, criticized contemporary egoists and emphasized that humans are in fact interrelated.

But before he chooses the best model for political rulers, he adds a fourth category, the patriarch who practices patronage, with all of his examples being from Africa (however, we know patronage is also practiced outside Africa). In his description of the early development of the patriarchs, they sound a bit like the philosopher-king. These leaders had rarified and extensive schooling, often abroad. They did not necessarily spring from the people's grassroots movements, but they knew how to catapult themselves into positions of leadership as they devised ways to get the colonizers to leave. A grateful populace was so impressed that they gave these first leaders a broad mandate. The leaders also took the opportunity to reject the constitutions and governmental models bequeathed to them by the departing colonizers because, after all, those colonizers had no legitimate authority. While Oruka again insists that this is a fourth category of rulership, different from the first three, we again see that the rulers are presuming themselves to be philosopher-kings; so if this is a fourth category, its only difference can be that they are false philosopher-kings (and then the second category is saved for who—the real ones?). This is what Oruka says about

Senghor, Nyerere, Nkrumah, Kaunda, and Kenyatta: they "show an attitude of a patriarch and a destined father who has the sole prerogative to initiate, evaluate and implement what he considers *right* and *good* for his nation" (116, italics in original). One sign of this patriarchal disposition is that they can't listen with an open mind to any internal criticism.

Oruka then gave concrete examples for each of the five leaders regarding internal criticism (and, Oruka implies, true shortcomings) that they neglected to acknowledge and address. While Senghor critiques Marxism and comes up with African socialism, he doesn't admit to any problems with implementing it in Senegal. Nkrumah couldn't admit that the personality cult around him skewed his vision of what the country needed. Nyerere's ideas of African socialism couldn't generate the wealth the country needed to distribute to all who needed it. Of special note is the way that he criticized the first president of Kenya, referring to his bad record of jailing his opponents, while at the same time asking everyone to remember his own years in jail. While Kenyatta claims to have spent his years in jail "without bitterness," why must he subject so many others to imprisonment (116)? While Oruka doesn't mention Kaunda's shortcoming here, he does so in another work, noting on the one hand that Kaunda upheld democratic government as the best form of government, but on the other hand, Kaunda banned one of the opposition parties and then transformed Zambia into a one-party state (1990c: 75–76).

While Oruka does not clearly choose which of the four outlined models of rulership is most just, or even most favored by himself for any reason, clearly he is against the patriarch, who seems to usurp power from both the legislative and judiciary branches of government. He also advances criticisms of the social contract theorists—if not in their ideal state, at least in practice, when their egoistic endeavors lead to a society in which there are "a class of super-rich and a class of paupers. From one you get 'dictators' and from the other 'the admirers of dictators'" (1990a: 113). One doesn't get a good sense of what Oruka is arguing in favor of until one gets to chapter 15, titled "Philosophy and Democracy." There, Oruka seems to advocate for democratic socialism as the form of government most likely to be egalitarian. After all, egalitarianism is a requirement for a just society, he argues (it is not only a "classical philosophical conception" but also the only government consonant with pre-colonial African traditions) (117, 122).

As Oruka cautions, democracy does not necessarily end up in egalitarianism. Democracy means that the people decide what they want. It doesn't necessarily mean that people will choose what is good for them. "A majority can just as well be a group of misguided robots making decisions which push their country to the rocks," he warns (121). If the people want life, a populist move will be to help them have life, but what if the people want death? (This may be hard to imagine, but we could ask, for example, what if the people prefer freedom of movement, even during a public health crisis that makes freedom of movement dangerous to health?) And so, while egalitarianism is a good, a democracy may decide it would rather have a socially stratified society with privileged and lower classes (122). In a democracy, it is up to people to decide what they want in life and what they want their government to provide (124). But Oruka argues that all people need both material and moral goods (125).

Most of the rest of the chapter is dedicated to Oruka's denouncing of elitism. While some argue that elitism is justified because there are some people who are morally and intellectually superior to others, Oruka insists that all persons have the potential to develop their moral and intellectual powers, and they just need the opportunity to do so. He also criticizes John Stuart Mill's theories of universal good that nevertheless make distinctions based on race, owing to Mill's acceptance of certain racist tenets of colonialism (122–25). As a worst-case scenario of elitism, he denounces "Aminocracy," no doubt a term coined to mean Ugandan dictator Idi Amin and any others who copy his leadership style (Oruka alludes to leaders of the Central African Republic and Equatorial Guinea as well.) Such a ruler will do anything that pleases him- or herself, without restrictions (122–23).

In his book on Odinga, Oruka (1992) asks Odinga about socialism. First, Odinga makes it clear that he is not a communist, despite having visited communist countries and having learned from them. But then Oruka presses him about socialism. Odinga says that even capitalist countries have practiced socialism in their welfare policies, and he cites the British Labour Party, Scandinavia, and even the United States as examples. He concludes that "socialism is a good thing.... It is an effective means to encourage sharing and discourage hoarding" (Odinga, in Oruka 1992: 89). Oruka then suggests that African practices of extended family support played a role similar to Western welfare systems (89). Odinga suggests that in the future Africa will need to develop socialism, in concert with the values of the extended family, but becoming more institutionalized in government. Odinga also reiterates a point made by Oruka in his *Ethics* chapters 14 and 15, that is, that Africans need to free themselves from African dictators. That is why Odinga started his own political party, FORD, and ran for president (96).

3. International Collaborations with Other Scholars

So far I have focused on Oruka's comments on social and political philosophy in the African context. But now I want to turn our attention to Oruka's interactions with a broader network of international scholars who helped to inform him and engage him on discussions of many philosophical issues, including social and political philosophy, with special concerns for the impacts of social inequality, racism, and the struggle for human rights. What follows first is the story of how Oruka engaged with a group of African American philosophers, led by Lucius Outlaw, Leonard Harris and others, in their project eventually called "Philosophy Born of Struggle." As Harris explains, he wanted to gather philosophers who philosophized under historical oppression, and offered resistance to that oppression, by exploring notions of freedom and dignity, exploring racism as a social event, and attempting to resolve conflicts in the social order (Harris 2015).

While Lucius Outlaw was at Morgan State University (1977 to 1980), he was engaged in a curriculum development project devoted to African and African American philosophy. He was searching for texts on African philosophy, and at this time he wrote to African scholars and asked them to send their books.[2] He received books by Wiredu, Sodipo, Hountondji, and others and received issues of the journal *Second Order* from Nigeria. It was then that Outlaw wrote Oruka for the first time, and Oruka responded with information about an upcoming conference at the University of Nairobi in summer of 1981. By then, Outlaw had been hired by Haverford College. Haverford paid to send Outlaw to the conference, and he spent two weeks in Kenya. The Inter-African Council of Philosophy had cosponsored the Afro-Asian Philosophy Association annual conference. Mourad Wahba and Ioanna Kuçuradi were the leaders of the association and the conference. This is where he met Wiredu, Hountondji, Sodipo, and Robert Murungi. (He would later meet Robert's cousin John, who taught philosophy at Towson State University back in Baltimore.) During a meeting at the conference, Oruka and others on the Executive Committee of the Inter-African Council of Philosophy endorsed Outlaw's idea of their all coming to Haverford College where they could have a conference that would allow more African American philosophy professors to get to know these African scholars. The event would be called the "International Research Conference on Africa."

Outlaw remembers going to dinner with the Canadian Jesuit professor Claude Sumner, who had been teaching and researching at Addis Ababa University. Sumner was looking for an American distributor who might publish (or distribute) his works on Ethiopian philosophy in the United States. While Outlaw didn't know how to help Sumner, he was able to carry home with him a large set of Sumner's books published in Ethiopia.

When Outlaw returned home, he began writing proposals to try to raise funds to bring the African scholars to the United States. His first attempt, at the National Endowment of the Humanities, was partly successful but didn't provide enough funds for the travel of the African participants. He got some additional funds from the Social Science Research Council and some private foundations he had researched. He tried the Ford and Rockefeller Foundations but didn't receive funding from them. But he was given a helpful piece of advice. The person at the Rockefeller Foundation noted that there was a branch of the Rockefeller Foundation in Kenya, and they suggested that Oruka apply there to get funds to attend the conference at Haverford. The plan worked, and Oruka attended the conference. The other African delegates similarly found funds in the local branches of these large foundations. The FISP in Paris funded Hountondji, and UNESCO and other institutions funded other scholars. Many African American scholars in several fields, as well as several African American philosophy graduate students, attended along with the African scholars for a weeklong conference.

Outlaw designed the conference so that participants could get the most out of their time together. Everyone sent presentations in advance, and these were reproduced and bound, with special covers. Presenters summarized their ideas for ten to fifteen minutes each, and there was ample time for discussion, as well as many meals and social events where the scholars could get to know each other better. They all stayed in one dorm at the Haverford campus, and these dorms were organized as suites, further facilitating socializing. Outlaw and several other faculty, including his colleague V. Y. Mudimbe, lived on campus near each other. Mudimbe was in the philosophy department at Haverford and attended sessions. "People were having fantastic conversations," Outlaw noted, due to all these opportunities to spend time with each other, even "into the wee hours of the morning."

Outlaw also got a glimpse of the kinds of struggles his African colleagues were going through. Wiredu wanted to fill his luggage with food staples that weren't available in Ghana—like flour, sugar, and powdered milk—and Outlaw's wife helped Wiredu gather these necessities. A white woman from the University of Delaware wanted to attend the conference and asked if it was okay to attend. Outlaw told her she was welcome. That was Sandra Harding. Through her meeting so many scholars at that conference, she was able to later invite several of them to the University of Delaware to give talks. This was some of the context of her subsequently writing the influential article, "The Curious Coincidence of Feminine and African Moralities: Challenges for Feminist Theory" (1987).

Based on their growing acquaintance from this conference, Outlaw was able to invite Oruka to come back to Haverford as a visiting professor for the spring semester. At the time Oruka was married to Millicent, who visited for part of the time. The faculty at Haverford were reading texts together in their homes once a week. While Oruka was there, they asked him to lead discussions on texts by Hountondji and Wiredu. Those were valuable discussions.

Outlaw reminisced about this period. He would jokingly call his Kenyan friend "H. Odera Oruka Dada!"—comparing him to Idi Amin Dada because Oruka had a tendency to order people (including Outlaw) around rather than ask them to do something. He was haughty and chief-like in his carriage, demeanor, and personality. Outlaw described him as "a classical, almost stereotypical African paternalistic male." And when he had a goal in mind, he would pursue it and not be dissuaded. A colleague at Haverford wanted to sell their Peugeot sedan, and Oruka got the idea that he wanted to buy it. Even though it was difficult to send the car to Kenya, he was determined to do it. He drove the car to New Jersey, and it was loaded onto a ship. Despite its having the steering wheel on the left side, intended for U.S. driving, he drove the car for many years in Kenya.

At the end of his time at Haverford, Oruka asked Outlaw to keep several manuscripts in safekeeping for him. He was worried about returning to Africa with texts that might be construed as controversial, and he was worried the authorities would search his belongings. Oruka's book, *Punishment and Terrorism in Africa*, had already been published, and Oruka said he was receiving pushback from political figures.

Outlaw later met up with Oruka again in Cairo, at the Third Afro-Asian Philosophical Association conference organized by Mourad Wahba in 1991. At this conference, Oruka and Outlaw differed with Hountondji on the value of "ethnophilosophy." And there were debates over whether you could have philosophy without writing. Oruka insisted that you could, while Hountondji said no. Outlaw notes, rightly, that Wiredu and Hountondji changed their views soon after discussions like these. Starting in the 1980s, Wiredu was already arguing that African philosophy should be written in African languages.

While Outlaw has shared a sketch of the Third Afro-Asian Philosophy conference from his memory, Mona Abousenna (1995) has written an article reflecting on the Association and its conferences. She notes that the conference co-founder, Mourad Wahba, held up enlightenment ideals. He advocated for the use of reason to "change reality for the benefit of the mass-man," noting that the gap between developed and developing nations could never be closed until Afro-Asian societies, which he thought were dominated by "mythos and cultural taboos" changed their ways and became more philosophically critical (129). Oruka shared some of these ideas and aspirations, of course. But at the third conference in 1991 he presented his book and ideas on sage philosophy. There he insisted that it is sages who tackle societal problems, whether they be Gandhi, Lenin, or Nyerere, and their wisdom should be heeded, whether or not society calls them philosophers (Oruka quoted in Abousenna,

130–31). But Abousenna shares her concern about Oruka's ideas. She thought he was proposing something rather religious, insofar as he mentioned that African societies may have intuition as their source for knowledge. That went against the secular focus of several participants. Abousenna was also concerned that Oruka was against Western society due to colonialism, and she thought he had "an antagonistic and defensive attitude against all the intellectual products of the assumed enemy"—that is, to Western philosophy (131). Abousenna thought it was wrong to consider philosophy as it has been taught as "Western" because it was a mere accident that philosophy began in the West. She herself was in favor of de-dogmatism, universalism, and acknowledgment of interdependence, developing a global consciousness and a futuristic vision. Abousenna thought Wahba would consider Oruka as practicing ethnophilosophy. She then covered Hountondji's ideas presented at their conferences more sympathetically (131–32). One can see that in certain philosophical circles, Oruka's proposal of sage philosophy was an uphill battle. The "trend" of professional philosophy, as he described it in his "Four Trends" essay (1990c: 18–20), was a large part of Oruka's own approach, but, he challenged himself to change from the ways of his academic training, to incorporate a new respect for the thoughts of African sages and their cultural knowledge.

Oruka was often able to invite high-profile keynote speakers to his conference. This often got him in trouble. Kenya was a one-party state, and President Daniel arap Moi had been in power since 1978 when the 1991 FISP conference on the environment was being held in Nairobi. As authors in the *Daily Nation* explain, Professor Mazrui, who had given his keynote paper titled "From Sun Worship to Time Worship: Toward a Solar Theory of Time," was found by reporters in the conference center, and he agreed to be interviewed at a press conference, doing so without the presence of Oruka and the other conference organizers. Then, according to one writer, Mazrui asked President Moi to resign. *The Daily Nation* published two differing views from their readership about Mazrui's comments. While Wilson Chelulo defensively replied that "Kenyans elected President Moi to lead them for as long as they wish," another writer, Rosemary Mutonyi, thinks that Oruka was too defensive in criticizing Mazrui for having made his remarks, and too jealous that Mazrui got all the press attention while other aspects of the conference were being ignored (*Daily Nation* 1991).

No matter how much Oruka felt marginalized for his political views in his home country, he knew he had a network of international scholars to collaborate with and who were willing to help as much as they could. He served for many years on the Human Rights Committee of FISP. There, and in the Afro-Asian Philosophical Association, he worked closely with İoanna Kuçuradi of Turkey.

They had a long collaboration. The important groundbreaking work of this society was chronicled by Abousenna (1995).

As two past Presidents of the International Development Ethics Association (IDEA), David Crocker and Nigel Dower (2022) have testified, Odera Oruka was one of their society's founding members. Dower also mentions that it was Oruka who first suggested to him (on one of Dower's visits to Nairobi) that he connect with David Crocker, because he knew of their similar scholarly interests. It led to a lifelong collaboration between the two. IDEA members participated in Oruka's 1991 conference, holding sessions of their society on development ethics there.

4. A Host of Pressing Social and Political Issues

Odera Oruka was an active member of the World Futures Studies Federation (WFSF). Just a few months before his death on December 9, 1995, he had organized and hosted the 14th World Conference of the WFSF, the first such conference to be held in Sub-Saharan Africa. The federation members were actively engaged, from a multiplicity of disciplinary perspectives, in calculating what the future would look like. Not being determinists, they realized that there was always a possibility of multiple futures, depending on which trends continued forward in uncontrolled momentum or were purposely changed by human decision making and commitment to goals. Such approaches to futures were particularly attractive to Oruka's own idea of his role as a philosopher.

At the end of the introduction to *Practical Philosophy* (1997), he dedicates the book "to the futures—to the future African philosophers and all future thinkers and workers for human justice and better environment." As he explains there, "Future is not one given, unalterable fate. There are always many possible futures. And depending on our actions today we can encourage the chances of some and diminish the chances of others." Insofar as future catastrophes can be predicted, he insists, humanity has the moral obligation to do everything it can to prevent such catastrophes (Oruka 1997: xvii).

As an academic philosopher and ethicist, Oruka would use reason to extrapolate the probable consequences of trends that he noticed in society at large. His approach, like the sages and prophets, was also intuitive, based on his own estimation of the signs of the times. But he also consulted statistical analyses of economic and sociological trends and at times carried out his own exhaustive studies of trends. But he did not consider himself a soothsayer or even a scientific know-it-all. He humbly stated that, despite his membership in WFSF, "we can only guess but we cannot rightly claim to know" what the future centuries hold.[3] His constant interest in the future was grounded in his concern for injustices existing in our world right now, and how best to encourage people to change the current destructive trends. As he explained in an interview with Kai Kresse in 1993, the philosopher has a special duty to "warn his/her people" so that they understand the implications of their present actions (Oruka 1997: 217). I therefore argue that not only was Odera Oruka a futurist and a prophet, but he also challenges all philosophers everywhere to take up their prophetic responsibility in regard to their respective communities and the planet as a whole.

Oruka was always coming up with a strong philosophical argument about why rich nations, no matter how reluctant, should change their ways. In his article "The Philosophy of Foreign Aid," he argues that if the world community agrees that humans have a right to life, then implicit in that right is the right to physical security, health, and subsistence. Such rights are inherent in the person as a person, not as a citizen of a certain country. A government's right to sovereignty cannot override the individual's right to life. Therefore, rich countries cannot argue that they have an option as to whether they will aid starving persons. Foreign aid is ethically obligatory and not just international charity. Therefore, individuals who accept it should not have to feel self-pity, nor should countries have to "pay back" such "favors" by giving rich nations their beneficial trade or ideological zones, since the aid is not a favor in the first place but rather a duty (in Graness and Kresse 1997: 47–60, esp. 49–51).[4]

Oruka definitely thought that the best motivation for filling the basic needs of others was a moral one. He tried to show through rational philosophical argument that we are all saddled with duties toward each other. Nevertheless, he realized that such motivation was not effective with all people. He therefore often appealed as well to self-interest as a motivator; and it was in this capacity that he most often turned to the pondering of possible future scenarios.

Oruka notes that not all people heed warnings of the future, no matter how scientifically proven the future dangers are. For example, he says, science has shown that cigarette smoking leads to cancer; nevertheless, people continue to smoke. In another scenario, he notes that, no matter how many times it is shown that fatal road accidents in Kenya and Nigeria are caused by carelessness, excessive drinking, and speeding, few drivers heed the warning based on such studies (Oruka 1997: 71–72). It is indeed a shame that some Kenyan drivers have not heeded such studies and reduced the rate of road carnage. Professor Oruka himself died on the roads in Nairobi in December of 1995, when a truck ran him over as he crossed the street. In the same month, five other University of Nairobi faculty and administrators also died in a car crash. With the rate of deaths on the road so high, it becomes difficult to sort out genuine accidents from planned collisions, making it ever so easy to knock off political dissidents.

In such a world seemingly oblivious to the dangers inherent in present action, what is the role of the philosopher? As he explains, in similar self-interested strategy, philosophers must work to ensure the survival of humanity because, citing Archie Bahm, philosophy has a future only if humanity has a future; therefore, there is an urgent need to create a philosophy of human survival. But what kind of special contribution can philosophy make to solving the world's problems? He explains that philosophy, with its unending search for truth, will strive to find solutions. Those solutions must avoid the trap of "scientism" by emphasizing both knowledge and values. Likewise, philosophy can use its communicative and dialogical method, if not to find consensus on conclusions, then at least to raise important topics for discussion. He suggests that philosophers must have an epistemological or axiological ground to their discourse if they are to contribute to discussion any more than the average person (1997: 101–105).

Indeed, Oruka insists, perhaps cynically, that people should turn away from religion and to philosophy to find solutions to the world's problems. Religion, he insists, has no vested interest in finding long-term solutions to people's problems, since religion survives and thrives by being something for people to turn to when they have unbearable problems. In other words, if religions were to succeed in providing the world with real solutions to its problems, they would put themselves out of business (75). In his essay "Philosophy and Humanism in Africa," Oruka states that what Africa needs is critical and dialectical philosophy, which would come up with tentative conclusions and experimental projects to improve Africa. Africa does not need ethno-religious solutions that tend toward dogmatism. He sees the main function of moral and social philosophy as applying rigorous analytical and synthetic reasoning to the moral problems of the day. Philosophers should devote themselves to liberating ARID (African Republic of Inhumanity and Death) or preventing its spread. How can they best do that? By postulating alternatives "to the current prevailing and dehumanizing ethics of political might" (144). As Reginald Oduor (2018) attempts to sum up Oruka's point here, saying that philosophy alone can't overthrow ARID, but "a culture of critical thinking in the citizenry" could "catalyze the process of liberation" (238).

Oruka, in his essay "Philosophy and Humanity Today," insists that humans need both instinct and insight to survive and to avoid either self-destruction or destruction from external factors. Back in the 1980s, he expressed concern that, given the rate of militarization and moral decay, humanity would be lucky to survive another fifty years. Therefore, the world needs to be humanized. Three main threats to freedom, as he sees it, are fear, greed (lack of fairness), and false pride (which is the basis of racism, sexism, and colonialism). He here expresses his prescriptions and hopes for the future. He suggests that a strengthening of the UN General Assembly could help the cause of world peace. And he hopes that the autocratic era of the 1970s and 1980s in Africa will soon be replaced by the rebirth of a global democratic spirit. He insists that philosophers should set themselves the task of bringing such a spirit to birth (Oruka 1997: ch. 12).

In an essay in which he reflected upon his life's calling as a philosopher ("My Strange Way to Philosophy"), Oruka (1997: 283–84) thematized his own interests in philosophy. He saw his goal as to clear current and future obstacles to philosophy, wisdom, and justice. He did this by exposing and analyzing three evils: socio-economic deprivation, cultural-racial mythology, and the illusion of appearance. His emphasis on the first, he explains, is because poverty and hunger are the greatest constraint to mental development and creativity. He means by the third evil those who pursue style rather than substance and are distracted and fooled by the glitter of surfaces. Masolo particularly appreciates how Oruka has explained that that socio-economic deprivation is "an encumberment on the freedom and expression of thought" (2018: 208) and Oruka's critique of a liberal world where only the rich and powerful are really free (205).

Nyarwath (2018: 281), drawing upon Oruka's ideas, elaborates on the many ways in which democracy is denied those with little financial clout. Some people sell their vote to get food to eat. Some may be busy looking for food and not have time to vote. Some may have no transportation to polls. Under such circumstances they can hardly make the best choice, even if they do manage to vote.

Oruka has indeed spent his intellectual energy on waging "philosophic war with factors and values which promote social and economic disadvantage and oppression" (Oruka 1997: 284). On the positive side, he names three vehicles to a fruitful philosophy: freedom of thought, inspiration (to solve the world's problems), and destiny, whereby he means not some preordained state-to-be but, rather, a concern with one's own origin and future, which will guide personal and community self-definition (286).

This concern for issues of justice stuck with him to the end. Just a few months prior to his death, in September of 1995 he gave a paper on "Mahatma Gandhi and Humanism in Africa." He had been invited to New Delhi to a conference organized by the Indian Council on Philosophical Research. There he reflected on the great loss of life of the Rwandan genocide the year prior. Reflecting back on how in 1978 he had described ARID, that is, the "African Republic of Inhumanity and Death," Oruka in 1995 admitted that he had painted a gloomy picture back then and had really hoped that history would prove him wrong. But unfortunately, things became even worse. "Arid became an inferno," he bemoaned, referencing not only Rwanda's tragedy but similar problems in Somalia and Liberia (Oruka 1995: 2).

Reviewing Gandhi's nonviolence in contrast to Fanon, Oruka felt confident that Gandhi's was the better course of action. He noted that Gandhi's emphasis on the interrelatedness of all of humanity was consonant with his own "Parental Earth Ethics." He also saw Gandhi's concern for poverty coinciding with his own insistence that there needed to be a moral minimum. He drew parallels to Leo Tolstoy's comments on the "Law of Love" (3). While Fanon advocated violence to attain Africa's liberation, Oruka said that such so-called acts of liberation were turning into vicious circles of more violence (4).

Interestingly enough, he wanted one departure from Gandhi. Gandhi, he noted, would always look for the truth in his opponent, and would not claim to possess truth himself. From Gandhi's perspective, he thought, "By making an argument against an adversary which is intellectually superior to his/her argument, one inflicts intellectual violence" (6). Oruka did not want to give up this practice of making the better argument. He said that it was needed as "a method for political-social change" (6). As long as this exception could be made to Gandhian nonviolence, Oruka would advocate for it. Now, whether making a superior argument really does count as "intellectual violence" or not could be debated. But clearly, such an argument could be delivered in such a way that it either intentionally or unintentionally creates harm or injury. But, perhaps also, such arguments could be delivered in a different way, so their ideas could take root in listeners (see Rooney, 2010; Presbey, 2000).

Few can parallel Oruka's ability to pinpoint the specific problems facing Africa and our globe. His tenacity in bringing up the moral and normative dimension of future trends is to be admired, and I suggest that few would be able to call his prescriptions into question. Indeed, which one of us can argue that the eradication of poverty, hunger, narrow-mindedness, environmental degradation, and injustice should not be the top priority of all individuals and communities?

But this message is not just for Africa; Odera Oruka challenges us all by asking us to look into our future and ask ourselves, what kind of a future world are we willing to work for? How will we re-prioritize our values and reorient our actions today? And for that "jolt" of prophetic questioning, we thank him.

5. Odera Oruka's Last Few Months, and Death

I was in Kenya in the 1995–96 academic year to work with Oruka further. I had also arranged, as he had requested, a visiting professorship to begin in January 1996 at my home institution. Unfortunately, he would not be able to take up the visiting position. While I was very appreciative of the time I was able to spend with Oruka, even going with him on his journeys to interview sages, I had no idea that it was in fact a last opportunity, since he would soon be killed—by a truck.

There was often an aspect of fear in the adventures of seeking sages—not the usual "wild animal" fear of elephants trampling us; rather, were the loyal KANU party members following him, stalking him in this "subversive" research? There were some grounds for these fears. Oruka had been interviewing Oginga Odinga, former first vice president of Kenya turned opponent of the ruling KANU party, throughout the years of repressive single-party rule. His research assistant, Chaungo Barasa, who accompanied Oruka to some of their interviews with Odinga, verified that they had sometimes been followed by shady characters and had to elude them on the roads.[5] Odinga was the kind of sage that Oruka liked best: he was *Ker*, a title meaning "cultural leader" of the Luo ethnic group (to which Oruka belonged), signifying that Odinga was an expert on the traditions of his community; but he was also an active politician devoted to an idea of ethical politics, opposed to authoritarianism and Machiavellian tactics. After leaving the vice presidency, Odinga became involved in organizing peasant farmers into cooperatives to protect them from exploitation by the sugar companies. Oruka was proud that his farms participated in Odinga's cooperative. Odinga had been pressuring the Kenyan government to reinstate multiparty politics long before the World Bank and IMF thought of such policies. When the first multiparty elections were scheduled for 1992, Odinga ran for president as a candidate for an opposition party, FORD-Kenya.

Elated that the oppressive climate had finally lifted, Oruka undertook new interviews with Odinga, and he published both the old and new interviews in a book released in Kenya. Oruka was greatly surprised and disappointed, as were many Kenyans, to find out that, despite multiparty elections, the former ruling party remained in power. Reasons for this maintenance of dominance are many, but briefly, the incumbent party had resources to buy votes (even going so far as to print extra money for the purpose), promising riches to those who remained loyal; and the opposition could not maintain a united front and quickly divided along ethnic lines, unable to capture a majority. Oruka soon realized that his candid support for Odinga and his confessions about his clandestine activities during one-party rule would not please the presidentially appointed district commissioner (DC) of Nyanza Province (Oruka's home area).

On a bus trip in 1995 that Oruka and I were taking to Kisumu, the town in Nyanza where his wife and children were living at the time, I proudly showed him the reading material I had brought along for the trip—a copy of his book on Oginga Odinga. "Put that away," he ordered me. I was surprised but did as he said. He explained quietly that the book was not liked by the DC in Nyanza, and he didn't want to endanger me by letting others on the bus notice that I had the book. I was quite surprised and actually a bit confused about how hiding the book could help me, considering I was traveling with the book's illustrious author. Other signs of the extent of Oruka's nervousness about the political situation showed themselves while we were on the road seeking out sages. At one point while driving, Oruka's car hood came flying up, temporarily blocking his view of the road. He pulled off safely and closed the hood. But he was quite frightened and began speculating whether someone had purposely sabotaged the car with hopes of killing him. At the time I thought the theory improbable, and I tried to reassure him that, since we had just stopped at the petrol station and the attendant had checked under the hood, the most plausible scenario was that she had not banged the hood shut properly. At this point in the journey, Oruka began to tell me the stories of the many times over the years when he felt certain he had been hounded and menaced by the authorities. (This sense of foreboding and fear for his life and work has been corroborated by the fact that I keep running into one more friend and colleague of Oruka's who mentions that Oruka had given them manuscripts for them to keep in safekeeping for him, since he had a fear for about two decades that Kenyan authorities might confiscate his manuscripts.)

On one occasion, we were seeking out a female sage, something that Oruka did not often do, but he did at my insistence. We were waiting at a petrol station along a major road, while we sent a local messenger into a residential area to locate the woman we were looking for. The longer we sat, the more Oruka thought about the fact that this woman's sons were in politics. He began to worry that the woman's political connections would be problematic. He always put things as his attempt to protect me from controversy and trouble. The longer we waited for the messenger to return, the more apprehensive he got about the meeting. He finally decided we should not meet the woman. But just then, the messenger returned with the information that the woman we were seeking was selling tea in the main market. We followed this person to the market and met the woman there. But by then, Oruka merely greeted her and politely said that he would return another day, and we left.

Signs that Oruka was concerned about his own safety were there, but he did not elaborate to any of us in the philosophy department. One day in early December, in his office, Prof. Oruka seemed particularly nervous and troubled. Junior faculty members from the philosophy department were just gathering on the next day in the Senior Common Room of the university with Professor Gilbert Ogutu of religious studies, Oruka's colleague and contemporary, to ask for his advice and help, when the news reached the group that Oruka had been hit and killed by a lorry while he was crossing the road on foot. The day was December 9, 1995. Oruka was only fifty-one years old. The whole group, including myself, made it to Ugenya, Oruka's rural home, for the burial. Just a few weeks prior to that I had been at Oruka's home with him, and he was explaining to me how he was preparing the house for his retirement.

There was much hushed debate at the wake at his house in Nairobi, at the memorial mass at the University chapel, and at the funeral in Ugenya as to whether the death was accidental or whether it was a disguised murder. Many people held different views on the subject. I listened for compelling evidence among the many stated opinions. Most arguments in favor of the theory of his killing cited precedents of other political killings in Kenya, also often made to look like accidents, suicides, or robberies. They also cited Oruka's own convictions that his life was in danger. Those holding that it was an accident argue that the lorry driver was innocent, not known for criminality, and that Oruka, absent-minded professor that he was, was known for walking out carelessly into traffic. Others argued that Oruka's involvement in politics was minimal compared to outspoken rabble-rousers like James Orengo (who, incidentally, spoke at Oruka's funeral), doubting that there could be enough of a political motivation to kill him. Oruka's wife noted to the press that the police had given her conflicting accounts of her husband's death (*Daily Nation*, December 13, 1995). This lack of clarity about the facts of the day he died was also troubling to many. The debate continues; I can't say I know who is right. There has been no further investigation into the circumstances of his death. We can say with certainty, however, that Oruka lost his life while he still had much to offer the world, and the world is poorer for his absence.

If there is a life after this one, one can be sure that Oruka, like Socrates stated in the *Apology*, (Plato, Apology 41a) is questioning and cross-examining all the great historical Kenyans he meets in that afterlife, as well as any of the international philosophers already taking up residence there in the next life. And hopefully he is there with his ancestors, receiving further counsel from his father, among others.

As is often the case with brave characters with pioneering ideas, their influence is felt beyond the grave. A new generation of scholars has continued to push forward his research agenda and his searching questions on the nature and substance of African philosophy. His book, *Sage Philosophy*, has been cited by hundreds of scholars. His other books and articles are often referenced. Students are studying sage philosophy as well as other aspects of his work at several universities. Masters and PhD theses have been written about him. A recent collection, edited by three philosophy professors at the University of Nairobi (Oduor et.al. 2018), includes sixteen articles on his philosophy. But this is not the only way to measure Oruka's ongoing influence. His ideas regarding protecting the environment, addressing hunger, eradicating racism, and promoting egalitarianism, while defending the dignity of many African traditions and wisdom from the continent of Africa, while promoting thoughtful change and modernization, are all projects that go beyond academia to influence activists and impact the everyday lives of many people in our world. As his works are better known and understood, I predict that his influence will grow.

Notes

Introduction

1   In his youth, in Sweden, and when he was first hired at the University of
    Nairobi, Oruka was known as Henry Odera. When he matured as a scholar,
    he decided to minimize the use of his Christian name and emphasize his
    African names. He used "H" instead of "Henry" and added his father's name,
    Oruka, becoming known as H. Odera Oruka. The people who knew him
    early on knew him as Henry Odera. All his published works are signed
    H. Odera Oruka. In the present work, I will refer to him by his last name,
    "Oruka"; in quotes from others I will retain their usage. For more on Oruka's
    name, and for a rationale for referring to him as "Oruka" instead of "Odera
    Oruka" please see Reginald Oduor et al., eds., 2018: 2–6.
2   Michael Krausz, with Odera Oruka's help, interviewed Tago Athieno, a
    Luo medicine man, on February 6, 1985. He included excerpts of the
    interview in the appendix of his book, *Rightness and Reasons* (Krausz
    1993: 167–169).
3   See Ochieng'-Odhiambo 1995–96, especially 18–19; a list of theses that
    Oruka directed appears on 20–21n11.
4   Oruka was a panelist on a Kenya Broadcasting Corporation show called
    "Press Conference," in an episode entitled "Philosophy and the Environment"
    chaired by Kipserem Maritim, in 1991.
5   Oruka was convinced that the past failure of outside experts in
    implementing family planning programs was due to misunderstanding the
    beliefs and desires of the members of the communities at issue. He was
    satisfied with the results of his extensive study, which he was sure would lead
    to a more effective family planning policy. Oruka finished this project just
    before his death.
6   In Bulgaria, he presented a critique of Hungarian Marxist historian Andre
    Sik's history of Africa.
7   The letter is undated, but known to be prior to July 1995. I was also fortunate
    to have a letter of reference from Oruka to the Fulbright Committee
    recommending me for research in Kenya. Although I did not receive a
    Fulbright grant at that time, but did so at a later date, I cherish this letter he
    wrote, which confirmed his confidence in myself as a researcher. On August
    3, 1994 he wrote

> Dr. Presbey intends to carry out a practical and concentrated
> investigation on the role of sages in these communities and the power
> plus ethnocentric factors that govern the relationship between men
> and women and inter-ethnic conflict and harmony in Africa.

Dr. Presbey's approach will have a special degree of significance and uniqueness: She is an academic professional American Philosopher with deep knowledge of western style societies who will be studying indigenous African communities in liaison with Professional African Philosophers. The outcome will be of immense value to both African and Western societies and universities.

During the year 1993 Dr. Presbey visited our University, gave a number of lectures and attended seminars with the established staff of the Department. Her lectures, contributions and personal touches were very highly appreciated by both students and staff. I warmly and strongly recommend her to you.

> Oruka to the Fulbright/CIES committee, August 3, 1994,
> in possession of the author

8   See for example, Barasa 1997, Ogutu 1995–96, Ochieng'-Odhiambo 1995–96

Chapter 1

1   Oruka mentions that his father had thirty-six children, (1991b: 118). See also Oruka 1990b: 39. Please note that this comment doesn't precede an interview when it is in 1990b.

2   In her thesis, Gichohi criticizes many of the notions of God put forward by many of the sages. She questions why Paul Mbuya Akoko says there must be one god to account for the orderliness of the universe. According to Gichohi, Mbuya is begging the question, for who is to say that many gods must take on a mischievous character? (1996: 89) She also notes that Mbuya says that no one really knows God, but later he affirms that God exists and rules nature. (1996: 91). She further is concerned that M'Mukindia Kithanje's interpretation of God as present at the biological process of procreation confuses the mysterious or marvelous with God. (1996: 94).

3   Interview by the author of David Felder, 2015, and personal correspondence, March 2022. Oruka's testimony at the S.M. Otieno trial will be covered in more detail in chapter 6.

4   While Parkin and other authors sometimes spell Mbuya as "Mboya," Oruka explains in an endnote his rationale for always spelling it "Mbuya." See Oruka 1991b: 159n10.

5   Nyando Ayoo Oguda died on 22 August 2000. (*Kenya Gazette*, July 22, 2005: 1570).

6   *The Kenya Gazette* (October 3, 1950: 818) records Nyando Ayoo as receiving a "non-spirituous liquor licence" at Sega Market, Central Nyanza in 1950.

7   There was a harsh famine (caused by drought) in Nyanza at the end of the First World War, followed by an influenza epidemic in 1919 (Ogot 1963: 260).

8 Humphrey Ojwang notes in correspondence dated 29 December 2011 that
   Filida Okaya died in 2011. Okaya comes from a different part of Nyanza
   Province than Oruka but is from the same Luo ethnic group.
9 These accounts by European travelers include statements by "Speke, Stanley,
   Decken, Peters, Lugard, Johnston, Baumann, Portal." (Cohen and Atieno
   Odhiambo 1989: 68)

Chapter 2

1 See news article "Abborremetare pa Rafsten," in *Uppsala Nya Tidning* August
   27, 1965, p. 1.
2 Mai Palmberg, now retired from the Nordic Africa Institute, where she had
   worked for twenty-seven years, contributed this memory of Oruka during a
   question-and-answer session at the European Conference on African Studies
   special panel on the philosophy of H. Odera Oruka, Uppsala University,
   16 June 2011.
3 Mutahi and Theuri 2003: 18. On Fanon, see Oruka 1997: 108, 143. See also
   Oruka's unpublished 1976 autobiographical novel, *In the Mother Africa (the
   Family Broke Down),* in possession of the author, 152.
4 "Immanuel Kant Biography," on the website of the European Graduate School,
   http://www.egs.edu/library/immanuel-kant/biography/ (accessed July 3, 2013).
5 Nordin 2004: 517. English translation appears in Andersson 2005.
6 For example, Walter Kaufmann clarified that Popper's reading of Hegel
   contains serious misconceptions and was based on too small and selective a
   reading of Hegel's works. Popper also quilted together quotations of Hegel
   that obscure the context, most notably quoting from students of Hegel's who
   held views that Hegel explained were erroneous. See Kaufmann, "The Hegel
   Myth and Its Method."
7 The U.S. magazine *The Saturday Evening Post* published an article in 1959
   attributing these social problems in Sweden to its welfare state. The article
   was republished in *Readers Digest,* and Eisenhower relied on this study in his
   remarks at a Republican National Committee breakfast on July 27, 1960
   (Einhorn and Logue 2003: 308–309).
8 Kaj Hansen explains that "3 betyg" literally means the third semester of the
   major of a Fil.Kant., which is roughly equivalent to work beyond a BA but
   less than an MA. "An '3 betygs uppsats' at that time meant an essay, the
   bachelor's project, written during the second half of the third semester of the
   major. At that time, the '3 betygs uppsats' was considered very important. For
   instance, a good '3 betygs uppsats' was needed to be accepted for the
   licentiate study." (Pers. commm, Kaj Hansen to Presbey, August 3, 2011)
9 I presume Oruka refers to the 1961 edition.
10 Pers. comm. Hedenius to Oruka, 27 June 1968, in Uppsala University archive.
   Kaj Hansen explains, "the grade '3' is the middle grade (pass without

distinction) in the Swedish grade system" (Pers. comm., Hansen to Presbey, August 8, 2011). On a related note, according to Svante Nordin, Hedenius wrote a letter to Ann-Mari Henschen-Dahlquist on 18 January 1969, which said that Oruka had become "like a son" to him. (Nordin 2004: 398, translation by Jennifer Hultén)

11 Strang 2010: 75. For example, see Källström 1986: chapters 3–5.

12 Strang explains: "In the years from 1932 to 1944 he tried a wide range of solutions, from opinion polls to an eclectic cultural analysis based on interviews and central written material, such as the Constitution and canonized fiction, in order to specify the values, or 'creed', of a society" (Strang 2010: 90). Strang explores this in depth in his 2007 paper, "Overcoming the Rift between 'Is' and 'Ought': Gunnar Myrdal and the Philosophy of Social Engineering"; see especially 157–77.

13 What is now known as Samaritan House in Uppsala was established as a Christian organization to help the vulnerable. It began in 1882 as a home for girl-prostitutes and then served many decades as a private hospital. It is now a guest house. See http://www.samariterhemmet.se/om-oss. Swedish friends of Oruka's who knew him when he attended Uppsala University said that Oruka had stayed in *Samariterhemmet* during part of his studies.

Chapter 3

1 Oruka's 1969 Master's thesis, "The Concept of Punishment and its Abolition: An Essay on the Philosophy of Punishment and Criminology," was submitted under the older form of Oruka's name, Henry T. Odera, and approved by Hedenius on Oct, 25, 1969. Oruka used material from his Master's thesis in his book *Punishment and Terrorism in Africa*.

2 The riots/rebellion took place in 1967.

3 All translations from Nordin 2004 are by Jennifer Hultén; translation in possession of the author.

4 Pers. comm., Hedenius to Sven Danielssen, January 14, 1969, quoted in Nordin, *Ingemar Hedenius*, p. 399, translated by Jennifer Hultén.

5 Nordin's book refers to a newspaper article published in *Upsala Nya Tidning* on January 15, 1970.

6 Similar comments about forty "holdups" can be found in Nordin (2004: 397).

7 How did he finish so quickly? A letter from Odera to Hedenius in the Uppsala library archive dated July 14, no year (but most probably 1969, from the context), states that Wayne State University was to give him some credit for the fact that he had studied beyond the usual BA degree in having done Bachelor Honours. After talking to Chairman Angell, Oruka wrote, "from him I learned that so far my grades amount to '3.72' which is, according to him, a very high score." So, Oruka continues, they will give him additional credits, "For the fact that F.K. is more than 'BA' and that I did some additional

work (3 betyg) after the FK. In this case, all that I would need to do in order to fulfill the MA requirement would be to complete the paper on punishment." (F.K. is short for Fil.Kant.) To get credit toward the Master's degree, he needed Hedenius to vouch for him with WSU, which he did.

8 Ann-Mari Henschen Dahlquist supplies the information that Hedenius developed his ideas into a book. While Hedenius' book was published in 1972, before Oruka's *Punishment and Terrorism* came out in 1976, Oruka only cites the 1969 WSU paper and not the 1972 book.

9 Sweden's rate of motor vehicle theft, according to United Nations statistics, remains high, at about twice the rate of its Scandinavian neighbors (and similar to U.S. rates), and much higher than Kenya's rate as well. Keep in mind that Kenya's rate of car ownership (24 per 1,000) is drastically lower than Sweden's (520 per 1,000). See UNODC 2011 and World Bank n.d.

10 This point is also made in a much more in-depth way by Hannah Arendt in her research into the use of terror in totalitarian governments. She argues that totalitarian methods were first practiced by European powers in Africa and other colonies and then used during the Second World War against European enemies. But Arendt goes a step further in arguing that, while violence and threat of violence can temporarily coerce the movements of a person, totalitarian governments advance their control of others through the use of propaganda. If one can change the mind of the other, then coercion is not needed. It was the use of propaganda that made totalitarian governments effective, because to rule through violence and threat of violence alone is difficult and taxing, as it requires constant application of pressure. See Presbey 2008 and Presbey 1992–93.

11 There are many accounts of this, but as one example I suggest *Pedro and the Captain: A Play in Four Parts,* by Uruguayan exile Mario Benedetti.

12 A case in point is the abduction, torture, and repeated rape of three women by a Cleveland, Ohio, man, who held the women prisoners in his house for ten years. See Martinez 2013.

13 Although Oruka does not cite this source, these first two statistics can be found in the (British) Colonial Office (1963) report, p. 80. The report also gives an insight into the British perspective on their actions. The report highlights British efforts at famine relief in Kenya, as well as education, farming, and political participation that newly included Africans.

14 Pers. comm., Oruka to Hedenius, July 3, 1974. Note that pages 1–47 and 90–92 of *Punishment and Terrorism* are basically the same as "The Concept of Punishment," meaning he added about seventy-five pages to the book during his time in Kenya. The first edition of *Punishment and Terrorism* included chapters 1 through 6, with chapters 7 and 8 added to the 1985 second edition.

15 This and subsequent quotes refer to an English translation provided to me on July 11, 2011, by Kaj Hansen. The article in Swedish was published in *Dagens Nyheter* (*Today's News*), May 3, 1977.

16 In the second edition of *Punishment and Terrorism* he lists eight book
reviews of which he is aware (Oruka 1985: xiv).

Chapter 4

1   Today's Wikipedia website notes that in Denmark, the *filosofie doktor* or Fil.
Dr. used to be an equivalent of a German-style habilitation, and the licentiate
was considered the equivalent of an American doctorate. Denmark made the
switch to calling their licentiates Ph.D's in 1989. It goes further to affirm that
the Swedish licentiate is equivalent to the Danish licentiate which is now
called a Ph.D. (http://en.wikipedia.org/wiki/Doctor_of_Philosophy),
accessed August 6, 2022. Ann-Mari Henschen-Dahlquist, whose husband
was a colleague of Hedenius' in the Philosophy Dept. at Uppsala University,
said that it was usual for other universities to consider it the equivalent of a
doctorate, since they held Swedish education in such high esteem. Personal
correspondence, Ann-Mari Henschen-Dahlquist to Gail Presbey, May 20,
2007, in possession of the author.

2   This was a widespread practice, also followed by other Uppsala-schooled
UON professors such as Prof. John Onyango Kokwaro who received a PhD
in Botany in 1969 from Uppsala. http://archive.uonbi.ac.ke/all_cvs/8010.pdf
(accessed Nov. 12, 2015).

3   Lubumbashi, Université Nationale du Zaïre, Département de Philosophie.
Oruka mentions in correspondence May 16, 1972 that this article was part of
the thesis he did for Hedenius. Uppsala archive.

4   It's not exactly clear when the last two chapters were really written. Although
the seventh chapter is entitled "Freedom, Independence and Development:
The First Three Decades," presumably covering from about 1961–1991 (when
this book was published), almost all the references are from works in the late
1960s to early 1970s. There is only one end note making a comment referring
to an event that happened in 1980. It is my theory that he wrote this chapter
at first in the early 1970s but clearly after the dissertation and Ph.Lic. At least
one page of this chapter mirrors closely writings to be found in the semi-
autobiographical novel he wrote in the mid 1970s. Clearly he did not wait for
three decades of freedom before writing this chapter. It may be that he wrote
it after one decade, and concluded two decades later that little had changed
and that his original claims were still valid and relevant.

5   Although the published book includes, at the very end of chapter 2, an extra
footnote to reference a 1982 article.

6   In fact, chapter 7 of the 1991 book mostly discusses developments in Africa
in the 1970s. Pages 86–97 were published in 1993 in a collection in Turkey,
and that shorter essay was included in *Practical Philosophy* 1997:106–14; but
the book *Philosophy of Liberty* (Oruka 1996) adds an additional fourteen
pages onto that shorter article, discussing Idi Amin and other dictators of

Africa, and offering his insights into the prevalent Army coups in Africa, but almost all within the context of 1970s events, despite the subtitle "The First Thirty Years" which refers to the first thirty years of African independence. There are two quick 1980 references, one to President Léopold Senghor of Senegal retiring in 1980—"May the Almighty reserve for him a special place an honorable place in the Cosmos," Oruka says (101n). The second 1980 reference is to developments in Ethiopian politics, but it is quite vague (107). And on page 107 he notes that by the 1990s, Somalia had lost its sovereignty.

7 See also Grendler (2006: 154–55).

8 See relevant parts of Oppenheim's definition in "Freedom," International Encyclopedia of the Social Sciences, 1968, http://www.encyclopedia.com/topic/Freedom.aspx

9 Perhaps Oruka was influenced here by a popular song by Gil Scott-Heron, "Whitey on the Moon" that was released in 1969, just as he was visiting the U.S. As A. D. Carson notes, the recent documentary "Summer of Soul" captures the mood of the Harlem music festival that took place during the 1969 space launch, and the mood of the crowd that sensed, as Heron's poem does, the "seeming wastefulness of the Moon trip" while others in the U.S. struggle against formidable daily problems that remain unaddressed. Those feelings are reignited in 2021 as billionaires Richard Branson and Jeff Bezos fly off into space. See Carson 2021.

10 Neill wrote that he thought Oruka was underqualified. Oruka always considered that an insult arising from Neill's preconceived idea that Africans couldn't philosophize. Clearly, from reading Neill's reflections on African philosophy, we can detect many negative prejudices. However, it could be that Neill was not convinced that the Fil.Lic. degree was a doctorate. To his credit, Neill relented after receiving letters attesting to the worth of the degree.

11 Joseph Donders, interviewed by the author, April 13, 2007, Washington, D.C.

12 Ibid.

13 Ibid.

14 There were two divisions, Cultural and Economic.

15 Taban lo Liyong, interviewed by the author, July 10, 2010, Kenya. While Liyong in 2010 described he and Oruka as working for the same goals of decolonizing the curriculum, Oruka published an essay, "Black Consciousness," (1973), in which Oruka criticizes Taban Lo Liyong as being too Eurocentric. He thought that Lo Liyong's attempts to synthesize Western and African sources still presumed the superiority of Western literary sources (20–21). The same article is republished in Oruka 1990c: see pp. 80–81.

16 Donders, interview.

17 Ibid.

18 Correspondence from Oruka to Hedenius dated July 3, 1974, in Hedenius papers collection, Uppsala University Library archive.

19 In correspondence from Tommie Zaine to Oruka dated May 22, 1978, Zaine acknowledges having received a letter from Oruka dated March 10, 1978, in which Oruka explained that the manuscript had been rejected by publishers for being "too realistic." If the autobiography was already submitted to and rejected by a publisher by March 10, 1978, chances are that it was written either during Oruka's sabbatical year or soon afterward.

20 Correspondence from Odera Oruka to Ingemar Hedenius, dated May 16, 1972, and September 12, 1972, in Hedenius papers collection, Uppsala University Library archive.

21 FESTAC is an acronym that refers to the Second World Festival of Black Arts and Culture which took place in Nigeria in 1977.

22 Oruka makes this same point in an article of his entitled "Ideology and Culture: The African Experience," in Oruka and Masolo 1983 (57–62). The same article can be found in Coetzee and Roux 2003 (69–75). See esp. 73, 75n3.

Chapter 5

1   Correspondence from Oruka to Ingemar Hedenius, June 9, 1972.

2   Okot p'Bitek, "Myths and Nation Building." In possession of author.

3   However, from reading the book's account, including the endnote, it sounds as if Nordenstam, not the student, drew the analogy to Aristotle's philosophy (Nordenstam 1968: 82, 228n8). Even if it were the student's analogy, though, considering how long a history the study of ancient Greek classics has in North Africa, we can't be sure that the reference to Aristotle was due only to the Norwegian philosophy professor's influence (Ormsby 1995).

4   Nordenstam mentions that he visited Oruka in Kenya in 1987. Oruka invited Nordenstam to his Nairobi house where they enjoyed a home-cooked meal that included dishes from his home region. During this evening, Nordenstam found out that Oruka shared portions of *Sudanese Ethics* with his Ethics students at UON. Nordenstam remarks, "that evening in his home we found that we largely agreed ... on how to develop philosophy for present-day needs." Correspondence from Tore Nordenstam to Gail Presbey, June 21, 2011 and quote, March 3, 2022.

5   The BLitt degree has been considered the equivalent of a Master's degree in literature since 2002. See University of Oxford, "Regulations for Degrees, Diplomas, and Certificates," last modified May 31, 2013, http://www.admin. ox.ac.uk/statutes/regulations/307-072.shtml#_Toc28140153

6   Imbo (2002, 14–15) quotes Ngugi wa Thiong'o's introduction to Okot p'Bitek's (1973: xii) *Africa's Cultural Revolution*. Imbo (2002, 15) also quotes E. S. Atieno Odhiambo (1973: 108–9).

7   In his book on the use of Akan proverbs, Kwesi Yankah (1989: 77–78) shows that proverbs used in royal court ceremonies in Ghana are always changing

through context; he gives the example of a queen mother who cited a proverb which suggested that she should be deferential to male chiefs only as a prelude to her disagreement with it, as she performed a ceremony usually presided over by men. Additionally, sometimes proverbs change. For example, Volta Hall, a women's dorm at University of Legon, has the hen as its symbol. It used to refer to a proverb, "The hen knows the dawn of day, yet she looks to the cock's crow," but now the proverb has been revised to, "The hen also knows the dawn of day." Another example regards the old proverb, "If the male bird does not fly, its wife and young ones sleep hungry." Now it is said: "If both mother and father birds do not fly, their young ones are hungry" (Yankah 1995: 70).

8 Hountondji's "African Philosophy: Myth and Reality" later became chapter 3 of the book by the same title.

9 He also criticizes Radin for saying that Africans consider the social world to be as independent from human action as the material world; thus intellectuals are unable to change the world. Hountondji 1996, 79–80.

10 Irele's preface is reprinted in the second edition of Hountondji's (1996) *African Philosophy*.

11 There is overlap between this paper and the introduction published in the 1991 ACTS edition of *Sage Philosophy* (Oruka 1991b).

12 This part also appears in *Sage Philosophy*, ACTS ed. (Oruka 1991b: 5).

13 The quote of Hountondji, *African Philosophy*, 86n32 is a close paraphrase of a famous quote from Edmund Husserl (1965: 71).

14 "Priest Seeks Police Help over Sacred Tree Threat." *Daily Nation* (Nairobi), January 7, 2002.

Chapter 6

1 See Presbey 2018: 105–14. The article can be accessed through Phil Papers at https://philarchive.org/archive/PREOOO. Also see Presbey 2022, available at https://digitalcommons.csbsju.edu/social_encounters/vol6/iss1/4

2 John Murungi argues against Stamp's account, saying that S.M. Otieno and Wambui married for individual, private reasons, and not as a political act to bring Kikuyu and Luo tribes together (Murungi 2013: 177–78). Be that as it may, Oginga Odinga was clearly concerned that a subtext of the trial was Kikuyu-Luo tension, and he wanted to address that tension. Considering he would launch a new political party in 1990 that would attempt to create an alliance of Kikuyu, Luo and Luhyia citizens to be able to win the presidency away from KANU, one can see why in 1987 Oginga Odinga would have been concerned about the subtext of ethnic animosity during the burial trial. For an overview of the background of Luo-Kikuyu tension, see Dickovick 2012: 214–18.

3 I will be quoting from a published version of the lecture in Oruka 1990a, 101–108 that Oruka states is the text of the two talks (see 101).

4   Oruka commented at a very early date on the topic of same-sex couples in
the United States. The same trend that he recognized and commented upon
in the 1980s has, twenty-five years later, resulted in more legal and social
recognition for same-sex couples in the United States. In 2013 courts ruled
that bans on same-sex marriages or discrimination against same-sex married
couples are wrong. See National Conference of State Legislatures 2014.
Oruka only mentions the American context here, although we know that
many African countries have passed legislation punitive toward same-sex
couples. For example, the Ugandan Parliament passed an Anti-
Homosexuality Act and Nigeria's President Goodluck Jonathan signed the
Same-Sex Marriage Prohibition Act (see Bowcott 2014).

5   We should note however, that it is not literally the case that colonial powers
wanted Africans to give up everything African and take on foreign values.
After all, as we pointed out, it is the colonial powers who set up the courts of
customary law. Rattray, the British anthropologist and colonial administrator,
said it was his goal to retain "all that is best in the African's own past culture"
(quoted in Mamdani 1996: 112). Mamdani thinks this seeming open-
mindedness to African custom had some of its motivation in the desire to
withhold European civil laws and freedoms from Africans.

6   In the Algeria context, Surkis explains that French colonizers thought that
title deeds should only be given to those who had "effective possession" of the
land through active farming. But French authorities decided that women and
minors could not have any effective possession of the land, categorically,
despite women going to court and pointing out their productive farmland,
with trees and crops that they had planted with their own hands. See Surkis
2019: 103, 107–108, 113–14.

Chapter 7

1   Oruka has three different articles on the environment (Oruka, "Ecophilosophy:
Environmental Ethics," in Oruka 1997: 243–54; "Parental Earth Ethics" in
Oruka 1997: 146–51; and "Ecophilosophy and Parental Earth Ethics: On the
Complex Web of Being," co-authored with Calestous Juma, in Oruka, ed., 1994:
115–29). However, as Oriare Nyarwath points out, Oruka published the
"Parental Earth Ethics" article three times: once in a journal, *Quest* in 1993,
once as an additional chapter in his revised edition of *The Philosophy of Liberty*
that came out in 1996, 111–22 (the original edition was 1991), and again as a
chapter in his collected works, *Practical Philosophy* which he was editing at the
time of his death (and that Oriare Nyarwath finished editing and had
published after Oruka's death) (Nyarwath 2018: 269). I cite the 1997 version in
this chapter. One could possibly surmise that his repeated publication of the
article/argument was a sign either of his estimate of the importance of his idea,
or of the importance of the issue of the environment.

2 See Attfield's 2012 article, in which Attfield speculates which of the subsequent global attempts at slowing climate change would have met with Oruka's approval, had he lived long enough to hear about them. This topic will be discussed at the end of the chapter.

3 Although, recognizing economic dependency doesn't stop egoists from leveraging their power in transactions to extract a greater share of the wealth for themselves. American consumers might need bananas, but they can ensure the bananas are at an incredibly low price because certain countries are very dependent on the need to sell their bananas, as Eduardo Galeano (1997: 109–10) as well as Schlesinger and Kinzer (1983) explain.

4 I don't intend to deny that some animals exhibit a sense of just reward and punishment, feel social shame, or engage in compassionate action; clearly some of them do. See part 1b, "Common Themes in Primate Ethics," in Singer 1994. Also see de Wall, 2012.

5 We might conclude, therefore, that Oruka's argument is circular. Think of a similar case. Elizabeth Spelman charges Aristotle for having a circular argument regarding the naturalness of men ruling women. He purports that his politics is based on the nature of individuals. But, he has packed his description of individuals with political categories. The soul has rational and irrational parts, and these different parts of the soul rule with despotic or constitutional powers. In this way, he politicizes the soul, and then uses this so-called description to come to political conclusions about the public (Spelman 2003). Oruka here has given a very politicized version of the family. In animal nature and in human families, inequalities are not usually that dramatic as the six children in his example. There might be one "runt" of a litter of puppies, or there may be one sibling who hits the lottery or becomes famous, or a sibling who struggles with addiction or a physical or psychological disadvantage, but as a whole and statistically on a large scale, rich families produce rich children and poor families produce poor children (with many factors contributing to this stagnation; it is not the family's fault, per se, it is just that parents and/or the part of society in which they live can provide opportunities, or not, that other families don't have) (Alexander et. al. 2014). Oruka knows this, so why did he emphasize this counter-example? Was it to make people feel responsible for the worse off, as they would for a sibling? But as Nyarwath and I point out, what he says subsequently seems to justify these inequalities, at least on occasion.

6 See Wangari Maathai Institute for Peace and Environmental Studies, n.d.

7 Saulo Namianya Manyonge, interview by author, December 27, 1998, Bungoma area. Translation on-site by Chaungo Barasa. Transcription and translation by tape, by Shadrack Wanjola Nasong'o. In possession of the author.

8 An interesting case study of a similar problem is written about French colonialism in Algeria. As Judith Surkis explains, French colonial government in Algeria wanted to break up communal lands, and give title deeds to those who "possessed" the land, and by that they meant, those who

actively lived on and farmed the land. But then in addition, they did not give the land to all of the family members, only the male heads of household. Some women farmers who were unmarried (or widowed) went to the courts to prove they possessed the land. One woman pointed out how she planted trees and grew crops, but she was not taken seriously by the French colonists, who presumed (despite any evidence to the contrary, even evidence relevant to their concept of possession) that it was impossible for women to possess the land. See Surkis (2019), 103, 113–14.

Chapter 8

1 "What Is Justice" had originally been given as a talk to the International Conference of Jurists (Kenya Chapter) Conference in Nairobi.
2 Lucius Outlaw, interview with the author, December 30, 2021. The following description of the conference derives from this interview.
3 H. Odera Oruka, "Philosophy and the Environment," opening address to the World Congress of Philosophy, Nairobi, Kenya, July 21–25, 1991, unpublished.
4 Also see Oruka 1997: chap. 8; and *Praxis International*, no. 8, January 1989.
5 Chaungo Barasa, personal communication, June 2001.

References

Abousenna, Mona. 1995. "Contemporary Philosophical Thinking in Africa and Asia in the Light of the Afro-Asian Philosophy Association (AAPA)." *Journal of Value Inquiry* 29, no. 1: 129–35.

Abraham, William E. 1962. *The Mind of Africa*. Chicago: The University of Chicago Press.

Abuya, Pamela. 2002. "Women's Voices on the Practice of *Ter* among the Luo of Kenya: A Philosophical Perspective." *Fabula* 43, nos. 1–2: 94–101.

Achebe, Nwando. 2020. *Female Monarchs and Merchant Queens in Africa*. Athens: Ohio University Press.

Adagala, Kavesta. 1992. "Mother Nature, Patriarchal Cosmology, and Gender." In *God, Humanity, and Mother Nature*, edited by G. E. M. Ogutu, 47–55. Nairobi: New Era/Masaki.

Adhikari, Mohamed. 2011. *The Anatomy of a South African Genocide: The Extermination of the Cape San Peoples*. Athens: Ohio University Press.

Agala, Seth. 2015. "Hear How Kenya's Largest Tea Producer Is Empowering Women Tea Workers." Ethical Tea Partnership, June 3. http://www.ethicalteapartnership.org/hear-kenyas-largest-tea-producer-empowering-womens-lives/ (accessed March 10, 2022).

Alexander, Karl, Doris Entwisle, and Linda Olson. 2014. *The Long Shadow: Family Background, Disadvantaged Urban Youth, and the Transition to Adulthood*. New York: Russell Sage Foundation.

Almeida, Lucio Flavio de, and Felix Ruiz Sanchez. 2000. "The Landless Workers' Movement and Social Struggles against Neoliberalism." *Latin American Perspectives* 27, no. 5: 11–32.

Andersson, Stefan. 2005. "Russell's Influence on Ingemar Hedenius." Review of *Ingemar Hedenius*, by Svante Nordin. *Russell: The Journal of Bertrand Russell Studies* 25, no. 1: article 7. http://digitalcommons.mcmaster.ca/russelljournal/vol25/iss1/7

Anonymous. 1999. "The War against Palmares: Governor's Report, 1675–1678." In *The Brazil Reader: History, Culture, Politics*, edited by Robert M. Levine and John J. Crocitti, 125–30. Durham, NC: Duke University Press.

Arendt, Hannah. 1968a. *On Revolution*. Reprint, New York: Penguin, 1985.

Arendt, Hannah. 1968b. "What Is Authority?" In *Between Past and Future: Eight Exercises in Political Thought*, 91–142. Enlarged edn. Reprint, New York: Penguin, 1985.

Atieno Odhiambo, E. S. 1973. "Atieno Odhiambo, Aloo Ojuka, Margaret Marshment, and George Heron: Okot and Two Songs, a Discussion." In *Standpoints on African Literature: A Critical Anthology*, edited by Chris Wanjala, 108–109. Nairobi: East African Literature Bureau.

Atieno Odhiambo, E. S. 2000. "Luo Perspectives on Knowledge and Development: Samuel G. Ayany and Paul Mbuya." In *African Philosophy as Cultural Inquiry*, edited by Ivan Karp and D. A. Masolo, 244–58. African Systems of Thought. Bloomington: Indiana University Press.

Atieno Odhiambo, E. S., and John Lonsdale. 2003. *Mau Mau and Nationhood: Arms, Authority, and Narration*. Columbus: Ohio State University Press.

Attfield, Robin. 2012. "Henry Odera Oruka, Ecophilosophy, and Climate Change." *Thought and Practice: A Journal of the Philosophical Association of Kenya (PAK)*, new series 4, no. 2: 51–74. https://www.ajol.info/index.php/tp/article/view/88139/77776 (accessed February 14, 2022).

Attfield, Robin. 2021. Interview by Gail Presbey, virtual. December 26.

Attfield, Robin, Johan P. Hattingh, and Manamela D. J. Matshabaphala. 2004. "Sustainable Development, Sustainable Livelihoods, and Land Reform in South Africa: A Conceptual and Ethical Inquiry." *Third World Quarterly* 25: 405–21.

Auma, Leonida. 1998. Interview by Gail Presbey and Humphrey Ojwang, Koru, Kenya, December 4. Transcript and translation by Robert Vincent Okungu.

Ayer, Alfred J. 1936. *Language, Truth, and Logic*. Reprint. London: Victor Gollancz, 1958.

Ayieko, Monica Awuor. 1995. "Household Allocation of Labor Time in Two Types of Smallholder Farming Systems in Rural Kenya." PhD diss., University of Illinois at Urbana-Champaign.

Ayoo, Nyando. 1995. Interviewed with H. Odera Oruka and Gail Presbey in Sega, Ugenya, Western Kenya on November 19. Translation to English done on-site by H. Odera Oruka. Transcription and translation of audio tape from Luo to English by Oriare Nyarwath. Audio tape and transcript in possession of the author.

Azenabor, Godwin. 2009. "Odera Oruka's Philosophic Sagacity: Problems and Challenges of Conversation Method in African Philosophy." *Thought and Practice: A Journal of the Philosophical Association of Kenya*, n.s. 1, no. 1: 69–86.

Azikiwe, Abayomi. 2013. "The Role of MI6 in the Assassination of Patrice Lumumba." *Global Research*, April 8. http://www.globalresearch.ca/the-role-of-mi6-in-the-assassination-of-patrice-lumumba/5330515 (accessed February 16, 2022).

Barasa, Chaungo. 1997. "Odera Oruka and the Sage Philosophy School: A Tribute." In Graness and Kresse 1997: 19–22.

Barasa, Chaungo. 2002. "Narrowing the Gap between Past Practices and Future Thoughts in a Transitional Kenyan Cultural Model, for Sustainable Family Livelihood Security (FLS)." In Presbey et al. 2002: 217–22.

Barker, Nicola. 2011. "Ambiguous Symbolisms: Recognising Customary Marriage and Same-Sex Marriage in South Africa." *International Journal of Law in Context* 7, no. 4: 447–66.

Bell, Richard H. 2002. *Understanding African Philosophy: A Cross-Cultural Approach to Classical and Contemporary Issues*. New York: Routledge.

Bello, A. G. A. 2004. "Some Methodological Controversies in African Philosophy." In Wiredu 2004: 263–73.

Benedetti, Mario. 2009. *Pedro and the Captain: A Play in Four Parts*, translated by Adrianne Aron. San Francisco, CA: Cadmus Editions.

Bewaji, Tunde. 1994. "Review of *Sage Philosophy: Indigenous Thinkers and Modern Debate on African Philosophy*." *Quest: Philosophical Discussions* 7, no. 1: 104–11. http://michiel.ipower.com/Quest%20PD%20Juni%201994.pdf

Boone, Catherine, Alex Dyzenhaus, Ambreena Manji, Catherine W. Gateri, Seth Ouma, James Kabugu Owino, Achiba Gargule, and Jacqueline M. Klopp. 2019. "Land Law Reform in Kenya: Devolution, Veto Players, and the Limits of an Institutional Fix." *African Affairs* 118, no. 471: 215–37. https://doi.org/10.1093/afraf/ady053 (accessed February 11, 2022).

Bowcott, Owen. 2014. "Nigeria arrests dozens as anti-gay law comes into force" *The Guardian*, January 14. https://www.theguardian.com/world/2014/jan/14/nigeria-arrests-dozens-anti-gay-law (accessed March 11, 2022).

Bustin, Edouard. 2002. "Remembrance of Sins Past: Unraveling the Murder of Patrice Lumumba." *Review of African Political Economy* 29, nos. 93–94: 537–60. http://www.jstor.org/stable/4006795

Card, Claudia. 2003. "Making War on Terrorism in Response to 9/11." In *Terrorism and International Justice*, edited by James P. Sterba, 173–85. New York: Oxford University Press.

Carnap, Rudolf. 1935. *Philosophy and Logical Syntax*. London: Kegan Paul.

Carson, A. D. 2021. "Why Gil Scott-Heron's 'Whitey on the Moon' Still Feels Relevant Today." *Conversation*, July 21. https://theconversation.com/why-gil-scott-herons-whitey-on-the-moon-still-feels-relevant-today-164681 (accessed February 16, 2022).

CDC (Centers for Disease Control and Prevention). 2002. "Policy Issues and Challenges in Substance Abuse Treatment." Substance Abuse Treatment Fact Sheet. February. http://www.cdc.gov/idu/facts/PolicyFin.pdf (accessed November 1, 2014).

Cekic, Miodrag. 1973. *Philosophy and Science*. Vol. 1 of *Proceedings of the XVth World Congress of Philosophy*. Varna, Bulgaria: Sofia.

Cesar, Dana. 2010. "Jane Addams and Wangari Maathai: Nobel Laureates on Educating and Organizing Women for Local Food Security." *Vitae Scholasticae* 27, no. 2: 123–41.

Chandler, D. J., and Njoki Wane. 2002. "Indigenous Gendered Spaces: An Examination of Kenya." *Jenda: A Journal of Culture and African Women Studies* 2, no. 1. https://www.africaknowledgeproject.org/index.php/jenda/article/view/71 (accessed February 10, 2002).

Cheeseman, Nic. 2020. "The Rise of Africa's New 'Old Men.'" *Africa Report*, September 17. https://www.theafricareport.com/42006/the-rise-of-africas-new-old-men/ (accessed March 7, 2022).

Chilisa, Bagele. 2012. *Indigenous Research Methodologies*. Los Angeles: Sage.

Churchill, Ward. 2003. *Perversions of Justice: Indigenous Peoples and Anglo-American Law*. San Francisco, CA: City Lights.

Ciarunji, Chesaina. 2005. "Cultural Attitudes and Equality of the Sexes: Forever Incompatible?" In *Social and Religious Concerns of East Africa: A Wajibu Anthology*, edited by Gerald Joseph Wanjohi and G. Wakuraya Wanjohi, 209–16. Nairobi: Fotoform.

Clark, Anna. 1995. *The Struggle for the Breeches: Gender and the Making of the British Working Class*. Berkeley: University of California Press.

Coetzee, P. H., and A. J. P. Roux, eds. 2003. *The African Philosophy Reader*. 2nd edn. London: Routledge.

Cohen, David William, and E. S. Atieno Odhiambo. 1987. "Ayany, Malo, and Ogot: Historians in Search of a Luo Nation." *Cahiers d'études africaines* 27, nos. 107–8: 269–86.

Cohen, David William, and E. S. Atieno Odhiambo. 1989. "The Hunger of Obalo." In *Siaya: The Historical Anthropology of an African Landscape*, 61–84. Athens: Ohio University Press.

Cohen, David William, and E. S. Atieno Odhiambo. 1992. *Burying SM: The Politics of Knowledge and the Sociology of Power in Africa*. Portsmouth, NH: Heinemann.

(British) Colonial Office. 1963. *Colonial Office Report on the Colony and Protectorate of Kenya for the Year 1961*. London: Her Majesty's Stationery Office. https://invenio.unidep.org/invenio//record/22875/files/KEN_C2049_2.pdf (accessed March 7, 2022).

Comaroff, John, and Jean Comaroff. 1991. *Of Revelation and Revolution: Christianity, Colonialism, and Consciousness in South Africa*. Chicago: University of Chicago Press.

Conversation. 2017. "Earthworms Are More Important than Pandas (If You Want to Save the Planet)." March 28. https://theconversation.com/earthworms-are-more-important-than-pandas-if-you-want-to-save-the-planet-74010 (accessed February 10, 2022).

Copleston, Frederick C., and Bertrand Russell. 1948. *A Debate on the Existence of God*. British Broadcasting Corporation. Transcript: http://www.philvaz.com/apologetics/p20.htm (accessed March 9, 2022).

Cotran, E. 1989. "The Future of Customary Law in Kenya." In Ojwang and Mugambi 1989: 149–65.

Crocker, David, and Nigel Dower. 2022. Comments during IDEA conference, via Zoom, Medellin, Colombia, July 15.

Cullors, Patrisse. 2018. "Op-Ed: My Brother's Abuse in Jail Is a Reason I Co-founded Black Lives Matter. We Need Reform in L.A." *Los Angeles Times*, April 13. https://www.latimes.com/opinion/op-ed/la-oe-cullors-los-angeles-sheriff-jail-reform-20180413-story.html (accessed March 6, 2022).

Daily Nation (Nairobi). 1991. "Prof. Mazrui: The Pros and Cons." August 3.

Daily Nation (Nairobi). 1995. "Scholar Dies in Accident." December 13.

Daily Nation (Nairobi). 2002. "Priest Seeks Police Help over Sacred Tree Threat." January 7.

Davidson, Basil. 1992. *The Black Man's Burden: Africa and the Curse of the Nation-State*. New York: Three Rivers Press.

Davis, Angela. 2012. *The Meaning of Freedom: And Other Difficult Dialogues*. San Francisco, CA: City Lights/ Open Media.

de Wall, Frans. 2012. "Moral Behavior in Animals," Ted Talk, https://www.youtube.com/watch?v=GcJxRqTs5nk (accessed Feb. 17, 2022).

Dewey, John, and Horace Meyer Kallen, eds. 1941. *The Bertrand Russell Case*. New York: Viking Press.

Dickovick, James Tyler. 2012. *Africa 2012*. The World Today Series. Lanham, MD: Stryker-Post Publications,

Dikirr, Patrick Maison. 1994. "The Philosophy and Ethics Concerning Death and Disposal of the Dead Among the Maasai." MA thesis, University of Nairobi.

Donders, J. G. 1977. "Don't Fence Us in: The Liberating Role of Philosophy." Eleventh Inaugural Lecture, University of Nairobi, Taifa Hall, March 10. Nairobi: Joseph Gerard Publication, University of Nairobi.

Donders, Joseph G. ("Sjef"). 2007. Interview with the author, April 13, Washington, D.C. Recording and transcript in possession of the author.

Eastman, Charles. (1911) 2020. *The Soul of the Indian*. Lincoln: University of Nebraska Press.

Eddy, Bill. 2019. *Why We Elect Narcissists and Sociopaths—And How We Can Stop*. New York: Penguin.

Einhorn, Eric S., and John Logue. 2003. *Modern Welfare States: Scandinavian Politics and Policy in the Global Age*. Westport, CT: Praeger Publishers.

Ekennia, Justin. 1996. "Committed Dialogue as a Response to Pluralism." *International Philosophical Quarterly* 36, no. 1: 85–96.

Elkins, Caroline. 2006. *Imperial Reckoning: The Untold Story of Britain's Gulag in Kenya*. New York: Henry Holt.

Enns, Elaine, and Ched Myers. 2009. *Diverse Christian Practices of Restorative Justice and Peacemaking*. Vol. 2 of *Ambassadors of Reconciliation*. Maryknoll, NY: Orbis Books.

Evans-Pritchard, E. E. 1937. *Witchcraft and Oracles among the Azande*. Oxford: Clarendon Press.

Eze, Emmanuel, ed. 1996. *Postcolonial African Philosophy: A Critical Reader*. London: Blackwell.

Eze, Emmanuel, and Rick Lewis. 2000. "African Philosophy at the Turn of the Millennium: Rick Lewis in Dialogue with Emmanuel Chukwudi Eze." *Polylog: Forum for Intercultural Philosophizing* 1, no. 1: 1–28.

Fanon, Frantz. 1967. *The Wretched of the Earth*. London: Penguin.

Ferdinand, Malcom. 2022. *Decolonial Ecology: Thinking from the Caribbean World*. Cambridge: Polity.

Forbes, Jack D., and Derrick Jensen [1979] 1992. *Columbus and Other Cannibals: The Wétiko Disease of Exploitation, Imperialism, and Terrorism*. Brooklyn, NY: Autonomedia.

Foucault, Michel. 1995. *Discipline and Punish: The Birth of the Prison*. New York: Vintage Books.

Friedman, Marilyn. 2000. "Impartiality." In *A Companion to Feminist Philosophy*, edited by Alison M. Jaggar and Iris Marion Young, 393–401. Malden, MA: Blackwell.

Gadamer, Hans-Georg. 1967–1972. *Kleine Schriften.* 3 vols. Tübingen: Mohr Verlag.

Galeano, Eduardo. 1997. *Open Veins of Latin America: Five Centuries of the Pillage of a Continent.* 25th anniv. edn. New York: Monthly Review Press.

Gallie, W. B. 1979. *Philosophers of Peace and War: Kant, Clausewitz, Marx, Engels, and Tolstoy.* Cambridge: Cambridge University Press.

Gathu, Wanja. 2014. "New Plan for Land Reform in Kenya." *Institute for War and Peace Reporting*, no. 395, July 25. https://iwpr.net/global-voices/new-plan-land-reform-kenya

Gbadegesin, Segun. 1997. "Current Trends and Perspectives in African Philosophy." In *A Companion to World Philosophies*, edited by Eliot Deutsch and Ron Bontekoe, 548–63. Oxford: Blackwell Publishers.

Geertz, Clifford. 2000. *Available Light: Anthropological Reflections on Philosophical Topics.* Princeton, NJ: Princeton University Press.

Gichohi, Wairimu. 1996. "Indigenous African Philosophical Knowledge: A Critique." MA thesis, University of Nairobi.

Gilbert, Erik, and Jonathan Reynolds. 2008. *Africa in World History: From Prehistory to the Present.* 2nd ed. Upper Saddle River, NJ: Prentice Hall/Pearson.

Gilmore, Ruth Wilson. 2006. *Golden Gulag: Prisons, Surplus, Crisis, and Opposition in Globalizing California.* Berkeley: University of California Press.

Goody, Jack. 1967. "Review of *Conversations with Ogotemmeli: An Introduction to Dogon Religious Ideas*, by Marcel Griaule." *American Anthropologist*, n.s. 69, no. 2: 239–41.

Gorsevski, Ellen. 2012. "Wangari Maathai's Emplaced Rhetoric: Greening Global Peacebuilding." *Environmental Communication: A Journal of Nature and Culture*, July: 1–18.

Graness, Anke. 2011. *Das menschliche Minimum: Globale Gerechtigkeit aus afrikanischer Sicht Henry Odera Oruka.* Frankfurt am Main: Campus Wissenschaft.

Graness, Anke. 2015. "Is the Debate on 'Global Justice' a Global One? Some Considerations in View of Modern Philosophy in Africa." *Journal of Global Ethics* 11, no. 1: 126–40. Doi: 10.1080/17449626.2015.1010014.

Graness, Anke, and Kai Kresse, eds. 1997. *Sagacious Reasoning: Henry Odera Oruka in Memoriam.* Frankfurt am Main: Peter Lang. Reprint, Nairobi: East African Educational Publishers, 1999.

Grendler, Paul F. 2006. *The European Renaissance in American Life.* Westport, CT: Praeger.

Griffiths, Anne M. O. 1997. *In the Shadow of Marriage: Gender and Justice in an African Community.* Chicago, IL: University of Chicago Press.

Gruver, Dusty. 1994. "The Earth as Family: A Traditional Hawaiian View with Current Applications." In Oruka 1994b: 301–305.

Gutema, Bekele. 2002. "The Role of Sagacity in Resolving Conflicts Peacefully." In Presbey et al. 2002: 207–16.

Gyekye, Kwame. 1995. *An Essay on African Philosophical Thought: The Akan Conceptual Scheme.* Rev. ed. Philadelphia: Temple University Press.

Gyekye, Kwame. 1997. *Tradition and Modernity: Philosophical Reflections on the African Experience.* New York: Oxford University Press.

Habibi, Don. 1999. "The Moral Dimensions of J. S. Mill's Colonialism." *Journal of Social Philosophy* 30, no. 1: 125–46.

Hallen, Barry. 2004. "Yoruba Moral Epistemology." In Wiredu 2004: 296–303.

Hallen, Barry. 2006. *African Philosophy: The Analytic Approach.* Trenton, NJ: Africa World Press.

Hallen, Barry. 2009. *A Short History of African Philosophy.* 2nd edn. Bloomington: Indiana University Press.

Hallen, Barry, and J. Olubi Sodipo. 1997. *Knowledge, Belief, and Witchcraft: Analytic Experiments in African Philosophy.* Stanford, CA: Stanford University Press. Mestizo Spaces/Espaces Métissés.

Halperin, Helena. 2005. *I Laugh So I Won't Cry: Kenya's Women Tell the Stories of Their Lives.* Trenton, NJ: Africa World Press.

Harding, Sandra. 1987. "The Curious Coincidence of Feminine and African Moralities: Challenges for Feminist Theory." In *Women and Moral Theory,* edited by Eva Feder Kittay and Diana T. Meyers, 296–315. Totowa, NJ: Rowman & Littlefield.

Harding, Sandra and Merrill B. Hintikka. 2003. *Discovering Reality: Feminist Perspectives on Epistemology, Metaphysics, Methodology, and Philosophy of Science,* edited by. Dordrecht, Netherlands: Kluwer Academic Publishers.

Hart, Herbert Lionel Adolphus. 1968. *Punishment and Responsibility.* New York: Oxford University Press.

Hart, W. A. 1972. "The Philosopher's Interest in African Thought." *Cahiers philosophiques africains/African Philosophical Journal,* no. 1 (January\–June): 61–73.

Harzing, Anne-Wil. 2007. "Publish or Perish." https://www.harzing.com/pop.htm

Hedenius, Ingemar. 1936. *Sensationalism and Theology in Berkeley's Philosophy.* Uppsala, Sweden: Almquist and Wiksells Boktryckeri.

Hedenius, Ingemar. 1937. "Studies in Hume's Ethics." In *Adolf Phalén in Memoriam: Philosophical Essays,* edited by Ingemar Hedenius, Konrad Marc-Wogau, and Harald Nordenson. Uppsala, Sweden: Almquist and Wiksells Boktryckeri.

Hedenius, Ingemar. 1941. *Om rätt och moral.* Stockholm: Tiden.

Hedenius, Ingemar. 1950. *Tro och Vetande.* Stockholm: Bonnier.

Hedenius, Ingemar. 1961. *Liv och nytta.* Stockholm: Bonnier.

Hedenius, Ingemar. 1963. "Retribution." In *Philosophical Essays Dedicated to Gunnar Aspelin on the Occasion of His Sixty-Fifth Birthday, the 23rd of September 1963,* edited by Helge Bratt, 35–45. Lund, Sweden: CWK Gleerup.

Hedenius, Ingemar. 1965. "The Welfare State and Its Ideals." In *Sweden Writes: Contemporary Swedish Poetry and Prose; Views on Art, Literature, and Society*, edited by Lars Bäckstrom and Göram Palm, 212–20. Stockholm: The Swedish Institute.

Hedenius, Ingemar. 1971. "Disproofs of God's Existence?" *Personalist* 52, no. 1: 23–43.

Hedenius, Ingemar. 1972. *Om människans moraliska villkor*. Goteborg: Forfattarforlaget.

Hedenius, Ingemar. 1973. "The Concept of Punishment." In *Modality, Morality, and Other Problems of Sense and Nonsense: Essays Dedicated to Sören Halldén*, edited by Sören Halldén, 13–30. Lund, Sweden: CWK Gleerup.

Heidegren, Carl-Göran. 2010. "Positivism before Logical Positivism in Nordic Philosophy." In *The Vienna Circle in Nordic Countries: Networks and Transformations of Logical Empiricism*, edited by Juha Manninen and Friedrich Stadler, 91–104. Vienna Circle Institute Yearbook. Dordrecht, Netherlands: Springer.

Hellsten, Sirkku K. 2018. "Punishment, Legal Terrorism and Impunity in Africa Reconsidered: Why is Oruka's Account Still Relevant to Present Day African Politics?" In Oduor et.al. 2018: 287–302.

Himmelstrand, Ulf, Kabiru Kinyanjui, and Edward Mbrurugu, eds. 1994. *African Perspectives on Development: Controversies, Dilemmas, and Openings*. London: James Currey.

Hoffman, Gerd-Rüdiger. 1984. "Faktoren und gegenwartige Tendenzen der Entwicklung nichmarxistischer Philosophie in Afrika." PhD diss., Leipzig University.

Holloway, Kali. 2021. "How Thousands of Black Farmers Were Forced Off Their Land." *Nation*, November 15.

Hord, Fred Lee, and Jonathan Scott Lee, eds. 1995. *I Am Because We Are: Readings in Black Philosophy*. Amherst: University of Massachusetts Press.

Horney, Karen. 1937. *The Neurotic Personality of Our Time*. New York: W.W. Norton.

Horton, Robin. 1967. "African Traditional Thought and Western Science." *Africa* 37: 50–71, 155–87.

Hospers, John. 1961. *Human Conduct: Problems of Ethics*. New York: Harcourt, Brace & World.

Hountondji, Paulin J. 1972. "Le mythe de la philosophie spontanée." *Cahiers philosophiques africains/African Philosophical Journal*, no. 1 (January–June): 107–42.

Hountondji, Paulin J. 1973. "La philosophie et ses revolutions." *Cahiers philosophiques africains/African Philosophical Journal*, nos. 3 and 4: 27–40.

Hountondji, Paulin J. 1974. "African Philosophy: Myth and Reality." *Thought and Practice*, o.s. 1, no. 2: 1–16.

Hountondji, Paulin J. 1992. "Daily Life in Black Africa: Elements for a Critique." In *The Surreptitious Speech:* Présence Africaine *and the Politics of Otherness,*

1947–1987," edited by V. Y. Mudimbe, 344–64. Chicago: University of Chicago Press.

Hountondji, Paulin J. 1996. *African Philosophy: Myth and Reality*, translated by Henri Evans and Jonathan Rée. 2nd ed. Bloomington: Indiana University Press.

Hountondji, Paulin J. 2002. *The Struggle for Meaning: Reflections on Philosophy, Culture, and Democracy in Africa*. Research in International Studies, Africa Series 78. Athens: Ohio University Press.

Husserl, Edmund. 1965., *Philosophie als strenge Wissenschaft, Zweite Auflage.* Frankfurt a.M.: Vittorio Klostermann.

Imbo, Samuel Oluoch. 2002. *Oral Traditions as Philosophy: Okot p'Bitek's Legacy for African Philosophy*. Lanham, MD: Rowman and Littlefield.

Janz, Bruce. 1998. "Thinking Wisdom: The Hermeneutical Basis of Sage Philosophy." *African Philosophy* 11, no. 1: 57–71.

Janz, Bruce B. 2009. *Philosophy in an African Place*. Lanham, MD: Lexington.

Johns, Sheridan, and R. Hunt Davies. 1991. *Mandela, Tambo, and the African National Congress: The Struggle against Apartheid, 1948–1990; A Documentary Survey*. Oxford: Oxford University Press.

Kabira, Wanjiku Mukabi, and Patricia Ngurukie. 1997. *Our Mother's Footsteps: Stories of Women in the Struggle for Freedom*. Nairobi: The Collaborative Center for Gender and Development.

Källström, Staffan. 1986. *Den gode nihilisten: Axel Hägerström och striderna kring Uppsalafilosofin*. Stockholm: Raben & Sjogren.

Kalumba, Kibujjo. 2004. "Sage Philosophy: Its Methodology, Results, Significance, and Future." In Wiredu 2004: 274–82.

Kanger, Stig, and Helle Kanger. 1966. "Rights and Parliamentarism." *Theoria* (Lund, Sweden) 32, no. 2: 85–115.

Kant, Immanuel. 1795. "Secret Article for Perpetual Peace." Second Supplement, *Perpetual Peace: A Philosophical Sketch*. http://www.constitution.org/ kant/2ndsup.htm

Karp, Ivan. 1989. "Notes on Iteso Moral Concepts." Paper presented at a seminar on anthropology and philosophy in Africa, Smithsonian Institute, April 17–20. Smithsonian Institution Archives, Washington, D.C.

Kaspersen, Lars Bo, and Johannes Lindvall. 2008. "Why No Religious Politics? The Secularization of Poor Relief and Primary Education in Denmark and Sweden." *European Journal of Sociology* 49, no. 1: 119–43.

Kathanga, Ngungi. 1992. "Philosophic Sagacity in Africa." MA thesis, University of Nairobi. http://erepository.uonbi.ac.ke/bitstream/handle/11295/18892/ Ngugi_Philosophic%20sagacity%20in%20Africa.pdf?sequence=3 (accessed March 10, 2022).

Kaufmann, Walter. 1980. "The Hegel Myth and Its Method." In *From Shakespeare to Existentialism: Studies in Poetry, Religion, and Philosophy*, 95–128. Princeton, NJ: Princeton University Press.

Kavan, Dana. 2008. "CeaseFire Gives Hope to Chicago's Violent Neighborhoods Despite Being Victim to State Budget Cuts." *Examiner*, August 14. http://

www.examiner.com/article/ceasefire-gives-hope-to-chicago-s-violent-neighborhoods-despite-being-victim-to-state-budget-cuts

Kekes, John. 1995. *Moral Wisdom and Good Lives*. Ithaca, NY: Cornell University Press.

Kelbessa, Workineh. 2002. "Logic in Ethiopian Philosophical and Sapiential Literature." In Sumner and Yohannes 2002: 109–16.

Kelbessa, Workineh. 2009. *Indigenous and Modern Environmental Ethics: A Study of the Indigenous Oromo Environmental Ethic and Modern Issues of Environment and Development*. Ethiopian Philosophical Studies 1. Washington, D.C.: Council for Research and Values in Philosophy. http://www.crvp.org/publications/Series-II/13-Contents.pdf (accessed March 10, 2022).

Kenya: White Terror. 2002. Broadcast televised on BBC 2, November 17. Currently on Kenya Digital Archives, https://www.youtube.com/watch?v=XV0udfKrzTQ (accessed March 10, 2022).

King, Martin Luther Jr. 1968. "A Christmas Sermon on Peace." In *The Trumpet of Conscience*, 68–75. New York: Harper and Row.

Kinyanjui, Mary Njeri. 2019. *The Sweet Sobs of Women in Response to Anthropain*. Newcastle upon Tyne, UK: Cambridge Scholars.

Kirwen, Michael. 1987. *The Missionary and the Diviner: Contending Theologies of Christian and African Religions*. Maryknoll, NY: Orbis Books.

Krausz, Michael. 1993. *Rightness and Reasons: Interpretations in Cultural Practices*. Ithaca, NY: Cornell University Press.

Kresse, Kai. 1996. "Philosophy Has to Be Made Sagacious: Interview with H. Odera Oruka at University of Nairobi, 16 August 1995." *Issues in Contemporary Culture and Aesthetics*, no. 3 (April): 5–14.

Kresse, Kai. 2007. *Philosophising in Mombasa: Knowledge, Islam, and Intellectual Practice on the Swahili Coast*. International African Library 35. Edinburgh: Edinburgh University Press.

Kresse, Kai and Oriare Nyarwath (Eds.). 2022. *Rethinking Sage Philosophy: Interdisciplinary Perspectives on and beyond H. Odera Oruka*. Lanham, MD: Lexington Books.

Ladha, Alnoor, and Martin Kirk. 2016. "Seeing Wetiko: On Capitalism, Mind Viruses, and Antidotes for a World in Transition." *Kosmos: Journal for Global Transformation*, Spring/Summer. https://www.kosmosjournal.org/article/seeing-wetiko-on-capitalism-mind-viruses-and-antidotes-for-a-world-in-transition/ (accessed March 8, 2022).

Lévy-Bruhl, Lucien. 1910. *Les fonctions mentales dans les sociétés inférieures*. Paris: Alcan.

Lewis, Rick. 1999. "African Philosophy: An Interview with Emmanuel Eze." *Philosophy Now* 23 (Spring): 9–12. Reprint. http://them.polylog.org/2/dee-en.htm

Liyong, Taban lo. 1966. "The Education of Taban lo Liyong." *Transition: A Journal of the Arts, Culture, and Society*, no. 24: 12–19.

Liyong, Taban lo. 1971. "Language and Literary Studies at University College Nairobi." *Research in African Literatures* 2, no. 2: 168–76.

Lölke, Ulrich. 1997. "Parental Care as a Principle of Development." In Graness and Kresse 1997: 219–32.

Lonsdale, John. 2003. "Authority, Gender, and Violence: The War Within: Mau Mau's Fight for Land and Freedom." In Atieno Odhiambo and Lonsdale 2003: 46–75.

Lopez, George. 2022. "A False Choice." *Morning* (newsletter), *New York Times*, March 6. https://www.nytimes.com/2022/03/06/briefing/crime-solutions-ukraine-war-books.html (accessed March 9, 2022).

Maathai, Wangari. 2007. *Unbowed: A Memoir*. New York: Anchor/Random House.

Maathai, Wangari. 2009. *The Challenge for Africa*. New York: Anchor/Random House.

Maathai, Wangari. 2010. *Replenishing the Earth: Spiritual Values for Healing Ourselves and the World*. New York: Doubleday.

Makinde, M. Akin. 1978. "Robin Horton's 'Philosophy': An Outline of Intellectual Error." Reading given at the University of Ife, Nigeria, June 20.

Makinde, M. Akin. 1988. *African Philosophy, Culture, and Traditional Medicine*. Athens: Ohio University Center for International Studies.

Makinde, M. Akin. 1989. "Philosophy in Africa." In *The Substance of African Philosophy*, edited by Campbell Shittu Momoh, 88–125. Auchi, Nigeria: African Philosophy Projects Publications.

Makoye, Kizito. 2013. "Widow Sexual Cleansing Ritual Continues." *AllAfrica*, October 4. https://allafrica.com/stories/201310040311.html

Makoye, Kizito. 2014. "Tanzania: Widows in Tanzania Struggle with Property Grabbing by Relatives." *AllAfrica*, January 20. https://allafrica.com/stories/201401201876.html?viewall=1

Mamdani, Mahmood. 1996. *Citizen and Subject: Contemporary Africa and the Legacy of Colonialism*. Princeton, NJ: Princeton University Press.

Mamdani, Mahmood. 2001. *When Victims Become Killers: Colonialism, Nativism, and the Genocide in Rwanda*. Princeton, NJ: Princeton University Press.

Maritain, Jacques. 1994. *The Person and the Common Good*. South Bend, IN: University of Notre Dame Press.

Martensen, H. L. 1878. *Den sociale Ethik*. Copenhagen: Gyldendals boghandels forlag.

Martinez, Michael. 2013. "As Ohio Women Remained in Captivity, Alleged Abductor's Life Crumbled." CNN U.S. website, last modified July 13, 2013. http://www.cnn.com/2013/05/12/us/cleveland-abductions-narrative

Maryknoll Institute of African Studies. 2013. "Sage Philosophy: The Root of African Philosophy and Religion." 2013–14 Course Catalog (accessed March 3, 2014). http://www.mias.edu/course24.htm. Archived at St. Mary's of Minnesota. https://catalog.smumn.edu/preview_course_nopop.php?catoid=18&coid=38592 (accessed March 2, 2022).

Masolo, D. A. 1981. "Some Aspects and perspectives of African Philosophy Today." Ph.D. dissertation. Rome: Instituto Italo-Africano.

Masolo, D. A. 1994. *African Philosophy in Search of an Identity*. Bloomington: Indiana University Press.

Masolo, D. A. 1997. "Conversations with Luo Sages." In "An African Practice of Philosophy," edited by V.Y. Mudimbe. Special issue, *SAPINA: A Bulletin of the Society for African Philosophy in North America* 10, no. 2: 249–64.

Masolo, D. A. 2004. "The Concept of the Person in Luo Modes of Thought," in Lee M. Brown, Ed. *African Philosophy: New and Traditional Perspectives*, New York: Oxford University Press, 84–106.

Masolo, D. A. 2005. "Sage Philosophy." *New Dictionary of the History of Ideas.* Farmington Hills, MI: Gale. http://www.encyclopedia.com/doc/1G2-3424300710.html (accessed June 6, 2014).

Masolo, D. A. 2006. "African Sage Philosophy." *Stanford Encyclopedia of Philosophy.* Spring ed. http://plato.stanford.edu/archives/spr2006/entries/african-sage/ (accessed June 6, 2014).

Masolo, D. A. 2010. *Self and Community in a Changing World.* Bloomington: Indiana University Press.

Masolo, D. A. 2018. "Oruka on the Role of Philosophy: An Interpretation." In Oduor et.al. 2018: 175–224.

Maweu, Jacinta Mwenda. 2012. "A Critical Assessment of Odera Oruka's Theory of Punishment." In "Odera Oruka: Seventeen Years On," edited by Reginald M. J. Oduor. Special issue, *Thought and Practice: A Journal of the Philosophical Association of Kenya*, n.s. 4, no. 2: 97–109.

Mazrui, Ali. n.d. "Language and the Rule of Law: Convergence and Divergence." https://zelalemkibret.files.wordpress.com/2013/02/language_and_the_rule_of_law.pdf (accessed March 2, 2022).

Mazrui, Ali. 1972. "The Written Word and Collective Identity." *East Africa Journal* 9, no. 5: 3–10.

Mbiti, John Samuel. 1969. *African Religions and Philosophy.* Nairobi: Heinemann.

Mburu, Michael Kamau. 2022. *Odera Oruka and the Right to a Human Minimum: An African Philosopher's Defense of Human Dignity and Environment.* Lanham, MD: Lexington Books.

Mbuya Akoko, Paul. 2001. *Paul Mboya's Luo kitgi gi timbegi / a translation into English by Jane Achieng.* Nairobi : Atai Joint Ltd.

McKenna, Erin, and Scott L. Pratt. 2015. *American Philosophy: From Wounded Knee to the Present.* London: Bloomsbury.

Mendes, Chico. 1992. *Fight for the Forest: Chico Mendes in His Own Words.* 2nd edn. London: Latin America Bureau (Research and Action) Ltd.

Merton, Thomas. 2004. *The Way of Chuang Tzu.* Shambhala Library ed. Boston: Shambhala.

Mill, John Stuart, and the East India Company. 1858. *Memorandum of the Improvements in the Administration of India During the Last Thirty Years, and The Petition of the East-India Company to Parliament.* London: Wm. H. Allen & Co.

Momoh, Campbell Shittu. 1981. "Modern Theories in an African Philosophy." *Nigerian Journal of Philosophy* 1, no. 2: 8–25.

Momoh, Campbell Shittu, ed. 1989. *The Substance of African Philosophy.* Auchi, Nigeria: African Philosophy Projects Publications.

Moore, G. E. 1993. *Principia Ethica*. Rev. ed. Cambridge: Cambridge University Press.

Mosima, Pius. 2016. "Philosophic Sagacity and Intercultural Philosophy: Beyond Henry Odera Oruka." Doctoral thesis. https://research.tilburguniversity.edu/en/publications/philosophic-sagacity-and-intercultural-philosophy-beyond-henry-od

Muhoho, Paul and Catherine Gicheru, 1987. "Lecturer Throws Light on Traditions." *Daily Nation* (Nairobi). February 6, 4.

Munyakho, Dorothy. 1990. "No Easy Road to Family Planning," *Daily Nation*, April 3, 21.

Murungi, John. 2013. An *Introduction to African Legal Philosophy*. Lanham, MD: Lexington Books.

Mutahi, Njuguna, and Mugo Theuri, eds. 2003. *We Lived to Tell the Nyayo House Story*. Nairobi: Friedrich Ebert Stiftung. https://library.fes.de/pdf-files/bueros/kenia/01828.pdf

Mutiso, G. C. M. 1975. "The Irrational as a System of Control." *African Thought and Practice* 2, no. 1: 49–52.

Muyia, Harrison Bwire. 1962. "Harrison Bwire Muyia." *Negro History Bulletin* 26, no. 1: 55–56, 82.

Nagel, Mechthild, and Seth N. Asumah. 2006. *Prisons and Punishment: Reconsidering Global Penalty*. Trenton, NJ: Africa World Press.

Nagel Mechthild E., and Anthony J. Nocella II, eds. 2013. *The End of Prisons: Reflections from the Decarceration Movement*. Value Inquiry Book Series/ Social Philosophy. Leiden, Netherlands: Brill.

Nation Newspapers. 1986. *S. M. Otieno: Kenya's Unique Burial Saga*. Kenya: Nation Newspapers.

NCSL (National Conference of State Legislatures). 2014. "Defining Marriage: State Defense of Marriage Laws and Same-Sex Marriage." January 7. http://www.ncsl.org/research/human-services/same-sex-marriage-overview.aspx

Ndaba, W. J. 1996. "Odera Oruka's Sage Philosophy: Individualistic vs. Communal Philosophy." In *Beyond the Question of African Philosophy: A Selection of Papers Presented at the International Colloquia, UNISA, 1994–1996*, edited by A. P. J. Roux and P. H. Coetzee. Pretoria: University of South Africa Press.

Ndulo, Muna. 2011. "African Customary Law, Customs, and Women's Rights." Cornell Law Faculty Publications. Paper 187. http://scholarship.law.cornell.edu/facpub/187

Neill, Stephen. 1991. *God's Apprentice: The Autobiography of Stephen Neill*, edited by E. M. Jackson. London: Hodder and Stoughton.

Neugebauer, Christian Michael. 1987. "Einführung in die akademische afrikanische Philosophie des anglophonen Raumes seit 1970." PhD diss., University of Vienna.

Ngugi wa Thiong'o. 1973. Introduction to *Africa's Cultural Revolution*, by Okot p'Bitek, xii. Nairobi: Macmillan Books for Africa.

Nicholls, Brendon. 2005. "The Landscape of Insurgency: Mau Mau, Ngugi wa Thiong'o, and Gender." In *Landscape and Empire, 1770–2000*, edited by Glenn Hooper, 177–94. Burlington, VT: Ashgate.

Nixon, Rob. 2006–2007. "Slow Violence, Gender, and the Environmentalism of the Poor." *Journal of Commonwealth and Postcolonial Studies* 13, no. 2, and 14, no. 1: 14–37.

Nixon, Rob. 2011. "Slow Violence." *Chronicle of Higher Education*, June 26. http://chronicle.com/article/Slow-Violence/127968 (accessed June 21, 2013).

Njambi, Wairimu Ngaruiya, and William E. O'Brien. 2005. "Revisiting 'Woman-Woman Marriage': Notes on Gikuyu Women." In *African Gender Studies: A Reader*, edited by Oyèrónké Oyĕwùmi, 145–66. New York: Palgrave MacMillan.

Nordenstam, Tore. 1968. *Sudanese Ethics*. Uppsala, Sweden: Scandinavian Institute of African Studies. https://torenordenstam.files.wordpress.com/2017/11/a-sudaneseethics.pdf (accessed March 2, 2022).

Nordenstam, Tore. n.d. "Tore Nordenstam—The Short Version." https://www.torenordenstam.se/ToreNordenstamE/index.htm (accessed July 22, 2013).

Nordin, Svante. 2004. *Ingemar Hedenius: En filosof och hans tid*. Stockholm: Natur och Kultur.

Nussbaum, Martha. 1996. "Compassion: The Basic Social Emotion." *Social Philosophy and Policy*, no. 1 (Winter): 27–58.

Nyandiga, David Obuola. 1998. Interview with Gail Presbey, March 2. Kamagambo, S. Nyanza. Translation on-site by Humphrey Ojwang. Transcribed from tape and translated by Robert Vincent Okungu.

Nyarwath, Oriare. 1994. "Philosophy and Rationality in Taboos, with Special Reference to the Kenyan Luo Culture." MA thesis, University of Nairobi.

Nyarwath, Oriare. 2009. "Odera Oruka's Philosophy: A Search for His Philosophical Commitment." PhD thesis, University of Nairobi.

Nyarwath, Oriare. 2012. "The Luo Care for Widows (Lako) and Contemporary Challenges." *Thought and Practice: A Journal of the Philosophical Association of Kenya*, n.s. 4, no. 1: 91–110.

Nyarwath, Oriare. 2018. "Oruka's Right to a Human Minimum as a Principle of Global Justice," in Oduor et al., 2018, 261–86.

Nzioki, Elizabeth Akinyi. 1993. *Effect of Land Tenure Reform on Women's Access to and Control of Land for Food Production: A Case Study in Mumbuni Location, Machakos District, Kenya*. IDRC Report. Nairobi: International Development Research Centre. https://idl-bnc-idrc.dspacedirect.org/bitstream/handle/10625/13522/100890.pdf?sequence=1 (accessed February 17, 2022).

Nzomo, Maria. 1994a. "'Wife-Inheritance' by Any Other Name Is Just as Repugnant." *Sunday Nation* (Nairobi), February 13.

Nzomo, Maria. 1994b. "Women in Politics and Public Decision Making." In *African Perspectives on Development: Controversies, Dilemmas, and Openings*, edited by Ulf Himmelstrand, Kabiru Kinyanjui, and Edward Mbrurugu, 203–17. London: James Currey.

Ochieng, Omedi. 2008. "The Epistemology of African Philosophy: Sagacious Knowledge and the Call for a Critical and Contextual Epistemology." *International Philosophical Quarterly* 48, no. 3: 337–59.

Ochieng, Omedi. 2011. "The Ideology of African Philosophy: The Silences and Possibilities of African Rhetorical Knowledge." In *Silence and Listening as Rhetorical Arts*, edited by Cheryl Glenn and Krista Ratcliffe, 147–62. Carbondale: Southern Illinois University Press.

Ochieng'-Odhiambo, F. 1995–96. "An African Savant." *Quest: Philosophical Discussions* 9, no. 2, and 10, no. 1: 12–21.

Ochieng'-Odhiambo, F. 1997. "Philosophic Sagacity Revisited." In Graness and Kresse 1997: 171–79.

Ochieng'-Odhiambo, F. 2002a. "The Evolution of Sagacity: The Three Stages of Odera Oruka's Philosophy." *Philosophia Africana* 5, no. 1: 19–32.

Ochieng'-Odhiambo, F. 2002b. "Some Basic Issues about Philosophic Sagacity: Twenty Years Later." In *Perspectives in African Philosophy: An Anthology on "Problematics of an African Philosophy: Twenty Years After (1976-1996),"* edited by Claude Sumner and Yohannes, 64–74.

Ochieng'-Odhiambo, F. 2009. "Philosophic Sagacity: Aims and Functions." *Caribbean Journal of Philosophy* 1, no. 1 (30 October) Online version of the article, stating it is a revised version of a paper delivered in Kingston, Jamaica at the ISAPS conference of 2004, is at http://ojs.mona.uwi.edu/index.php/cjp/article/viewFile/289/189 (accessed March 10, 2022).

Ochieng'-Odhiambo, F. 2006. "The Tripartite in Sagacity." *Philosophia Africana* 9, no. 1: 17–34.

Ocholla-Ayayo, Andrev B. C. 1976. *Traditional Ideology and Ethics among the Southern Luo*. Uppsala, Sweden: Scandinavian Institute of African Studies.

Odeny, Manuel. 2013. "Free Houses for Widows in Migori." *AllAfrica*, June 7. http://allafrica.com/stories/201306070086.html

Odinga, Jaramogi Oginga. 1969. *Not Yet Uhuru: An Autobiography*. New York: Hill and Wang.

Oduor, Reginald M. J., ed. 2012. Special issue entitled "Odera Oruka: Seventeen Years On." *Thought and Practice: A Journal of the Philosophical Association of Kenya*, n.s. 4, no. 2.

Oduor, Reginald M. J., Oriare Nyarwath, and Francis E. A. Owakah, eds. 2018. *Odera Oruka in the Twenty-First Century*. Kenyan Philosophical Studies II. Cultural Heritage and Contemporary Change, Series II, African Philosophical Studies, vol. 20, Washington, D.C.: Council for Research in Values and Philosophy.

Ogola Onyango, Peter. 2002. "A Continuing Study of Sage Philosophy: Emphasis on Jaramogi Oginga Odinga." In Presbey et al. 2002: 239–43.

Ogot, Bethwell. 1963. "British Administration in the Central Nyanza District of Kenya, 1900–60," *Journal of African History* 4, no. 2: 249–73.

Ogot, Bethwell A. 1971. "Men of the People." *East Africa Journal* 8, no. 6: 14–16.

Ogot, Bethwell A. 1995. "The Construction of a National Culture." In *Decolonization and Independence in Kenya, 1940-1993*, edited by B. A. Ogot and W. R. Ochieng', 214–36. Athens: Ohio University Press.

Ogutu, G. E. M. 1995–96. "Weep Not: Philosophers Never Die." *Quest: Philosophical Discussions* 9, no. 2, and 10, no. 1: 5–11.

Ogutu, Gilbert, Pentti Malaska, and Johanna Kojola, eds. 1997. *Futures beyond Poverty: Ways and Means out of the Current Stalemate, Selected Papers from the XIV World Conference of the World Futures Studies Federation* (Nairobi, 1995). Helsinki: World Futures Studies Federation.

Ojwang', H. J. 2005. "Towards a Social Philosophy of the African Leviratic Custom: How the Luo Marriages Survive Death." In *African Philosophy at the Threshold of the New Millennium*, edited by Bekele Gutema and Daniel Smith, 58–77. Addis Ababa: Addis Ababa University Printing Press.

Ojwang, J. B., and J. N. K. Mugambi, eds. 1989. *The S. M. Otieno Case: Death and Burial in Modern Kenya*. Nairobi: Nairobi University Press.

Okaya, Filida. 1999. Interviewed with Gail Presbey, February 28, Kamagambo, S. Nyanza. Translation on-site by George Opiyo. Later transcription from tape and translation by Robert Vincent Okungu.

Okech-Owiti, M. D. 1989. "Some Socio-Legal Issues." In Ojwang and Mugambi 1989: 11–29.

Okin, Susan Moller. 1998. "Justice as Fairness—for Whom?" In *Social and Political Philosophy: Classical Western Texts in Feminist and Multicultural Perspectives*, 2nd edn., edited by James P. Sterba, 444–56. Belmont, CA: Wadsworth.

Okowa, Duncan. 2020. "Land Reforms in Kenya: Achievements and the Missing Link." Institute for Law and Environmental Governance, May 21. https://ilegkenya.org/2020/05/21/land-reforms-in-kenya-achievements-and-the-missing-link/ (accessed February 11, 2022).

Oladipo, Olusegun. 2000. *The Idea of African Philosophy*. 3rd edn. Ibadan, Nigeria: Hope Publishers.

Olúwọlé, Sophie Bọ̀sẹ̀dé. 2017. *Socrates and Orunmila: Two Patron Saints of Classical Philosophy*. Third ed. Lagos, Nigeria: ARK Publishers.

Oppenheim, Felix E. 1961. *Dimensions of Freedom: An Analysis*. New York: St. Martins.

Ormsby, Eric. 1995. "Arabic Philosophy." In *World Philosophy: A Text with Readings*, edited by Robert C. Solomon and Kathleen Marie Higgins, 120–44. New York: McGraw-Hill, Inc.

[Oruka], Henry Odera. 1968. "Political Ethics: Democracy and the Notion of Human Rights." Three betyg [honors] thesis, Uppsala Institute of Philosophy, June. Copy in possession of the author.

[Oruka], Henry T. Odera. 1969. "The Concept of Punishment and Its Abolition: An Essay on the Philosophy of Punishment and Criminology." Master's thesis, Wayne State University.

Oruka, H. Odera. 1971. Review of *Sudanese Ethics*, by Tore Nordenstam. *East Africa Journal* (June): 37–38. https://www.yumpu.com/en/document/read/28935628/east-africa-journal-june-1971-book-reviews (accessed March 2, 2022).

[Oruka], H. Odera. 1972a. "The Meaning of Liberty." *Cahiers philosophiques africains/African Philosophical Journal*, no. 1 (January–June): 144–71.

Oruka, H. Odera. 1972b. "Mythologies as African Philosophy." *East Africa Journal* 9, no. 10: 5–11. Reprinted in Graness and Kresse 1997: 23–24.

[Oruka], H. Odera. 1973. "Black Consciousness." Joliso: East African Journal of Literature and Society. 1/1, 13–24.

Oruka, H. Odera. 1974. "Philosophy and Other Disciplines." *Thought & Practice* 1, no. 1. Reprinted in Graness and Kresse 1997: 35–46.

Oruka, H. Odera. 1975. "The Fundamental Principles in the Question of 'African Philosophy.'" *Second Order: An African Journal of Philosophy* 4, no. 1: 44–55.

Oruka, H. Odera. 1977. "Punishment and Terrorism in Africa." Paper presented at the Lagos Festival, January 15–February 12, unpublished, in possession of the author, and archived online. http://alkalimat.org/festac/pdfs/Oruka.pdf (accessed March 7, 2022).

Oruka, H. Odera. 1978. *In the Mother Africa (The Family Broke Down).* Unpublished manuscript, in the possession of Tommie Zaine and the author.

Oruka, H. Odera. 1979. "On Elections and the Common Good: The Great Race to Get into Parliament." *Sunday Nation* (Nairobi), November 4.

Oruka, H. Odera. 1979[?]. "The Philosophical Roots of Culture in Western Kenya." Grant proposal, in possession of the author. (For corroboration of the date, see Ochieng'-Odhiambo 2002a: 29).

Oruka, H. Odera. 1980. "Philosophy and the Search for a National Culture." *Sunday Nation* (Nairobi), August 31.

Oruka, H. Odera. 1981. "Paul Mbuya the Sage Philosopher." *Sunday Nation* (Nairobi), May 17.

Oruka, H. Odera. 1983. "Sagacity in African Philosophy." *International Philosophical Quarterly* 23, no. 4: 383–93.

Oruka, H. Odera. 1985. *Punishment and Terrorism in Africa.* 2nd edn. Nairobi: Kenya Literature Bureau.

Oruka, H. Odera. 1988. "Grundlegende Fragen der Afrikanischen Sage-Philosophie." In *Vier Fragen Zur Philosophie in Afrika, Asien und Lateinamerika,* edited by Franz M. Wimmer, 35ff. Vienna: Passagen.

Oruka, H. Odera. 1989a. *Ethics, Beliefs, and Attitudes Affecting Family Planning in Kenya Today.* Report. Nairobi: Institute of Population Studies, University of Nairobi.

Oruka, H. Odera. 1989b. "Philosophy and Anthropology in African Thoughts." Paper presented at a seminar on anthropology and philosophy in Africa, Smithsonian Institute, April 17–20. Smithsonian Institution Archives, Washington, D.C.

Oruka, H. Odera. 1989c. "Traditionalism and Modernisation in Kenya: Customs, Spirits, and Christianity." In Ojwang and Mugambi 1989: 78–88.

Oruka, H. Odera. 1990a. *Ethics.* Kenya: Nairobi University Press.

Oruka, H. Odera, ed. 1990b. *Sage Philosophy: Indigenous Thinkers and Modern Debate on African Philosophy.* Leiden, The Netherlands: Brill. This work was reprinted with slightly different contents in 1991. See Oruka 1991b for publication details.

Oruka, H. Odera. 1990c. *Trends in Contemporary African Philosophy*. Nairobi: Shirikon Publishers.

Oruka, H. Odera. 1991a. "Sagacity in African Philosophy." In *African Philosophy: The Essential Readings*, edited by Tsenay Serequeberhan, 47–62. New York: Paragon House.

Oruka, H. Odera, ed. 1991b. *Sage Philosophy: Indigenous Thinkers and Modern Debate on African Philosophy*. Reprint, Nairobi: ACTS Press. This work was first published with slightly different contents in 1990. See Oruka 1990b for publication details.

Oruka, H. Odera. 1992. *Oginga Odinga: His Philosophy and Beliefs*. Nairobi: Initiatives Publishers.

Oruka, H. Odera. 1994a. "Commentaries." *Sunday Nation* (Nairobi), January 23.

Oruka, H. Odera, ed. 1994b. *Philosophy of Nature and Environmental Ethics*. Vol. 1 of *Philosophy, Humanity, and Ecology*. Nairobi: ACTS Press, African Centre for Technology Studies (ACTS) and the African Academy of Sciences.

Oruka, H. Odera. 1994c. "Why the Future Will Judge Us Harshly." *Sunday Nation* (Nairobi), December 11.

Oruka, H. Odera. 1995. *Ethics, Beliefs, and Attitudes Affecting Family Planning in Kenya Today: A Final Report*. Report commissioned by USAID. Nairobi: University of Nairobi, Institute of Population Studies.

Oruka, H. Odera. (1991) 1996. *The Philosophy of Liberty: An Essay on Political Philosophy*. Rev. ed. Nairobi: Standard Textbooks Graphics and Publishing.

Oruka, H. Odera. 1997. *Practical Philosophy: In Search of an Ethical Minimum*. Nairobi: East African Educational Publishers.

Oruka, H. Odera, and Calestous Juma. 1994. "Ecophilosophy and Parental Earth Ethics: On the Complex Web of Being." In Oruka 1994b: 115–29.

Oruka, H. Odera, and D. A. Masolo, eds. 1983. *Philosophy and Culture: Proceedings of the Second Afro-Asian Philosophy Conference, Nairobi, October/November 1981*. Nairobi: Bookwise.

Oseghare, Anthony. 1985. "Sagacious Reasoning in African Philosophy." PhD thesis, University of Nairobi. Abstract available at University of Nairobi Digital Repository. http://erepository.uonbi.ac.ke:8080/xmlui/handle/11295/23580

Oseghare, Anthony. 1992. "Sagacity in African Philosophy." *International Philosophical Quarterly* 32, no. 1: 95–104.

Østergård, Uffe. 2011. "Lutheranism, Nationalism, and the Universal Welfare State." In *Europeans and Global Christianity: Challenges and Transformations in the 20th Century*, edited by Katherine Kunter and Jens Holger Sohjøring, 78–89. Oakville, CT: Vanderhoek and Ruprecht.

Otieno, Paulina. 1998. Interviewed with Gail Presbey, March 1, Rongo, S. Nyanza. Translation on-site by John Ogola. Transcribed from tape and translated by Robert Vincent Okungu.

Otieno, Wambui Waiyaki, and Cora Ann Presley. 1998. *Mau Mau's Daughter: A Life History*. Boulder, CO: Lynne Rienner Publishers.

Parkin, David. 1978. *The Cultural Definition of Political Response: Lineal Destiny among the Luo.* London: Academic Press.

P'Bitek, Okot. 1972. "Myths and Nation Building." Paper presented at a seminar at the Department of History, University of Nairobi, February.

P'Bitek, Okot. 1973. *Africa's Cultural Revolution.* Nairobi: Macmillan Books for Africa.

P'Bitek, Okot. 1974. *The Horn of My Love.* London: Heinemann.

P'Bitek, Okot. 1979. *African Religions in Western Scholarship.* Nairobi: Kenya Literature Bureau.

P'Bitek, Okot. 1983. "On Culture, Man, and Freedom," in Oruka and Masolo eds., 105–19.

P'Bitek, Okot. 1986. *Artist, the Ruler: Essays on Art, Culture, and Values.* Nairobi: East African Educational Publishers.

P'Bitek, Okot. 2011. *Decolonizing African Religions: A Short History of African Religions in Western Scholarship.* New York: Diasporic Press.

P'Chong, Lubwa. 1986. "A Biographical Sketch." In P'Bitek 1986: 1–12.

Peden, Creighton. 1994. "F. E. Abbot and the Environmental Crisis." In Oruka 1994b: 285–90.

Plantinga, Alvin. 1967. *God and Other Minds: A Study of the Rational Justification of Belief in God.* Ithaca, NY: Cornell University Press.

Plato, Apology. Project Gutenberg ebook. https://www.gutenberg.org/files/1656/1656-h/1656-h.htm (accessed Jan. 16, 2023).

Plum Village. n.d. "The Order of Interbeing." https://plumvillage.org/about/order-of-interbeing/ (accessed February 10, 2022).

Pollock, Joycelyn M. 2014. "The Rationale for Imprisonment." In *Prisons: Today and Tomorrow*, edited by Ashley G. Blackburn, Shannon K. Fowler, and Joycelyn M. Pollock, 3–20.

New York: Jones & Bartlett Learning. http://samples.jbpub.com/9781284020212/15963_CH01_Pass3.pdf (accessed March 7, 2022).

Presbey, Gail M. 1992-93. "Hannah Arendt on Power, Consent, and Coercion: Some Parallels to Gandhi." *Acorn: Journal of the Gandhi-King Society* 7, no. 2: 24–32. http://acorn.sbu.edu/fall%2092/fall92-hanna.pdf

Presbey, Gail M. 1996. "Ways in Which Oral Philosophy Is Superior to Written Philosophy: A Look at Odera Oruka's Rural Sages." *APA Newsletter on Philosophy and the Black Experience* (Fall): 6–10.

Presbey, Gail M. 1997. "Who Counts as a Sage? Problems in the Further Implementation of Sage Philosophy." *Quest: Philosophical Discussions* 11, nos. 1–2: 53–65.

Presbey, Gail M. 1999. "The Wisdom of African Sages." In "The Dimensions of African Philosophy: Ethics, Politics, and Culture." Special issue, *New Political Science* 21, no. 1: 89–102.

Presbey, Gail M. 2000. "Contemporary African Sages and Queen Mothers: Their Leadership Roles in Conflict Resolution." In *Peacemaking: Lessons from the Past, Visions for the Future*, edited by Judith Presler and Sally Scholz, 231–45. Amsterdam: Rodopi.

Presbey, Gail. 2002a. "African Sage Philosophy and Socrates: Midwifery and Method." *International Philosophical Quarterly* 42, no. 2: 177–92.

Presbey, Gail M. 2002b. "Philosophic Sages in Kenya Debate Ethnicity's Role in Politics." In *Ethnicity in an Age of Globalization*, edited by D. Carabine and L. L. Ssemusu, 161–83. Nkozi: Uganda Martyrs University Press.

Presbey, Gail M. 2004. "Sage Philosophy and Critical Thinking: Creatively Coping with Negative Emotions." *International Journal of Philosophical Practice* 2, no. 1: 1–20. https://npcassoc.org/journal/table-of-contents/vol-2-no-1 (accessed March 2, 2022).

Presbey, Gail M. 2007. "Sage Philosophy: Criteria That Distinguish It from Ethnophilosophy and Make It a Unique Approach within African Philosophy." *Philosophia Africana* 10, no. 2: 127–60.

Presbey, Gail M. 2008. "Arendt on Language and Lying in Politics: Her Insights Applied to the 'War on Terror' and the U.S. Occupation of Iraq." *Peace Studies Journal* 1, no. 1: 32–62. http://peaceconsortium.org/peace-studies-journal/archives

Presbey, Gail M. 2011. "War against Terrorism." In *Encyclopedia of Global Justice*, vol. 2, edited by Deen Chatterjee, 1139–43. Dordrecht, Netherlands: Springer. doi:10.1007/978-1-4020-9160-5_667

Presbey, Gail M. 2012. "Kenyan Sages on Equality of Sexes." In "Odera Oruka: Seventeen Years On," edited by Reginald M. J. Oduor. Special issue, *Thought and Practice: A Journal of the Philosophical Association of Kenya*, n.s. 4, no. 2: 111–45.

Presbey, Gail. 2013. "Women's Empowerment: The Insights of Wangari Maathai." *Journal of Global Ethics* 9, no. 3: 277–92.

Presbey, Gail M. 2014a. "Attempts to Create an Inter-ethnic and Inter-generational 'National Culture' in Kenya." *Diogenes* 59, 3–4: 48–59

Presbey, Gail M. 2014b. "Sage Philosophy," *Internet Encyclopedia of Philosophy*, September. http://www.iep.utm.edu/afrsage/

Presbey, Gail. 2015. "Odera Oruka and Mohandas Gandhi on Reconciliation," *Polylog: Forum für interkulturelles Philosophieren*, 34/2, 187–208.

Presbey, Gail. 2017a. "Die Arbeiten von Odera Oruka: Fortlaufende Inspiration fur eine neue Generation von Wissenschaftlern." Review of *Philosophic Sagacity and Intercultural Philosophy: Beyond Henry Odera Oruka*, by Pius Mosima. Translated into German by Britta Saal. *Polylog: Zeitschrift für interkulturelles Philosophieren* 37: 143–48.

Presbey, Gail M. 2017b. "Oruka and Sage Philosophy: New Insights in Sagacious Reasoning." In *Handbook of African Philosophy*, edited by Toyin Falola and Adeshina Afolayan, 75–96. New York: Palgrave MacMillan.

Presbey, Gail M. 2018. "Odera Oruka on Culture Philosophy and its role in the S.M. Otieno Burial Trial" in Odera Oruka in the Twenty-First Century, ed. by Reginald M. J. Oduor, Oriare Nyarwath and Francis Owakah. Washington, D.C.: Council for Research in Values and Philosophy, 2018, 99–118.

Presbey, Gail M. 2022. "Women's Rights in Kenya since Independence: The Complexities of Kenya's Legal System and the Opportunities of Civic

Engagement," *Journal of Social Encounters*, thematic issue on Democracy and Political Change, 6/1, 32–48.

Presbey, Gail M., Daniel Smith, Pamela A. Abuya, and Oriare Nyarwath, eds. 2002. *Thought and Practice in African Philosophy*. Nairobi: Konrad Adenauer Foundation.

Primoratz, Igor. 2013. *Terrorism: A Philosophical Investigation*. Cambridge, U.K.: Polity Press.

Quinton, A. M. 1954. "On Punishment." *Analysis* 14, no. 6: 133–42. doi. org/10.1093/analys/14.6.133

Raab, Francis V. 1963. "The Relevance of Morals to Our Denial of Responsibility." In *Morality and the Language of Conduct*, edited by Héctor Neri Castañeda Calderón and George Nakhnikian, 351–62. Detroit, MI: Wayne State University Press.

Radin, Paul. (1927) 1957. *Primitive Man as Philosopher*. New York: D. Appleton and Co. 2nd rev. edn. New York: Dover Publications.

Ranger, Terence. (1983) 2003. "The Invention of Tradition in Colonial Africa," 211–62, in Eric Hobsbawm and Terence Ranger (Eds.), *The Invention of Tradition*. Eleventh printing. Cambridge, U.K.: Cambridge University Press.

Rawls, John. 2009. *A Theory of Justice*. Rev. ed. Cambridge, MA: Harvard University Press.

Rigby, Peter. 1971. "Review of *African Religions in Western Scholarship*," by Okot p'Bitek. *Mawazo* 3, no. 1: 65–67.

Roberts, Dorothy E. 2022. *Torn Apart: How the Child Welfare System Destroys Black Families—and How Abolition Can Build a Safer World*. New York: Basic Books.

Rodriguez, Alex. 2007. "Russian Dissidents Called Mentally Ill: Soviet-Era Practice Revived, Activists Say." *Chicago Tribune*, August 7. https://www. chicagotribune.com/news/ct-xpm-2007-08-07-0708070053-story.html

Rooney, Phyllis. 2010. "Philosophy, Adversarial Argumentation, and Embattled Reason." In "Reasoning for Change." Special issue, *Informal Logic: Reasoning and Argumentation in Theory and Practice* 30, no. 3: 203–34.

Routley, Richard. 1973. "Is There a Need for a New, an Environmental, Ethic?" *Proceedings of the XVth World Congress of Philosophy* 1: 205–10.

Ruddick, Sara. 1995. *Maternal Thinking: Toward a Politics of Peace*. Boston, MA: Beacon Press.

Russell, Bertrand. 1929. *Marriage and Morals*. New York: Liveright.

Russell, Bertrand. 1969. *Autobiography of Bertrand Russell: The Middle Years; 1914–1944*. New York: Bantam.

Santos, Boaventura de Sousa. 2012. "Public Sphere and Epistemologies of the South." *Africa Development* 37, no. 1: 43–67.

Sarkin, Jeremy. 2008. "Prisons in Africa: An Evaluation from a Human Rights Perspective." *Sur: Revista internacional de direitos humanos* 5, no. 9., 23–50, https://sur.conectas.org/wp-content/uploads/2017/11/sur9-eng-jeremy-sarkin.pdf (accessed March 10, 2022).

Scheiber, Noam, Farah Stockman, and J. David Goodman. 2021. "How Police Unions Became Such Powerful Opponents to Reform Efforts." *New York Times,* June 6, 2020, updated April 2, 2021. https://www.nytimes. com/2020/06/06/us/police-unions-minneapolis-kroll.html

Schlesinger, Stephen, and Stephen Kinzer. 1983. *Bitter Fruit: The Untold Story of the American Coup in Guatemala.* Garden City, NY: Anchor Books, Anchor Press/Doubleday.

Schmitz, Christiana. 2008. "Shootings Increase after CeaseFire's Budget Cut." *Chicago Reporter,* July. https://www.chicagoreporter.com/shootings-increase- after-ceasefires-budget-cut/

Serequeberhan, Tsenay (Ed.), 1991. *African Philosophy: The Essential Readings.* New York: Paragon House.

Simon, Joseph Irungu. 1992. *Daily Nation* (Nairobi), August 24.

Singer, Peter. 1994. *Ethics.* Oxford: Oxford University Press.

Sloan-Lynch, Jay. 2012. "Domestic Abuse as Terrorism." *Hypatia* 27, no. 4: 774–90.

Snow, Nancy E. 1991. "Compassion." *American Philosophical Quarterly* 28, no. 3: 195–205.

Sodipo, J. O. 1973. "Notes on the Concepts of Cause and Chance in Yoruba Traditional Thought." *Second Order: An African Journal of Philosophy* 2, no. 2: 12–20.

Spelman, Elizabeth V. 2003. "Aristotle on Politicization of the Soul," in Harding and Hintikka, 17–31.

SPLC (Southern Poverty Law Center). n.d. "Garrett Hardin." https://www. splcenter.org/fighting-hate/extremist-files/individual/garrett-hardin (accessed February 10, 2022).

Stamp, Patricia. 1991. "Burying Otieno: The Politics of Gender and Ethnicity in Kenya." In "Women, Family, State, and Economy in Africa." Special issue, *Signs* 16, no. 4: 808–45.

Steward, Dugald, James Mackintosh, John Playfair, and John Leslie. 1835. "On the History of Metaphysical and Ethical, and of Mathematical and Physical Science." Edinburgh: Adam and Charles Black. n.p. Internet Archive. https://www.archive. org/stream/dissertationsonh00stewrich/dissertationsonh00stewrich_djvu.txt (accessed May 30, 2014).

Sterba, James. 1981. "The Welfare Rights of Distant Peoples and Future Generations: Moral Side-Constraints on Social Policy." *Social Theory and Practice* 7, no. 1: 99–119.

Stromberg, Bertil. n.d. "Filosofi och lingvistik, Umea Universitet." http://www. umu.se/philos/personal/stromberg2.htm (accessed July 29, 2010).

Strang, Johan. 2007. "Overcoming the Rift between 'Is' and 'Ought': Gunnar Myrdal and the Philosophy of Social Engineering." *Ideas in History* 2, no. 2: 143–81.

Strang, Johan. 2010. "History, Transfer, Politics: Five Studies on the Legacy of Uppsala Philosophy." PhD diss., University of Finland. Available at https:// helda.helsinki.fi/bitstream/handle/10138/19461/historyt.pdf?sequence=2

Sumner, Claude. 1995. *Proverbs, Collection, and Analysis.* Vol. 1 of *Oromo Wisdom Literature.* Addis Ababa: Gudina Tumsa Foundation.

Sumner, Claude, and Samuel Wolde Yohannes, eds. 2002. *Perspectives in African Philosophy: An Anthology on "Problematics of an African Philosophy: Twenty Years Later."* Addis Ababa: Addis Ababa University Press.

Sunday Nation (Nairobi). 1981. "World Scholars End Seminar." August 23.

Surkis, Judith. 2019. *Sex, Law and Sovereignty in French Algeria, 1830-1930.* Ithaca, NY: Cornell University Press.

Sutton, Jane. 2013. "Military Doctors Urged to Refuse Forced Feeding at Guantanamo." Reuters U.S. edition website, last modified June 12. https://www.reuters.com/article/idUSBRE95C01D20130613

Swai, Elinami. 2010. *Beyond Women's Empowerment in Africa: Exploring Dislocation and Agency.* n.p.: Palgrave MacMillan.

Táíwò, Olúfemi O. 2021a. "Public Lecture with Olufemi O. Taiwo, 'Reconsidering Reparations.'" Harvard University, Edmost J. Safra Center for Ethics. YouTube video, October 18, 59.07 min. https://www.youtube.com/watch?v=lS1taGQsHrU (accessed February 17, 2022).

Táíwò, Olúfemi O. 2021b. *Reconsidering Reparations.* New York: Oxford University Press.

Tempels, Placide. 1945. *Bantu Philosophy*, translated by Colin King. Paris: Présence Africaine.

Tingsten, Herbert Lars Gustaf. 1947. "Review of *The Open Society*, by Karl Popper." *Dagens Nyheter* (Stockholm), August 21.

Tosh, John. 2015. *The Pursuit of History: Aims, Methods, and New Directions in the Study of History.* New York: Routledge.

Towett, Taita. 1959. "Le role d'un philosophie Africain." Special issue, *Présence Africaine* 27–28 (August–November): 108–28.

Tragardh, Lars. 1997. "Statist Individualism: On the Culturality of the Nordic Welfare State." In *The Cultural Construction of Norden*, edited by Bo Stråth and Øystein Sørensen, 253–85. Oslo: Scandinavian University Press.

Tragardh, Lars. 2012. "The Swedish Model Is the Opposite of the Big Society, David Cameron." *Guardian*, February 10. https://www.guardian.co.uk/commentisfree/2012/feb/10/swedish-model-big-society-david-cameron/print

Twining, William. 2010. "Normative and Legal Pluralism: A Global Perspective." Duke Journal of Comparative and International Law, vol. 20, 473–517.

UNODC (United Nations Office on Drugs and Crime). 2000. "Preventing Crime … and Cutting Its Costs." *Tenth United Nations Congress on the Prevention of Crime and Treatment of Offenders Press Kit*, Backgrounder no. 2. Vienna: United Nations Department of Public Information, February. http://www.un.org/events/10thcongress/2088c.htm

UNODC (United Nations Office on Drugs and Crime). 2008. *Handbook for Planning and Action for Crime Prevention in Southern Africa and the Caribbean Regions.* New York: United Nations. https://www.unodc.org/documents/justice-and-prison-reform/CPhandbook-120109.pdf

UNODC (United Nations Office on Drugs and Crime). 2011. "Motor Vehicle Theft at the National Level: Number of Police-Recorded Offences." December 12, 2011. *Crime and Criminal Justice Statistics.* https://www.unodc.org/unodc/en/data-and-analysis/statistics/crime.html

UNODC (United Nations Office on Drugs and Crime). 2018. "Victims of Intentional Homicides in Cities." *UNODC Homicide Statistics.* https://dataunodc.un.org/data/homicide/Homicide%20in%20cities (accessed March 6, 2022).

Van Binsbergen, Wim. 2003. *Intercultural Encounters: African and Anthropological Lessons towards a Philosophy of Interculturality.* Münster: LIT Verlag.

Van Hook, Jay M. 1995. "Kenyan Sage Philosophy: A Review and Critique." *Philosophical Forum* 27, no. 1: 54–65.

van Voren, Robert. 2016. "Ending Political Abuse of Psychiatry: Where We Are at and What Needs to Be Done." *BJPsych Bulletin* 40, no. 1: 1–3. doi:10.1192/pb.bp.114.049494

Wahba, Mourad, ed. 1978. *Philosophy and Civilization: Proceedings of the First Afro-Asian Philosophy Conference.* Cairo: Ain Shams University.

Waldron, Jeremy. 1991. "Homelessness and the Issue of Freedom." *UCLA Law Review* 39, no. 2: 295–324.

Wangari Maathai Institute for Peace and Environmental Studies, n.d. https://wmi.uonbi.ac.ke/index.php/basic-page/about-us (accessed March 13, 2022).

Wanja, Judy. 2013. "The History of an Epidemic." *Destination Magazine*, July 26. http://allafrica.com/stories/201307270023.html

Wanjala, Chris, ed. 1973. *Standpoints on African Literature: A Critical Anthology.* Nairobi: East African Literature Bureau.

Wanjala, S. C. 1989. "Conflicts of Law and Burial." In Ojwang and Mugambi 1989: 101–15.

Wanjohi, Gerald. 1997. *The Wisdom and Philosophy of African Proverbs: The Gikuyu World-View.* Nairobi: Paulines Publications Africa.

Wikipedia, n.d. "Swedish Humanist Association." Last modified April 11, 2013. http://en.wikipedia.org/wiki/Swedish_Humanist_Association

Wiredu, J. E. Kwasi. 1972. "On an African Orientation in Philosophy." *Second Order: An African Journal of Philosophy* 1, no. 2: 3–13.

Wiredu, J. E. Kwasi. 1974. "What Is Philosophy?" *Universitas* (Accra) 3, no. 2: n.p.

Wiredu, J. E. Kwasi. 1978. "Philosophy, Mysticism, and Rationality." *Universitas* 2, no. 3: 97–106.

Wiredu, J. E. Kwasi. 1980. *Philosophy and an African Culture.* Cambridge: Cambridge University Press.

Wiredu, J. E. Kwasi. 1996. *Cultural Universals and Particulars: An African Perspective.* Bloomington: Indiana University Press.

Wiredu, J. E. Kwasi, ed. 2004. *A Companion to African Philosophy.* Malden, MA: Blackwell Publishers.

Wiredu, J. E. Kwasi. 2011. Introduction to *Decolonizing African Religions: A Short History of African Religions in Western Scholarship,* by Okot p'Bitek, xi–xxxvii. New York: Diasporic Press.

The World Bank. n.d. "Motor Vehicles per 1000 People." *World Development Indicators.* Last modified July 2, 2013. http://data.worldbank.org/indicator/IS.VEH.NVEH.P3

Worthington, Nancy. 2003. "Shifting Identities in the Kenyan Press: Representations of Wangari Maathai's Media Complex Protest." *Women's Studies in Communication* 26, no. 2: 143–64.

Yankah, Kwesi. 1989. *The Proverb in the Context of Akan Rhetoric: A Theory of Proverb Praxis.* New York: Peter Lang.

Yankah, Kwesi. 1995. *Speaking for the Chief: Okyeame and the Politics of Akan Royal Oratory.* Bloomington: Indiana University Press.

Young, Iris Marion. 1990. *Justice and the Politics of Difference.* Princeton, NJ: Princeton University Press.

Index

Note: Page numbers followed by *f* indicate a figure.